Praise for *One-Legged Mongoose*

"There are pivotal years in life when everything changes and comes into focus. In this touching memoir, Marc Straus reaches back to two eventful years in his childhood and retells them in rich and vivid detail. There are secrets and accidents and illnesses and, most of all, awakenings. Ultimately, *One-Legged Mongoose* is about how a sometimes abused, sometimes loved, and always bookish boy becomes a man. It is a moving story that will make readers think about their own journeys."

— **Ari L. Goldman**, professor of journalism, Columbia University, and author of *The Search for God at Harvard*

"Marc Straus, writing as his ten-year-old self, tells us 'Memories often stay in me as though they might be now,' and that is why reading **One-Legged Mongoose**, utterly enthralled, is to live two catastrophic years in the now of this lovable, wise kid, down to the finest details. In this prodigious act of memory, one imperfect family in the America of the '50s is seen through the clear gaze of an acute student of reality who captivates us with his matter-of-fact profundity, his brave refusal to look away. The book is a wonder, as close to recovered experience as language can provide, and the title is an apt metaphor for the fearmongering that drives so much of history, then and now."

— **Eleanor Wilner**, MacArthur Award-winning author of *Before Our Eyes: New and Selected Poems*

"In **One-Legged Mongoose**, Marc Straus boldly assumes the point of view of the preadolescent boy he was in the early 1950s, when his story takes place. Because his recall is so remarkably vivid and detailed, and because the young Marc was so keenly aware of the historical and personal violence that shaped his character, the result is a riveting and insightful account of an American Jewish childhood in the shadow of the Great Depression and the Holocaust."

— **Matthew Sharpe**, author of *Jamestown* and *The Sleeping Father*

"Marc Straus has written an astonishing memoir full of humor and hilarity, heart and vision. This year's sleeper hit, I predict. A must read!"

— **Mary Karr**, author of *The Liars' Club* and *Lit*

"Marc Straus's **One-Legged Mongoose** is a wry and insightful memoir of a bright, resourceful New York boy who survives polio, endures a four-hour daily commute to a yeshiva in Queens, and tells no one about the secret abuse he suffers at home. A great addition to the lore of New York in the era following WWII."

— **Dan Wakefield**, author of *New York in the Fifties* and *Spiritually Incorrect*

Dec 30 2021
For Warren Lawrence
with Thanks
Marc Straus

One-Legged Mongoose

Secrets, Legacies, and Coming of Age
in 1950s New York

MARC J. STRAUS

One-Legged Mongoose

Secrets, Legacies, and Coming of Age
in 1950s New York

MARC J. STRAUS

GREENPOINT PRESS
NEW YORK, NY

One-Legged Mongoose
Secrets, Legacies, and Coming of Age in 1950s New York

by Marc J. Straus

"Sugar Ray," "The Vow," and "Wheelchair" were previously published in slightly different form in *F&M Alumni Arts Review*...

All poems were previously published, some with different titles and in slightly different form, in the journals and periodicals *Judaism*, *Poetry East*, *JAMA*, *Jewish Affairs*, *Journal of Medical Humanities*, *Fan Magazine*, and *Passager*, and in the collections *Uncharted Lines*, *Symmetry*, and *Not God: A Play in Verse*, the last two by Marc J. Straus.

ISBN: 978-1-7346740-4-0

Library of Congress Cataloging-in-Publication Data pending

Book Designer: Robert L. Lascaro
LascaroDesign.com

Greenpoint Press
A division of New York Writers Resources
greenpointpress.org
200 Riverside Boulevard, Suite 32E
New York, NY 10069

New York Writers Resources
• newyorkwritersresources.com
• newyorkwritersworkshop.com
• greenpointpress.org
• prisonwrites.org

Printed in the United States on acid-free paper

To Stephen Ezra Straus, MD (1946–2007)

A brilliant man, a leading scientist,
a true friend for life, my brother

And to Livia Selmanowitz Straus, PhD

The most talented educator on the planet
and the love of my life
since the first day of ninth grade

"But man is not made for defeat," he said. "A man can be destroyed but not defeated."

—Ernest Hemingway, *The Old Man and the Sea*

AUTHOR'S NOTE

THE ONLY WAY I KNEW to tell this story was in the voice of the boy who lived it, as he lived it—to let my younger self speak. This was possible because my memory of the times and events I relate in this memoir is acute. I came to realize early in life that I can often visualize scenes in their entirety and recount conversations verbatim, my brain spooling out the minutia. But my recall is not perfect, so while I wrote from memory, my editor and I also did our best to verify all content. It was impossible to confirm everything—some names, establishments, locations, and events were simply too long ago and too obscure. In these cases, I relied on memory. The events, people, and places I write about are all real. Most names are also real. Some, however, I couldn't check and don't recall exactly. Others I've changed to protect privacy. Readers who'd like more specifics are invited to contact me at marcjstraus. com. I regret that I don't precisely recall the name of Mrs. Mahoney. She was my safe harbor in many a storm, and I'll never forget her, even if I can't remember her name.

CONTENTS

PART ONE

CHANGING SCHOOLS

CHAPTER 1

Van Wyck

I HOLD MY BREATH as a cloud of smoke encases my face. Then Mom pulls deeply again on her Old Gold, turns her head quickly to the open window, and exhales another long tentacle of gray smoke, which quickly arcs back at me in the passenger seat.

She is a chain-smoker, Old Golds now, and burns through three packs a day, while Dad is a moocher. If a customer lights up in the store, Dad asks for one. But Dad doesn't count that as smoking and denies he ever inhales.

But back to the car and why I am here in Mom's 1951 gray Dodge Wayfarer without air conditioning on a brutally hot June 14th, a Sunday, just 12 days after I turned ten. I am transferring to a religious school in September in Queens, New York.

Of course, it makes no sense. Five years at Chestnut Street School in West Hempstead and now I'm transferring to Yeshiva of Central Queens, and not because we are religious. We are not. And not because Chestnut Street is a bad school. It is. But it doesn't take five years to figure that out.

I entered Chestnut Street School in kindergarten with Mrs. O'Connor. I started three days late because I had had a bad sore throat and when I came to her class she said it was already full. The principal made her take me and it was all downhill from there. I had already read *Tom Sawyer* and *Huckleberry Finn*. Mrs. O'Connor spent three weeks teaching the letters A and B and no doubt I made my displeasure understood. I remember having an itching attack.

In any event, I soon discovered I could fit under the baby grand Steinway piano sitting on a small stool. That's how I was punished almost every day. That year I learned to create stories in my head. I learned to identify every kid by their shoes and gait. But I was never made to sit in the dunce seat. I think she knew I would have refused. That's pretty much how kindergarten went. Most years that followed, school was no better.

Yesterday Jim Peters ran the marathon in record time: 2 hours 18 minutes.

That's the good news. The bad news: Mom is driving me all the way to Queens for my first Hebrew lesson to get ready for the new school. And more bad news, mostly for Dad, is that the Rosenbergs are scheduled to be electrocuted as Russian spies.

Dad and Mom never explained why Stephen and I have to go to a religious school. At home Mom decides almost everything, but then there are these rare times she has no say. I think going to this school is one.

I'm not sure why I have to go to this new school but I have a big clue. Every Saturday morning, I go with Dad to Temple Beth Israel. During services he mouths a few prayers and mostly talks with his friends. Recently I overheard Morris Gerson say, "Sam, Solly Berkowitz's son didn't get accepted to a good college." Mr. Gerson always knows all the news. He also mentioned that Al Landman's son dropped out of NYU after two years.

Dad said nothing, but his face scrunched up and his jaw tightened. I know what that means because I work in the store with Dad almost every Sunday. Dad probably made the decision right then. Mr. Berkowitz came to the U.S. from Ukraine a few years before Dad. He owns a textile mill and lives in a large house in Hempstead not far from the Temple. I think that like Dad he moved his family to Long Island thinking it would be nice to have a private house in the suburbs and now his son can't get into a decent college. Dad decided the schools in West Hempstead are not good enough. That's an understatement. I think he also started to worry about our Jewish education. He's not really religious but he's a strong Jew, always raising money for Jewish things.

We moved from Brooklyn to a town with few Jews and Dad has no clue about being a Jewish kid here. He works six days a week and I doubt he has ever set foot on Hempstead Avenue.

He knows nothing about my fights and how much Stephen gets

picked on. The house and what goes on in the neighborhood would be Mom's territory, but Stephen has never said anything, and I won't.

The principal of the yeshiva, Rabbi Charny, met with us last week. He is tall and built really solid, as though he might have been an athlete once. His hair is black with gray along the sides and he has soft pouchy brown eyes. He had teachers test me in English and Hebrew.

For English Mrs. Feldstein asked about books I had read and she didn't believe me at first when I said I'd read *The Call of the Wild*, *The Count of Monte Cristo*, and *Gulliver's Travels*. That is until she quizzed me about Gulliver in Lilliput. And I didn't tell her about all the other books, almost two a week from the Hempstead Public Library.

"Well this is really unusual," she said. "Some of these are not even in the high-school curriculum."

Mrs. Eliafson asked me to read Hebrew. I have been going to Beth Israel Sunday School since I was six and I can read Hebrew pretty well. Then she tested me to see if I understood Hebrew words. We never learned that in Sunday school. She told me that at Yeshiva Hebrew language is taught from first to fourth grades but if I am accepted I would be entering fifth grade when the boys study Talmud all morning, so I would need to catch up.

Dad's Uncle Itcha learns Talmud every day. It is 63 books of Jewish law written nearly 2,000 years ago. I never studied Talmud. What is the point of spending a half a day on ancient laws? They didn't have modern tools or weapons then. It was pretty much swords. And no phones and electricity or cars.

I was really hoping they wouldn't accept me. It would be almost four hours of travel a day and to a foreign country like Mongolia where they probably eat lizards and raw chicken.

Then Mom and I waited for the edict and of course, my bad luck, Rabbi Charny said he really wanted me in the school and he would pay close attention and make certain it is a good experience. He told me he would make sure I am in Mrs. Sonnenberg's class in English. "She will love having such a strong reader in her class," he promised. But he couldn't make a final decision until I studied Hebrew all summer with Mrs. Eliafson, who would then recommend whether or not to accept me.

THIS WILL BE MY SECOND Hebrew lesson. Mom exhales thick curlicues of smoke. She holds the cigarette aloft between her right index and middle fingers, swings it to her mouth, and pulls in deeply again. Her fingernails are all bitten down so low there is hardly any nail left.

We are on the Belt Parkway nearing the Van Wyck exit in Queens and the car shoots up a quick incline and hits a big bump. My stomach lifts with it, acid quickly backing into my throat.

I am terribly nauseated and taste my breakfast eggs.

"Humph," Mom says, blasting onto the Van Wyck. She drives really fast where Dad drives like a toad, and whenever we are on a family outing he goes even slower and she is always yelling at him to stay in one lane and not to take *that* exit.

By now I think he will do the opposite of anything she says.

We are seated at Mrs. Eliafson's small round glass kitchen table in a tiny kitchen. She is several inches taller than Mom's five foot five and much thicker-hipped and wears a baggy long cotton dress, brown with several flowers imprinted. Her hair is frizzy gray, pulled up high in a tight bun. She is 45 years old, as I saw on a document on her library shelf, but she looks almost as old as Grandma Katy, who is 65. Some adults age much faster than others. I see that working in Dad's store. Dad looks ten years younger than Uncle Ira, but their age difference is only four years.

She begins almost immediately.

"Let's see how you did on your homework," she says. Mom is sitting nearby.

"Can you tell me what *Abba* means?"

"Sure. Father," I answer.

"*Talmid*?"

"Student."

"Great. How about *Mahair*?"

I am stumped.

Mom grimaces and I say, "That is not in the lesson book."

"True," she says, "but I was checking to see if you studied ahead."

I see the deal now and this is going to be a tough summer. Then I get several questions right and with a wide smile Mrs. Eliafson claps. "Let me ask a question about your English reading. The report says you've read several Joseph Conrad books."

"Yes."

"How about *Heart of Darkness*?" she goes on.

"Not yet, but I know the main character transports ivory down the Congo River."

"It's an important book with a profound message," she explains.

"Racism and imperialism." Then she is quiet, writing a few notes on a pad and Mom is all tight, thinking Mrs. Eliafson will discontinue my lessons.

Mrs. Eliafson then looks slowly and carefully at me and I feel like a bug under a microscope.

"You see, Marc. I don't have much time, really. I am terribly busy tutoring and I don't begin anything that is wasted. Do you know what I am saying?"

"I think so," I answer, not daring to look at Mom.

"Why should I do this?" She pauses. She is wearing a long beaded necklace made with red and yellow stones and only one smaller green one near the bottom of the loop. "I never ever take on a student who doesn't succeed. Do you understand what I mean?"

"Yes."

"We won't fail. I assure you. But I require your promise that every single day this summer you give me one hour of studying on your own. One hour. Will you do that, Marc?"

"Yes," I respond, confused in a remote part of my brain. I absolutely mean yes. But I don't want to be transferred and I don't want to study Hebrew and travel four hours a day to a religious school. Yet I just answered that I agreed.

"This must be your word. No pushing from your mother. I will take you and we will succeed if you are certain and I have your word."

"Yes," I say again firmly, knowing I will do exactly as I promise without any pressure from Mom or from anyone.

"Wonderful," she claps. "Then we begin in earnest on Tuesday." She turns to Mom and says, "Dora, Sundays at noon and Tuesdays at one p.m. That's what I can give you. There's less traffic I imagine for you midday and on the weekend, and I don't work on Shabbat."

I can't recall anyone ever setting the terms for Mom.

Maybe I said yes not because Mom would be angry if I didn't. I know the consequences and I am not afraid. I think I agreed because they expect more from me. Not like Chestnut Street where they don't care if you are still reading *Dick and Jane*. Or *Babar*.

Dad was forced to leave school in Poland at age 11. He never speaks about that either. I think he is ashamed he didn't have a good education but everyone in the store knows he is the smartest. He remembers every customer and everything they ever purchased. But that isn't enough for him. The proof of success is to be a professional, a doctor everyone looks up to. That's his plan for Stephen and me but he doesn't say so directly.

Only now has it begun to sink in that if I'm accepted at this new school I'll have to go to class for half of every Sunday. Sunday is the time I am with Dad in his textile store. And yet I just promised Mrs. Eliafson.

ON TUESDAY WE ARE on the way to Mrs. Eliafson again. I studied the Hebrew books, not an hour a day but closer to two hours. They are worse than *Dick and Jane* but I guess everyone starts at the beginning.

Mom is focused and says nothing. Her bleach-white skin is speckled with sweat and her red hair looks orange, as if ignited by the hot sun.

We're almost on the Van Wyck, steaming hot, windows rolled down the entire way and smoke wafting across my face. I had forgotten the large traffic bump and Mom exits as always at 60 and up the ramp and then whomp, a huge bounce, and I lift several inches above my seat and crash down, my head almost hitting the dashboard, and Mom never brakes for a second.

"Pull over quickly!" I yell.

"Just do it out of the window," she responds, head locked forward.

"I am going to vomit!" I plead.

Mom quickly pulls onto the right grass.

I bend over at the knees and waves of vomit gush, horrible large yellow streams with chunks of cereal and eggs, and seeing this makes me vomit more. Mom is rushing me but I keep retching and finally pull myself back in.

"Don't sit down if you are still going to vomit," Mom orders, never looking at me.

"I'm finished," I answer.

"Good then." She reaches to her left and finds a paper towel in her car door and hands it over. "Wipe up your face and mouth. You stink."

"I can't go now," I protest. "I just vomited. I stink."

"Oh, you will go," Mom says. "You will go and sit there and review your studies. You can vomit or not. That's your problem. We will go there twice a week and you will get accepted to that school."

Next lesson on Sunday I vomit again, the same bump and the

same place on the grass. Mom never slows down and I know now this is going to happen every time so I will just have to skip breakfast.

It won't matter either way, and in September I will be starting religious school in Queens. ▪

CHAPTER 2

Markell's Shoes

HUMPHREY PLANT WAVES. He is washing his father's black De Soto in their driveway across the street. The sky is full of large white cotton balls and heat curlicues are rising off the black macadam of Lindberg Street. On the corner, at Plymouth, is the tall steel pole with spread wings on top. It's for Charles Lindbergh's solo flight across the Atlantic.

I don't know why our street, named after Lindbergh, dropped the H at the end. In any event Dad should have thought twice before buying this house on a street named for a man he says is a fascist.

Stephen is walking with me as we turn left on Plymouth. His head is buried in an electronics diagram. He is probably adding resistors to a radio board he is building in his mind. I don't even know what resistors do and I have no interest in soldering little pieces for days on end for a radio that may or may not work.

In his six-and-a-half-year-old brain everything has a purpose. His large wooden structures in the garage are made with total concentration. I have no idea what they are but I get all his wood and nails for him from the last of the building sites on Woodfield Road. Mostly leftovers.

If Stephen were marooned on an island like Robinson Crusoe, he would build a house with lots of rooms. If I were marooned, I would be lucky to have a lean-to.

His red hair is lighter than mine and I am ruddy compared to him.

We are redheads, as is Mom, and Miriam, three years older than me. But with Stephen and me the resemblance mostly ends there. I am stocky and thick with a large torso and short legs. Dad's side of the family. Stephen is paper thin, long-legged, and small on top: Mom's side.

My tenth birthday was just over a month ago and the only present I got was another pair of pajamas from Grandma Katy. She bought me a puppy five years ago, which was quickly banished by Mom because it wasn't housebroken and it barked.

How else do dogs talk?

But the next year I got Twinkie, my Wirehaired Terrier, when she was two.

"Queen Elizabeth's coronation was on my birthday," I tell Stephen. He barely grunts an acknowledgement. He is probably putting transistors on that board now.

It's a good thing I bought him those beginner electronic magazines. He reads them as quickly as comic books. He usually doesn't go shopping with me but today Mom's list is long and I have to go to the Associated Food Store down Hempstead Avenue.

We are walking as slow as worms. Stephen is wearing a blue and white polo shirt. Brown thin cotton pedal pushers come down to his ankles, below which are thick brown leather shoes. His outfits never make sense. I wouldn't be caught dead in pants like that, but then I have similar shoes. There is no avoiding Mom's rule that we wear sturdy shoes to support our arches. No cheap Keds for us. It's hot heavy high-laced brown leather shoes on a blazing hot day. Shoes Mom will buy only at Markell's in Rockaway, a store with thick gray carpet, metal contraptions to measure your foot length and width, and a big machine to X-ray your feet. Once when I stuck my feet in the slot and looked through the viewer at my bones I thought I was having a preview of what I would look like when long dead.

Markell's. I have an E width and even though Stephen is so tiny he is double E, and if I ever teased him, which I don't, I would tell him his feet are so wide he can wear his shoes sideways.

I have even played football a couple of times in these shoes. But no one would dare tease me. I guess by now every kid knows my reputation for fighting. I don't lose and I make certain when it's over they will never want a rematch.

Rocky Marciano beat Jersey Joe Walcott for the Heavyweight Championship. I watched in the basement on our new 12-inch Du-

Mont, and then six weeks ago Walcott made the mistake of fighting a rematch and that bout didn't last even three minutes.

Fighting has been my life since I started kindergarten at Chestnut Street School. My red hair, my shoes, and some kids found out we are Jewish. And then by second grade the number of fights seemed to slow—until Stephen started school when I began third grade.

Some kids are just picked on for no good reason. They would be picked on no matter what they wore, though the way Mom dresses Stephen doesn't help. Kids smell when you are afraid. And no one is more afraid than Stephen. He cringes and cries before he is even hit, and the worst of the kids are merciless.

I have my spies. If any of my friends learns that Stephen was beat up there is a huge price. I find the kids who did it and it ends. Stephen is embarrassed when I beat the kids up in front of him, so I have to bide my time. He wishes he could fight back but he is not made that way. He can't help it.

He learned fear well before he ever went to school, and that is something we never speak of.

For me it is simple. There is a line, and when it is crossed there is no turning back, and I am someone else. Not like Superman. I don't duck into a phone booth and make a quick change. I am ten, average size. What I mean is I tunnel my mind down into a private place where fear and pain are gone. I feel lighter and free. Invincible.

In that moment I see everything in slow motion just like Ted Williams sees a fast ball coming to the plate. He can even see the rotation of the ball.

Once it begins, there is no stopping until they are defeated and will never want such a day again.

In this neighborhood they know now.

Stephen looks up softly at me.

"Yes, I have extra money with me," I say.

He knows what I mean. At Hempstead Avenue a few doors up is Mackie's Candy Store and Stephen loves those Tootsie Pops and the bags of little candies with sprinkles.

At the Associated Mom has an account so I don't pay anything. At Mackie's I need money and I always have some. I get two dollars for every Sunday I work at Dad's textile store. And this past winter was really snowy, and I made almost $200 shoveling driveways and stoops.

Stephen smiles. He rarely says much. This will be our secret, just a small one in comparison to some.

On Plymouth, then right on Spruce. The trees are denser here than on Lindberg. Mostly old oaks and sycamores. In front of our house is a silver maple now five years old. Almost all the streets are named for trees that don't actually grow on those blocks. The houses here are deeply shaded, some brick, many white clapboard.

Dad went to Manhattan but not directly to his store. He is going to another rally at City Hall. He is still angry they electrocuted Ethel and Julius Rosenberg two weeks ago and Dad says he expects as many as 10,000 protesters. He doesn't believe the Rosenbergs were Russian spies. The government chose a Jewish judge, he says, because they knew a Jew wouldn't be lenient with the Rosenbergs.

We pass the Littletons' house on the left. Up ahead is Sal's Barber Shop, a tiny place with the same old five chairs with ripped plastic red seats.

Stephen suddenly turns to me and I know what it means instantly.

His face has pulled in and his eyes widen in fear.

Where? What?

A few feet up the next driveway are two boys about a year or so older than me.

Stephen has stopped now and is terrified.

He is far better than me at detecting danger. He feels it. He anticipates the pain even if there will be none. When Dr. Fallis visits for one of our many bouts of tonsillitis, usually mine, Stephen is already shrieking before the syringe and needle are out of the black leather bag. It doesn't matter that it's me getting the shot. Stephen thinks we are all lying and he will be the victim of that needle.

I stop now as well. The two boys are staring at us, mostly the taller one with dark eyes and a shallow chin. His dark brown hair is longer than mine and drops in all directions without a part.

The slightly open mouth and parted teeth leering at me tell me that unfortunately Stephen is right.

He is half-clapping and starts to move toward us.

I don't know who he is or why he wants to fight but there is no running. Not with Stephen here, and I don't run fast. Most kids my age could catch me and then again there are these heavy shoes.

Stephen is half-turned behind me unwilling to look at them and I can hear the soft whimpering begin. I push him with my left hand further behind and whisper, "Just let me take care of this."

They are about ten feet in front of us now. The other boy is thinner, with a Yankee cap on. He is enjoying this. He is a follower and will gladly be a bully as long as he is assured of success. And that assurance comes from the taller kid who is now chuckling to himself. A head taller than me and maybe 20 pounds heavier.

There is no sense saying anything. I will find out soon enough.

"You don't recognize us, Straus, do you?"

I don't respond.

"A couple of years ago on Plymouth you sucker-punched me and broke my bike apart."

My mind reaches out across almost half my life. I remember every face I ever see. I remember whole pages in books I read. But we were little kids then and there have been many fights since.

"Ah well, it doesn't matter. The only important thing is that I will beat your brains out and when I am done then it's that pipsqueak behind you."

I should know who he is. He must have moved away or I would have seen him in school or in the neighborhood.

Perhaps reading my mind, he says, "We moved back, and I waited, and today it's my turn and you won't ever forget again."

"Kenny," I say quietly.

"Good. Good for you," he rasps. "Not as stupid as I thought. Not like that monkey behind you with ridiculous pants."

I hear Stephen half-ducked behind me whimpering more loudly.

Kenny and Donny. That's who they are. Kenny the leader then as well. By keeping my hands down, I suckered him into dropping his guard and took him out with one left uppercut and then stomped on his bicycle spokes.

It is more complicated with Stephen here. It is hard to protect him and take on both of these kids, and Kenny now with a reach so much greater than mine.

I know not to move and to hope they make an error. Just one error in my favor.

Kenny orders Donny, "Take that shrimp out. I don't need any help with this piss-ant Hebe. And Jesus and Mary look at those ridiculous shoes their mommy dressed them in."

Any of those taunts would have been enough on their own for me to start a fight with one kid his size but this is far more difficult, and I have no chance if I am careless. It has been months since a fight and a tiny voice in my head is telling me that today is the day

I might lose and I can't listen. Fear means defeat and that means Stephen will be beaten badly.

I push every thought into a deep recess in my mind. Thoughts that I have not been fighting enough. Thoughts that I am over the hill. The great Joe Louis fought too long and lost. Sugar Ray Robinson got knocked to a knee by Rocky Graziano and then lost to Joey Maxim and that was it for him. Such thoughts are dangerous and I begin to brace myself. I take a slow short breath and let everything inside submerge as though I am floating down into a wide cool ravine. The air lightens and everything comes into sharp focus.

Kenny takes two steps toward me. He is better at this now. His feet are planted solidly at a 45-degree angle. His hands are both fisted chest high. He won't make the same mistake again. He is practiced and confident.

He waves Donny to step around me in a wider arc to get at Stephen. Kenny knows that if I turn to stop Donny, he will be on me and have complete advantage.

I wait and time stretches out. I turn slightly to the left with my left foot now behind. This would be the stance for a southpaw, which I am not, and I doubt Kenny would remember.

Donny is now three feet behind me to my left and just out of reach. In any event, from my angle my only chance at him is a left hook and not a good angle, but that is not my plan.

By now Stephen couldn't be any smaller, huddled down below my thighs.

Kenny waits. He wants Donny to attack Stephen first and hopes I then make an error by turning.

Donny cautiously closes the circle, now mostly behind me and nearer to Stephen.

I don't look. I feel it. I am staring at Kenny's chin. I will know from his face what his body and hands will do.

Donny is only about two feet behind my left foot. He takes a short step in and then it happens.

Without turning, I extend my left leg out, lifting slightly, and then I slam it down, my heavy leather shoe hitting Donny's right shin. My weight and the acceleration of my foot hit him full force as his leg collapses toward the ground and I hear a crack.

My left leg now quickly swings around to the front and I pivot into a right-hand boxing stance.

Kenny had only that brief moment to attack but he was too startled and that has enabled me to recover and set myself.

He is really fast and a clean right jab hits the left side of my face. It is like a steel anvil and it brings my left hand higher, where it should have been.

He jabs again but grazes my arm. And again.

I know now sooner or later I will be outdone by his long reach so I must do something I have never done before.

I quickly pivot my right foot forward and he instinctively takes a half step back. Then I lunge at him full force, right shoulder leading. The force and my weight propel us both to the ground, me on top of him. I tuck my face deep into the left side of his neck and I reach my right arm tightly behind his neck until my fingers grip his throat. My left arm keeps his right arm pinned back.

Kenny starts to punch furiously with his left arm, fist against my side and ribs, fist against my right kidney. Over and over again and I take punishing hits.

And then he softens. He gasps. There is no air coming in. Panicking, he hurriedly reaches with his left hand to pull my fingers off his neck. As he does that my left fist crashes into his chin and his head jolts back.

When I softly pull Stephen up and against me I don't want him to see. Kenny is rolled on his side making choking noises, white foam pouring from his mouth.

I untuck Stephen and he first looks up. Past four houses up the street, Joe's Pharmacy is on the corner of Hempstead Avenue. As we near it, to make light conversation, I say, "The Library Annex is right past Joe's."

Stephen looks. A Lionel train set is fortunately set up near the window inside Joe's, and that has his attention.

"I think we deserve two treats each at Mackie's. What do you say, Stephen?"

He breaks out in a wide smile and his wet eyes shine. ▪

CHAPTER 3

Interregnum

JULY INCHED ALONG and now mid-August. No one has said anything about Twinkie, my six-year-old Wirehaired Terrier. She is my dog and when I am in school in Queens who will take care of her? Stephen has nothing to do with her and I don't think Miriam knows she exists. When I got Twinkie of course a requirement was that the dog be already housebroken. Sometimes I believe that Miriam, Stephen, and I came out already potty-trained.

Twinkie was a secondhand dog. Her owners had a child and didn't want a dog around. Maybe Twinkie missed them but soon she began spending all her time with me. She is usually with me when I go to schoolyards to flip baseball cards, and even when I bike to the Hempstead Library. I don't have a leash for her. All I have to say is, "Twinkie, sit next to my bike until I come out," and nothing will move her, not even if she sees a cat.

Until Twinkie comes back into the house she can go wherever she chooses and I won't change that. It's the same for me. Since I've been little I leave and am gone for hours: my friends, schoolyards, my hideout, the library. There are no rules until the second I set foot again in the house and then everything has to follow Mom's regulations.

Twinkie, only 16 pounds, is without fear. I have seen 100-pound German Shepherds back down. She nips their ankles a thousand times until they give up. And I have never seen another animal outrun her. Still, she has yet to catch a cat, and not for lack of trying.

It is no exaggeration to say Twinkie is a genius dog. Even Mom knows it and secretly admires Twinkie. I tried to see how many words Twinkie understands and it's about 200. To make the test fair I said each word with the same tone. Like, "Twinkie, there's a cat in front of the Davis house," and off she went like a rocket. I hadn't even looked that way.

When I am not with her she is out on her own about four or five hours and then heads home. I know it is dangerous but she is careful crossing streets and if she didn't have freedom then she would be unhappy all the time.

Twinkie doesn't even care if she eats dog food and she never begs. That would be demeaning. Like me she loves to be out discovering things.

Twinkie knows things are changing. She has watched me with sad eyes when I leave in Mom's car and I have a feeling she knows soon we will see very little of each other.

My lessons have ended and in two weeks school begins.

Anyway, it means no more Chestnut Street School. In *Crime and Punishment*, the main character, Raskolnikov, is an impoverished student. He plans a murder. He probably had in mind my kindergarten and second-grade teachers.

It's the start of the interregnum. I just read a book about the monarchies in England. The Interregnum was the 11 years from the time the British Parliament beheaded King Charles I in 1649 until Charles II was installed. During those 11 years England was in constant danger from its enemies since it was like a ship without a rudder. In the end, it went back to a monarchy.

Eleven years is the time until I'll be finishing college and then I will be out of our home for good. Nothing at home ever changes, not since the first I can remember. I will endure it and bide my time and when I go to college I want to go far away. But I already worry about leaving Stephen behind.

The strongest British monarch was Henry VIII, a Tudor. He killed his wives if he didn't like them and when the church complained he changed the church. Then his daughter Queen Elizabeth I, the last Tudor, was just as tough. She didn't want to have a husband or family interfere with her reign, which is smart if you are going to be that ruthless. And there has been no other Elizabeth until Elizabeth II was coronated this June.

I spend more time with Twinkie but soon the rain clouds gather.

I have learned there is no use worrying about what is coming. If you do, you are defeated in advance.

I'VE HAD A CHANCE to work in Dad's store three days in a row. I know I will miss it. Roman Cotton Goods is on the corner of Grand and Eldridge Streets on the Lower East Side of Manhattan and I've long since known every item: towels, bedspreads, rugs, and curtains. Sundays are for retail customers who come because prices are much lower than in the department stores. Yesterday I spent most of the morning helping a customer who buys goods and sells them overseas to Arab countries, primarily Syria where he is from. Dad once even sold a truckload of textiles to King Saud of Saudi Arabia. Dad says that Israel and the surrounding countries are due for another war, but in our store the only war is bargaining, and no one bargains better than customers from the Middle East. You get used to it.

Today is Friday and I expect to work a few more times, but once school starts I may have no chance since I will have classes most Sundays.

The heat of the summer has taken a pause and you can feel the days getting shorter.

Miriam, who turned 13 in May, is off with her best friend, Rhoda Stopnick, and Stephen is tinkering in the garage as always. I shouldn't say tinkering, as everything he builds is purposeful. It's just that we have no idea what it is.

In two weeks Stephen and I will be headed off like Moses and Aaron on a long journey in the desert. But at least they kept going in one direction. For us it's going to be back to the starting point every day.

Why not Miriam, I have wondered. Because my parents expect less from a girl? Not many girls go to medical school or law school. But more likely because going into eighth grade she would never catch up in Hebrew, and besides Miriam never said anything about wanting to switch schools. She said she can't wait to be in Hempstead High School with Rhoda Stopnick and her other best friends. Stephen won't say anything. He knows we will be commuting together and I will watch out for him.

Everything is about to change. Now, like Dad, my only day off will be Saturday. That's when he reads his newspaper in the afternoon in the easy chair near the left front window and listens to the

RCA Victrola. It's the only time we are allowed in the living room or dining room. These are Mom's rules and she is a better detective than Charlie Chan. Any footprint in the carpet is immediately detected. She always knows who it is—me! And I pay the severe price.

But since I was four, Mom has let me sneak into the living room when she is practicing on the Steinway. Her practicing has become much more infrequent. Still, the baby grand is tuned every month by Mr. Orenstein, a man much older and skinnier than Dad. He has a small leather case with a single wrench-like tool that he uses to adjust the bolts connected to the strings. He hunches over on the piano stool and concentrates, listening really hard as he strikes each key firmly and rapidly tugs the wrench right or left until the sound is correct. Then Mom pays him before he leaves.

That's his work. He always tells Mom that her piano has the most beautiful soundboard he has heard.

The famous soundboard is a large unstained piece of wood, a light reddish color with glued seams. Holding it in place are thicker wooden crossties set in small brass corner sockets around the inner frame. And on a front wooden crosstie is a thin black metal plaque with gold lettering: Steinway & Sons 1889.

Until I was five Mom played the piano almost every week and then by the next year she had almost stopped. She used to yell at herself when she made mistakes and then played less and less. I know she was a prodigy. I saw the medal she got at Carnegie Hall at age 12 in a citywide youth competition. She was second place, and Mr. Cava, her piano teacher, who made no headway with me, said she could have been the best in the world. He once sadly told me only a few teachers in their lifetime ever have a student like Mom. He said Mom would even have been better than Myra Hess, who is now the highest-paid woman pianist.

Mom quit her piano lessons before she was 15 and I think it was because she had to leave high school and work during the Depression. But no one ever really said.

When she does sit down to play it is often Chopin but this morning it is a Liszt sonata, which I like even more. I quietly walk in and stand a few feet away. Of course, she knows I am there.

I don't know how fingers can move that fast. When she reaches the beginning of the second section her eyes tighten and her mind is somewhere else and she sees each note and key in her head. Liszt is no match for her large powerful hands rippling across the keyboard in a blur. I imagine the soundboard is on fire. The notes thump in and out of me in waves and today she doesn't make a mistake. If she did, likely she would refuse to continue. I would tell her that everyone makes mistakes if they don't practice. "It's too late," she would answer angrily. After Liszt today I tell her that no one can play Chopin and Liszt this well and she has to keep practicing. She stares at me, pulls in her lower lip, quickly closes the keyboard and hurries away. Maybe had she continued playing piano life would be very different for me. ▪

CHAPTER 4

The Annex

FROM THE LONG ISLAND RAILROAD station on Sutphin Boulevard, I walk Stephen to the main school building on 150th Street and Jamaica Avenue, or occasionally we take the subway one stop. After I drop Stephen off it is three more subway stops for me to my fifth-grade class in the Annex at 104th Street.

The five-story building must have been a large home at one time but now seems stranded in the middle of a nice residential neighborhood of small houses and stoops. It is part cinderblock covered with a dull yellow stucco and part wood with old cedar siding, a building whose construction appears to have been started and stopped several times. Perhaps it was meant to have been a mansion since the main entrance opens into a large wood-paneled hallway and to the right is a large rectangular room that was likely a grand library. The small rear backyard is a jumble of discarded furnishings. The shops are a block up on Jamaica Avenue.

In West Hempstead Miriam, Stephen, and I are among the few kids who are Jews and the only redheads. Now Stephen and I are going to an all Jewish school where I expect we will fit in even less. We don't follow Sabbath rules and we even eat at unkosher restaurants.

At Chestnut Street School I was called Carrot Top, Fire Engine Head, Christ Killer. I guess the last isn't relevant now. But more importantly I was watching out for Stephen and now he will be two miles away from me. What if he is hit? Who will tell me? And

Queens is more dangerous, with plenty of gangs. I warned Stephen he can't leave after school until I am back to pick him up.

The Annex is for one class each from grades five through eight. Kids are streaming in and we go downstairs to the assembly.

Folding metal chairs are arranged around a dozen or so folding tables with large pitchers of orange juice and platters of bagels and cream cheese on them. This is where we will have breakfast and lunch. There is one torn basketball hoop; this is also the gym, and all the way to the left is a raised stage, because this is also the auditorium.

A man in a tight blue polo shirt and tan shorts up on the stage blows a shrill whistle. Students are still milling about noisily, many greeting each other after a long hot summer. Another whistle and hard taps on a microphone.

"I am Mr. Birenbaum." He is short and very thick and totally bald. "Everyone take your seats and be still." Some adults are seated at the sides. "Please don't eat anything until we make a *motzi*."

A poppy seed bagel is eyeing me.

Boys and girls," he says, tapping a few more times and making the sound system screech. "Welcome to YCQ. I am the head of the athletic program and assistant English principal, and I already know most of you and will soon know all the newcomers. This is the gym..."A big boy at my table muffles his laugh. Mr. Birenbaum finds him like radar and the boy blanches. I am guessing there is much more to know about Mr. Birenbaum.

"Your teachers are all here and after *motzi* and a little breakfast we will introduce our headmaster, Rabbi Charny," he continues, "and then you will line up by class with your teachers."

Rabbi Charny is wearing a white shirt, thin blue tie, a dark blue suit, and a black knitted yarmulke. Most of the men in this room have beards, but he is clean-shaven. It seems as though he has no distinctive feature. Like a big nose or a black mole on his cheek. He is tall and thick, and his hair is pitch black with sprinkles of white on the sides.

Rabbi Charny is at the podium and calls to one boy, "Ira, come up here and say a *motzi*."

Ira, about my age but taller, happily goes up to the microphone and in a high-pitched voice rapidly says the Hebrew prayer used before you eat, and then hundreds of hands flash forward for bagels and before I can react the poppy seed is gone.

Here all the boys wear leather shoes. That's what we have in common. Otherwise kids here look different, dress different, and even smell different than the kids at Chestnut Street. There are no towheads in Yeshiva—blonds with spiky strands always sticking up, like my friend Howie, who moved away during kindergarten. The kids in West Hempstead are taller, stringier, more blue-eyed, but nothing could be more different than the clothing the kids wear in one school versus the other. Here the boys almost all have black leather shoes, white shirts much too large, and thick wool pants. No jeans, polo shirts, loud socks, or sneakers.

I think I am caught by the smell most of all. Perhaps I didn't notice this before. Kids in Chestnut Street smelled as if scoured with soap and polished off just before they went to class. Here some of the boys smell like rye bread and sour cream and the girls like starch and occasionally little bits of perfume.

Rabbi Charny says, "Students, we meet here first every morning at eight-thirty for juice and bagels and go over any announcements, and then class starts at eight forty-five. I am going to introduce each of the teachers. We are very fortunate that our wonderful teachers have all returned this year."

My fifth-grade morning class will be studying Talmud for the first time. Rabbi Berkowitz, our teacher, is pot-bellied with mostly gray hair, a long wiry beard and mustache. He wears a worn black fedora, shiny black worn wool suit, rumpled white shirt with some buttons ready to pop near his belly, and no tie. He looks like the picture of Dad's father we have in the den, only fatter.

My English teacher is Mrs. Sonnenberg and a thin girl nearby seems to be elated. Mrs. Sonnenberg waves when introduced. She has very light brown hair pulled back in a rounded bun. She is probably about 40 and not yet gray and somewhat overweight everywhere, including her face and neck and even her little hands. Her skin is almost as white as mine.

I am about to go to my Talmud class on the fifth floor when Rabbi Charny comes over to me.

"Marc, can you please come into my office? It's on the first floor, and when you go in, tell Mrs. Fishman that I wish to see you."

I nod my head okay, watching the other kids spill out of the room like cheese doodles from a broken bag.

Now I am reminded of Dad's Uncle Itcha, whose apartment always smells of foods, leather, and wool. Many of these Jewish kids have clothing that is perhaps worn a few days too long. I suppose no one in this school has ever seen a Roy Rogers or John Wayne movie. Wayne often wears a leather vest. Hopalong Cassidy's felt hat is black with a perfect deep middle crease. In Yeshiva many of the male teachers have old black hats seated much too high on their heads.

Everything feels strange. I am like Flash Gordon arriving on the planet Mongo, where there are strange humanoids. And it took me more than two hours to get here.

Dad had in mind that Stephen and I get a better education. Be stronger Jews. But I can do that without Talmud. What does Talmud have to do with biology, chemistry, and physics, all necessary if we are to go to medical school? I could use the four hours of travel learning something useful instead. And why will I be a better Jew hanging around with these kids? Dad is a strong Jew and he was in Sambor, where Jews were beaten in school. It's not good to be picked on but when you are almost the only Jew in your class you get tougher. You are tested. I will fit in here less well than in West Hempstead.

The outer office is very small and Mrs. Fishman seems to know who I am.

"Just wait a minute," she says over narrow glasses. "Rabbi Charny will be out shortly."

I see an old typewriter, two four-drawer metal file cabinets with badly chipped white paint, and a huge cup with hundreds of pencils. She looks over long sheets of lists with names, probably classes and students, and fills in blank boxes in a soft-covered blue-ruled book.

Rabbi Charny pops his head from behind the rear wooden door and beckons me in with his finger. Inside he sits in a wide wooden chair behind a narrow desk and points lightly to the chair in front of it.

"Sit, Moishe," he says, using my Hebrew name.

"No. Stand up again," he orders quietly. "I don't think you have *tzitzis* under the shirt."

I don't respond.

"Do you know what they are?"

I wag my head noncommitally.

"It's like a *tallis*," he goes on, "but worn under the shirt so that an observant Jew always has it on with the four corners of the fringe with God's name near him."

Of course I have seen Hassidic Jews walking in Brooklyn with fringes hanging out under their jackets but no one said it was required here or that it was worn under the shirt.

Rabbi Charny smiles broadly and motions me to sit down.

"Look, Moishe. I know your family is not religious. I know you don't wear *tzitzis*, which for me is no problem. A Jew can be a good Jew without *tzitzis*, without being religious, so long as they are kind and care about other human beings. But it is good if a Jew acquires the language with which we have been able to survive for thousands of years, by studying, by applying the mind, and that is why I accepted you. Your mind, Moishe. We will have a very good time together. I will try to help you. So really I don't personally care if you do or don't wear them, but if you don't I'll tell you what will happen. Unfortunately, some teachers will see this and make you go to the principal's office. That's me." He laughs loudly. "Me, and then you will come in here and maybe say, 'Rabbi Charny, you said you didn't care.' But it will be back and forth and if you would just wear them, then when you come in here it can be for other things. We can speak about what you are doing, your studies and how I can help."

He pauses. "And if you go to Essex Street, close to your dad's store there is a shop that sells very thin *tzitzis* that don't make you sweat. Buy those. Is that okay?"

I nod my head yes but wonder how will they know what's under my shirt.

"So we have a deal?" He reaches over with his large firm right hand and we shake the way Cary Grant would do.

"Next order of business. I understand that you take your younger brother, Shlomo, by train and drop him off at the main building before you come here."

I guess Mom met with him separately.

"That is an enormous responsibility," he continues, "but if your mother has entrusted you then she knows what she is doing. Very smart woman." And as if reading my mind, he adds, "Don't worry. I will watch out for Stephen, and by the way I have my library there and I would like to see you about every two weeks, just the two of us, and we might chat about studies, maybe a little baseball and Talmud." He chuckles.

I would be surprised if he knows much about baseball. I could ask him what Ty Cobb's lifetime batting average is, or Grover Alexander's win-loss record. I've stopped collecting baseball cards but my 2,212 are carefully stored in alphabetical order, 552 in mint condition, from 1908 to 1912.

"Which brings me to a more difficult topic," he continues.

Now I am worried. The shoe is about to drop. All this nice chatter building me up for something I won't like. If it is too bad, then I won't do it.

I am making up my mind when he says, "Mrs. Eliafson says she was thrilled to be your tutor. You know she is our best and she said she never had a student who learned as quickly as you. She wished that there was time to study English subjects and quite frankly you are so far ahead of fifth grade. But she made a recommendation that in Hebrew it would be a mistake to begin you in fifth grade because really the whole morning is now Talmud, which isn't even in Hebrew. It's in Aramaic. But before you can study Talmud you need more basics."

I wait; the shoe is dangling.

"So she recommends you start Hebrew in first grade. She says it will be easy, and within two weeks you move on and keep advancing grades until you are ready for Talmud, and she will meet with you and decide on each progression."

He raises his chin and is silent. This was the shoe. It was inevitable. Jean Valjean was on the run for 19 years pursued by his nemesis, Inspector Javert. You never get free. There is always a catch.

Flash Gordon had it far easier. He used his super-thrusters and was off to a new asteroid in an uncharted galaxy. I have to travel four hours a day on a slow, smelly, squealing train, and then what? Back to first grade. And when I come home nothing there will change.

I WALK OUT OF THE ANNEX and take the subway again. I get off on 150th Street and enter the main building across from Rufus King Park. It is a two-story tan cinderblock building with Hebrew writing across the overhang saying Yeshiva Central Queens. The school is 12 years old and the student population has already outgrown different locations including this new building so they opened the Annex last year.

I walk to the second floor of the main building with gray tile walls and look for Room 203, which has a heavy wood door with a small window. Inside are babies at tiny desks. I timidly open the door. Little faces turn around.

"Oh, come in," Mrs. Aronson beckons. "Marc, we have saved you a seat here in the second row." They are waifs like Fantine, they are midgets and dwarfs, stupid kids who probably can't even read the alphabet. I squeeze my frame into the miniature chair connected to the little desk that slopes down and opens toward my lap.

"Welcome then, Marc. We are reviewing alphabet letters and then some Hebrew words. Whenever possible I will use the Hebrew word. *Talmid* is student. *Moreh* is teacher."

There is one boy who is really big, almost as big as me. Perhaps it is the bushy hair and big shoulders and big legs. He will be very tall, far taller than me in time, but right now he is a first grader. There is a little girl with a pathetic sorrowful face and bright teary eyes. She is already afraid and struggling with the letters. School is not for her and might never be. She reminds me of my friend Charlie Aber in our first year at Chestnut Street School. He struggled with the alphabet and spent much of the year in the dunce seat. My punishment was sitting on a tiny stool under the piano.

Now I am stuck again, in a miniature chair in first grade. If I have children it will be different.

No one laughs, thank goodness, for if they did perhaps I would burn the room, throw gasoline everywhere and toss a lit match to begin an inferno. I might do that but first I would have to pry myself out of my tight seat. ▪

CHAPTER 5

Greenpea

THE GRAY PAINT HAS MOSTLY flaked off the long narrow wooden bench, and freshly incised on its middle surface in large block letters are the initials JK. Who is he? Perhaps it is Jonathan Kaufman, or Jayson Kravitz in sixth grade. A lowly coward hiding his identity. In any event the old bench will be painted soon enough.

I detest cowards and that's why I'm in the locker room, because I will have a fight with Robert Greenberg.

I can't ever recall a time without fights. Now six weeks in this school and not a fight. No word that anyone picked on Stephen. I know a part of me misses it, the thrill that ignites in every bone, muscle, and nerve. When my fist meets someone's face a current snaps on. My hands are blurs punching left-right-left. Even if I get hit it will do no good—I won't feel it. You have no chance with someone like me. No chance. I am invincible.

Lately I have been cutting more classes and playing handball at the schoolyard near the Annex.

But handball never has the exhilaration of fighting. Nothing does.

So today is my day for a fight and Greenberg deserves what's coming.

He goes into the boys' locker room and I follow. No one else is there. A large dank cement room behind the basketball court with two rows of back-to-back rusted metal lockers and two wooden benches in front, a room that stinks worse than the rat-infested wharf streets in *David Copperfield*. Here the odors are rooted and permanent and worsen with each sweated T-shirt and reused sock, each boy dripping and coughing, and peeing in the long yellow-stained porcelain urinal in the next room. Everything reeks horribly and contradicts the idea that real athletes use this room. And so does the fact that the gym outside only has one torn basketball hoop.

The girls' adjacent locker room is similar to the boys' except for the standup urinals. I know because I sneaked inside once. They have five metal stalls and everything is a bit neater. I can picture the girls coming in to change, especially the eighth graders, especially Sandra Feldman, whose boobs are mountainous and soft.

But back to Greenberg. He is almost six inches taller than me, though about the same weight. He is stringy with thin arms and legs. His hair is shoe polish black, he has black eyes and a skinny face.

In fairness, he is good-looking except for the acne on his face and neck. There is nothing athletic about Robert but then there is nothing athletic about most of the boys here. Some play chess. A few play at basketball, which is hilarious. None play football.

I don't think I am a particularly good athlete; I barely made first string on the Little League team. But I am good at fighting.

What they do well here is verbal combat. They can argue you under a table. They can rank you out in cold blood and turn your position upside down. They are as competitive as any kids I ever met, but all with talk. They learn that in Talmud class and at home. Their parents say one thing and mean something else. One has an opinion about President Eisenhower and the other disagrees. They are jousting like the Knights of the Round Table but with words rather than long pointed sticks.

On Grand Street where Dad's store is, Jews have a way of mocking each other. They debate about everything. And usually it is all in jest.

Greenberg is the best among us. With his high-pitched nasal voice, he has wounded half the kids in class. Sometimes he cuts them down with word cleavers. He is not a very good student but at verbal combat he is unequaled. This was okay until he made the grave error of aiming his insults at me. He mocked me repeatedly in the first weeks of class: my clothing, my red hair, my Long Island accent, my haircut. Always in front of others.

I am not sure why I found this so difficult. I guess because I am not like the other kids. They are religious. They are mostly puffy boys who wear baggy wool pants and prayer shawls under their white shirts. I am an outsider with bright red hair and clothes from Harry's on East Broadway and shirts from Orchard Street. Most don't even follow any sports.

I just can't get used to this.

I tried to fire back. I always hated green peas, which is probably why I started calling him Greenpea, hoping to upset him, but he found it funny. How do you win when the opposition is not offended?

I am good at arguments but Greenpea is a pro. Compared to him I am bush league. When I make fun of his hair, his acne, his awkward walk, none of it sticks.

"Sure I have acne," he says, "So what? It will go away and you will still have that ridiculous hair."

In West Hempstead things are clearer. You tease me enough, or you hit my brother, you will wind up fighting me sooner or later.

Nothing with Greenberg has worked, and in the last few days I watched for my opportunity. That day is now, a dreadfully hot day in a stinking locker room where he is changing slowly and no one else is here.

"Ah, Greenpea," I say coming closer. "We are alone." He barely glances at me and continues with his socks and shoes.

"We are alone now," I repeat, "and it is time to end what was started."

He lifts his befuddled face.

"What?" he asks guardedly.

"To finish, Greenpea."

"Finish what?" he asks, his voice quivering slightly.

"You make fun of me and tease me and we will finish it."

"I don't understand," he says.

"We will fight."

"Fight?" he repeats. "Why?"

"Because you keep doing it."

"Why fight?" he asks, as his lips and cheeks tremble with fear.

I have seen this many times. When the opposition is frightened before you begin it makes it much easier to win.

"That is what you do," I say firmly. "You fight and someone wins and someone loses."

"No, no," he cries. "I was just joking."

"It's not a joke when you make fun of people."

"It's what I do," he pleads. "I do this with everyone. I don't mean anything."

"It is nasty and you wouldn't stop."

"And you call me Greenpea. It's the same."

"It's not the same. And I won't argue about it. Stand up and we will have a fight, Greenberg." I almost say Greenpea.

His whole body is shaking now, and he says, "I will never do this again. Never."

"It's too late."

"It won't happen again, I promise."

"Let's go over there," I point behind me. "There's more room."

"But I don't fight," he pleads.

"What do you mean?"

"I never fought. I never fight. I just say things. That's all. I don't mean harm. I didn't know."

"Too late."

"I am sorry. It will never happen again."

"Good. Then we will have one fight there and it's over."

"No! I won't fight! You want to hit me? I won't fight back."

I look more carefully at Greenberg now, the red acne spots, a large new open one on his chin. His hair is hanging in tangles over his ears.

I have never encountered anyone like him. Boys fight. The idea is to never have to do it twice. You have to win convincingly. The older they are, the more humiliated when they lose. Once I fight them they stay away from Stephen and me. It is how things are ended. Perhaps I will hit him really hard just on his shoulder and he will never forget.

He is slumping further down on the bench. Then he stares up right into my eyes and I feel really uncomfortable.

I turn and walk out. ▪

CHAPTER 6

Sugar Ray

THE TREES IN EARLY NOVEMBER seem to accept their fate. Leaves fall down even before all yellow.

I've just finished Hebrew with the fourth graders. My last grade jump and soon I am out of there. But now I have about an hour and a half till fifth-grade English at the Annex, 40 blocks away. Why not walk? A new route.

Atlantic Avenue is so much quieter than Jamaica Avenue, which rumbles and screeches with the overhead subway. A couple of older men in shirtsleeves sit in front of a bar smoking Camels. Many of the storefronts are boarded up. In front of a two-story building a young Negro man passed out in a doorway coughs like a chainsaw.

Near Lefferts Boulevard four Negro boys are standing by the light pole laughing heartily. As I come near they stop their banter and turn to me as one. The shortest one, about my height, with the longest hair, has a deep frown. I've seen that look too many times. But I'm not going to change my path; that never does any good.

"Hey, Whitebread," he says pointing at me when I am about five feet away. "What you thinking you be doing here?" he says laughing.

I stop. No use running. Negro boys run much faster. Like Jesse Owens in the 1936 Olympics. I say nothing and look at him more closely, at the same time taking in all four, who are likely about two years older than me. This kid has on worn black chinos and a very soiled red polo shirt, much too large. His hair is knotted in several places.

"Whitebread," he says ever so slowly, getting a good laugh from his pals. "I don't think you been here before."

I extend my hand. "I'm Marc."

He almost reaches out and pulls back quickly. "Shit. What you think you doing?"

"Shaking your hand."

"Shit," he repeats, guffawing, and the one to his immediate left mumbles, "I ain't seen nuttin'."

"Shut the fuck up!"

The largest boy pushes out in front. He's the leader. More than a head taller than me, with skin so black it looks tinged with purple. Acne on his cheeks and long, long fingers and his oversize pants held up with a wide black leather belt.

He steps within arm's length, a distance I ordinarily wouldn't tolerate, but there is still uncertainty here.

"Fucking redhead from Mars," he chuckles loudly.

"Yeah, pretty rare," I agree, "even in my school."

"Are you staring at me, Whitebread?" he says, tightening his mouth into a hard line.

"I guess so," I say. "I never had a Negro in any of my schools."

"That be me. A Nee Grow."

I don't respond.

"But you a Whitebread who not be afraid."

"No, I'm not afraid," I say, mostly truthfully, now wondering if I came this way hoping for a fight.

"Then you be a very stupid kid, Mr. Redhead." He laughs like an old lawn mower starting up.

But my odds here are really bad. "I'll fight if you want," I offer. "But you're older and way bigger than me so how about one-on-one?"

Only one car has gone by and all four boys are sneering. I've invaded their territory, which is a cracked cement sidewalk in front of a store with a tattered red awning.

"Shit, Whitebread. We should just all beat your skinny white ass for coming here."

"But then what?" I answer, getting close to him. "You'll tell your friends that four boys twice my size beat me up? I'll fight you and my skinny ass will show you how a redhead fights!"

I take a half step closer and he jolts a half a step back.

A calm slow feeling seeps in like when I am standing chest deep in the ocean at Rockaway Beach and ahead a new wave begins to build.

"I go to a school on 104th Street," I say, "and classes start in an hour so I'm walking this way. Actually, I hate going there. It's a religious school. And I have to travel four hours a day."

"Oh, shit," another one chimes in, a boy with a shaved head glistening in the sun. "Shit, four fuckin' hours. Insane, my man."

"Two trains and I have to take my younger brother and the classroom stinks. The gym has only one broken hoop."

"Oh man, I wouldn't go," he says. "And I don't," he adds proudly.

"Yeah, well some days I don't either. I hang out and play handball."

"Whitebread plays handball?" the tallest one says, hiking both shoulders up.

"Good left and right," I brag.

"Whitey, you want to play for some bread?"

I look at him.

"Money, boy. Two bucks! Then if you win I don't beat you up."

"I don't have money with me," I say. "It's in my locker at school. But I'll play you. Do you have a ball?"

"You shitting me?" he asks. "A hard Negro ball."

Everyone laughs.

"I'm going to win," I say. "And I don't like sore losers."

"You don't have to worry 'bout that," says the fourth boy. He's got khaki pants and a thin black bandana knotted around his neck.

"I'm Marc," I say to the tall one, the leader.

He extends his hand, large, with small calloused from lots of handball. This won't be easy.

"Skull," he says grinning ear to ear.

"And you?" I ask the shortest.

"Sugar Ray," he says, raising his chin two notches.

"Sugar Ray," I repeat. "The finest boxer in history."

"Still Champeen of the World."

"He retired," I correct. "But he beat LaMotta five times."

"Of course he beat that White Boy."

"You get that ball," I say to Skull. "And watch a White Boy beat you."

"Oh this is goin' be fun," Skull laughs. "Mr. Marc. This is goin' be great fun," and everyone is laughing, and we turn right on Lefferts. ∎

CHAPTER 7

Chess

A ROUTINE HAS SET IN. The commute, the subway. Stephen seems to be okay.

I am back in English class five minutes before it begins. Kenny Siegel and Paul Slater are in the rear playing chess. Paul is unaware he is three moves away from checkmate and there is only one possible move to avoid that fate and even then it would be a hard slog back into the game. Kenny's face furrows up slightly and just as Paul misses the correct move, Mrs. Sonnenberg walks in.

Kenny says, "Okay, Paul, let's put it away?"

"We can finish later," Paul pleads.

"Naw," Kenny says in his tin-can voice that I now easily recognize. "Let's call it."

"I play chess," I tell Kenny casually as we take our seats.

"Really." He smiles. "Are you any good?"

"Enough to know you were three moves away from mating Paul."

"Yeah," Kenny guffaws. "He still doesn't see it."

"Do you play every day?"

"I wish. It's hard to get a good game. There is a sixth grader I often play."

"Okay then," I respond. "Let's see how I do."

"I never see you here at recess," he says smiling brightly.

I don't respond.

"Okay, let's play tomorrow," Kenny quickly suggests as Mrs. Sonnenberg begins writing on the blackboard.

Kenny is slightly taller than me with light wavy brown hair and a very pale complexion. He looks like he was never out in the sun even though he could probably tan. He is one of the quieter kids in class. He is a really good student but doesn't call attention to himself and he hardly gets called on in class, and when he does he often begins by saying, "I think the answer is...."

He is also cautious playing chess. Against Paul he took his time building up a strong defense and it's difficult to beat a good defensive player.

No one played chess at Chestnut Street School. Whenever we went to Brighton Beach Baths in the summer I played Dad and some of the older kids. I have read a few chess books Mrs. Mahoney loaned me from the Hempstead Library but often I have to play against myself.

Brighton Beach Baths is a private club where all the members are Jewish immigrants. The men play chess and pinochle all day. Many of the adults have blue tattoo numbers on their forearms. I didn't know what that was at first but of course now I do. I remember staring too long at one older woman with deeply tanned skin wrinkled from all the sun. She had only five numbers, 19332, the fewest I had seen. She looked up and smiled, "It's a lucky number I guess."

MOM'S OLDER BROTHER, Uncle Hy, told me that before Dad she dated Samuel Rashevsky, the U.S. chess champion, who wanted to marry her. I can imagine that if they were married he would have a hard time practicing chess at home. She would always be smoking, cleaning, and vacuuming under his feet.

I don't know how Dad got to be so good at chess. But he is the best at Brighton Beach and I still can't beat him after hundreds of games. Recently I have been reading about various strategic defenses, which are different depending if you play Black or White. The Sicilian Defense only works well when White opens with the king pawn advancing two rows.

I am getting close now and once I win it will be curtains for Dad.

I drop Stephen at the main building the next day. I get the subway as soon as Hebrew ends and am in the Annex an hour before English classes start. Kenny is waiting as we agreed, the board set up. He looks happy to see me and as I approach he takes a white pawn and puts his hands behind his back and then extends them in front. I tap his left. No pawn and Kenny opens his right hand with the pawn.

"I take White," he says.

I ease myself into a small chair. Kenny is concentrating and we haven't moved yet. He opens with his king pawn: 1e4, the most common opening on the planet, and I follow immediately with the Sicilian Defense and move the bishop pawn on the queen side: 1c5. Kenny is baffled at first but counters for a quick checkmate, which works if Black isn't careful, but that opens him up to lose a pawn in the middle.

Then the game really slows down and I have to hold myself back from making a hasty mistake. Fifty minutes pass and neither of us has said a word. By now several classmates surround us. No one has ever given Kenny a good game. When he finally makes another move, Ira Bernstein clicks his tongue and Kenny looks up and shouts, "Just shut up or move away!"

Mrs. Sonnenberg is in and everyone moves to their seats. Kenny says, "I can keep the board as it is and we can finish tomorrow."

"That's okay," I tell him. "Let's start a new game tomorrow."

Kenny smiles widely and takes his seat in the far left row, third seat.

In West Hempstead the kids my age frequently talked about baseball. They all rooted for the Yankees and Micky Mantle was their hero. No one spoke about books or current events. I doubt many knew the name of the President. Certainly, none knew who the Vice President was. The Korean War was never mentioned, nor the Rosenbergs.

In Yeshiva the kids came from families like mine. As I come to know them I learn most have small businesses like Dad's. Many like him are immigrants. Kenny's father was born in the U.S. and owns a small printing business near the Queensboro Bridge and they live in Westbury, Long Island. Kenny is driven to school each day by his dad.

All the Yeshiva families are deeply interested in Israel. Many of the kids hope someday to go to Israel to study. There are noisy kids and quiet kids like Kenny and most are smart like him.

Over the next weeks I usually come back as quickly as I can to the Annex to play chess with Kenny rather than playing handball with my friends Skull and Sugar Ray. By now Skull and I are an unbeatable doubles team. I am on the left up front and Skull plays deep and to the right. He is tall and moves like liquid. Everyone laughs that his partner is a smaller white kid. Until they lose. ▪

CHAPTER 8

Charlie and
The Squirrel

IN ONE WEEK, THANKSGIVING. This evening, darkening quickly, I read *Wuthering Heights*, which has no excitement, no battles, no war, no land of the giants, no landing on an uncharted island where no one can find you and you have to survive. The book was recommended by Mrs. Mahoney at the Hempstead Library, who usually knows what I will like, but this book is as slow as my train ride.

Time ticks so slowly it almost stands still. As monotonous as Mom's metronome on the Steinway piano.

Somehow, I always know the exact time. I awaken a minute before I am supposed to. When I was two years old and living in Borough Park, Brooklyn, Mom would send me outside right after breakfast and tell me to return for lunch at exactly 12:15. I couldn't tell time when I was two. I rode around the same streets on my tricycle and returned to the apartment building exactly on time.

Now the four hours of commute a day is routine but painful. I hate getting up early. It is up at 5:30 a.m., catch the 6:22 train at Lakeview, drop Stephen off at school at 7:40, Hebrew class for me at 8:15 a.m. Leave at 11:00, maybe play handball or chess for an hour, then English in the Annex at 12:45 p.m.

I have campaigned to skip breakfast and save 15 minutes. I hate soft-boiled eggs and oatmeal anyway. But no luck.

On the return trip we are picked up by Mom at the Lakeview station or we walk 20 minutes. We arrive home close to 7:15 p.m. and then dinner and a shower and by then Stephen is fast asleep.

By now Miriam is a ghost; we whisk by each other now and then. I miss talking to her even though it's always about new boys in school.

Last May, when Miriam turned 13, Mom decided that Miriam was old enough to be our babysitter. That was fine with me because most of the babysitters were 15 and clueless. What Mom didn't know was that as soon as we were left alone Miriam would get panicky and tell me I had to go to the basement and make sure there was no bogeyman.

"What if there is?" I would ask her. "Then he is going to kill me."

"Just go now. Hurry!" she'd say, flapping her hands and half-covering her eyes. And if I didn't go she would never let up.

Checking for the bogeyman means going downstairs to the basement coal room with our large furnace. It will never matter how many times I report back there is no one there.

Mom mentioned at breakfast this morning that Saturday night she and Dad have to go to a dinner party, so Miriam will be babysitting. Miriam looked at me with her squinty eyes. If only Mom knew Miriam is the biggest scaredy-cat and it's me always watching out for her.

I hardly ever see Grandma Katy, Mom's mother. I don't even have time with Twinkie. I am getting less sleep than Huck Finn on Jackson's Island in the Mississippi. At least the Yankees beat the Dodgers in the World Series—Mantle hit a two-run homer and a grand slam.

On the train Stephen is always deep in his thoughts so I give him some easy readers to take. He is small for his age and even lighter skinned than me. Everything about him is slight. I have dark brown eyes like Dad's, but Stephen's are aqua blue exactly like Mom's. He looks a lot like her and Grandpa Max, who died when Stephen was two.

We have been commuting now for more than two months and he never complains. I know he has opinions but with him they are tucked in a deep crevice. Unlike me, he takes no chances. He will rarely try something new unless I can assure him it's safe, and I can't lie because then there would be no one for him to trust.

Stephen is the quietest kid I know. What I worry about is if he is being picked on. I don't think he is. There are several kids at YCQ who are quiet like Stephen and I am thinking it might be better for him in this new school.

At least Stephen isn't in a lower grade in Hebrew.

At the start of the school year, Mom went with us to the Long Island Railroad station on Sutphin Boulevard and bought us one-month passes. Now I do this by myself. Two tickets for children under 12.

Public school is free and Yeshiva means paying tuition and the cost of the trains. Mom has been trying to get West Hempstead to pay for private transportation for us the same way it does for kids who go to Catholic school. I hear her on the phone one afternoon with her best friend, Adele Small.

"The Catholic Church has the power," Mom says. "Sam went to the school board, and they just made excuses. Believe me I am not done with them."

The school board has no idea that sooner or later they will lose. For two years now Mom has been the head of Hadassah at Temple Beth Israel. She organized the chapter's first rummage sale and the other women made the mistake of telling her that a rummage sale would never work, people wouldn't spend money on stuff stores no longer wanted or used items people donated.

It was a huge success.

Dad usually eats dinner alone because he gets home so late. One night he is concentrating on the *New York Post* and sucking on a chicken bone and Mom says, "Their damn rule is that the other school has to be within ten miles of home and they say they measured and the yeshiva is twelve-point-two miles." Dad seems not to have heard her. He laughs at something Leonard Lyons wrote.

"Damn it, Sam. They made the rule because a couple of Catholic kids go to a school in Elmont."

"Yeah, where all the cemeteries are," Dad mumbles.

"I am going to fight this."

"That's the rule," he says, "and they won't make an exception."

"When I finish with them they will."

Dad looks up briefly and says, "Find a shortcut."

I think the shortcut is we move to Queens, but no one discusses that.

It was Dad's idea we switch schools but now it's Mom's problem to solve.

Since I was five and working in Dad's store, traffic to the city has steadily been getting worse, and Dad is always looking for new shortcuts. Once we got stuck on a dead-end street in Queens.

Three days later Mom announces to Dad at dinner, "I have it down to ten-point-three miles now."

Dad hardly looks up. "Draw a straight line on a map and see how far that is."

Mom is really angry but the next night she announces, "I did it! Damn them all. I have it down to nine-point-eight miles and I did it twice." Dad is reading his *Post* and Mom yells, "And you didn't do a damn thing!"

Dad fights back by ignoring her. I am not sure he cares whether we go by train or bus.

A school board official then makes the trip with Mom in his own car using Mom's route, in case our odometer is *Jewed up*. But sure enough, his odometer also measures 9.8 miles.

I am surprised Mom doesn't punch him. If she did they would need to start over with another school official.

Mom then hires a man named Charlie to take us to school in his van. But the matter still isn't settled. The school district requires that there be at least six kids in the van and that means Mom has to find four more who go to the yeshiva. Finally, Mom is able to get the four, but only three mornings a week. The other two mornings, the train.

I am hoping I can sleep later now but no such luck. We get picked up first, and then one by one, in a complicated route, four more kids come on. The trip is now 20 minutes longer and there is not much money saved since we were already saving money by buying monthly kids' tickets.

Maybe Dad guessed all this. But now that she has permission for the van, Mom will never back down.

Worse yet, I can't read in the van because I get nauseous and would vomit.

IT'S BEEN ALMOST TWO WEEKS with the van. This morning I quickly put out Twinkie's food and grab Stephen, hardly awake, when we hear the honk in front of our house.

Charlie's tan van was made for deliveries but now he has put in six extra seats he can easily remove. This way he does his deliveries and makes extra money driving kids. Stephen and I scoot into the two seats behind Charlie. There are three seats behind us and one in front next to him and lots of storage space behind the last row.

There is a thin sheen of dew on our front lawn and the sky has a glimmer of first sunlight on the deep black. The days are short and as we board Charlie's van for the fifth time we wish we could sleep but I have never fallen asleep in a car or a train and Stephen is the same.

Charlie turns left down Dogwood Avenue and then right on Fenworth toward Franklin Square. I know his route now but instead of going another two blocks he turns right and slows down. This street is much older than ours in West Hempstead; the trees are tall and bare of leaves. Huge oaks and maples rising several stories above homes much larger than ours, each one different, some gabled. Finally, Charlie comes to a stop under a red oak on the left side. There are no cars leaving for work, no dogs being walked.

Charlie moves his head right to left as though he is a periscope on a submarine. Then he turns to me and says, "I need to take a three-minute break."

"Okay," I agree, thinking he needs to take a quick pee. What else is there to do but go on the side of the van near the wide-trunked tree?

It is still only Stephen and me, and Charlie reaches and opens his large glove compartment. I wonder why they call it a glove compartment when I have never seen gloves kept there.

Charlie retrieves something with his right hand and does nothing to disguise it. It is a black pistol. He balances it in his hand, seeming to check its weight.

"It's a pistol," he says. Then waits. "I shoot squirrels. I am not the kind of person who does this just for sport. I shoot them and then eat them."

He is looking at me but I am partially frozen staring at the gun.

Until now, he has probably not spoken ten words to us. Charlie is about Dad's age, perhaps a few years older, and just as dark, and his hair is also black, but much blacker if that is possible, and his seems thicker and is longer over the neck and ears.

His eyes are deep blue beneath very thick eyebrows and above a full nose, thin lips, and a cleft chin. I don't really know how tall he is. Today he wears a checked wool shirt and thick brown cord pants with a brown belt.

Stephen is frozen-faced staring at the gun. He might cry. Charlie loads something into the pistol handle and turns a screw.

"I shoot squirrels," he says, "and I don't miss. I don't like to injure them and then leave them to die."

I don't respond.

"Look," he explains, "I have to do this quickly while there is little light, and I can't be late getting all of you to school or I lose my job."

He hesitates. "Are you okay? Is it okay if I go out and shoot a squirrel?" Stephen is still petrified. "If you don't want me to I won't, but if you say it's okay then I need your promise."

"What's that?" I respond.

"That you don't tell anyone, none of the other kids. That you tell your brother not to talk. If anyone finds out, you know your mother will fire me or worse. So only if you are okay with this. I mean the Indians only killed animals for food, not like the White Man who butchered almost all the buffalo. I eat them and really it's not so strange. I like squirrel and I save money on food."

He waits and perhaps it is only seconds but it feels so slowed down. I want to think about shooting an animal. No one in my family ever did that. We went fishing at times off Captain Jack's boat out of Sheepshead Bay in Brooklyn but even then I would not pull a hook out of a fish's mouth. I couldn't stand seeing the mouth gaping and the fish dying out of the water. Charlie is different than us, just like Indians are, and cowboys who drive cattle in Montana. But then we are different than almost everyone in West Hempstead. Mr. Mitchell next door owns a shotgun and Robbie Davis told me his dad has three pistols and a rifle. "Jews don't have guns," Dad once said, and so far as I know it's true, but no one has explained why.

"Okay," I say, looking squarely at him.

Charlie looks grateful. "And your brother won't tell?"

"No, he won't," I promise, looking at Stephen.

It is a promise I can keep. Stephen is seven in a week and will not go against me. It is a matter of trust. I never break my word with him, and he has seen worse than this and never speaks about it.

"You can come out and watch if you wish," Charlie coaxes me.

Charlie quickly opens his door and goes behind the van, looking around again, and I open our door and step out as the sky is brightening with thin orange streaks.

"Up there," he points with his left index finger. I see nothing.

"The electric wire past that tree," he continues, and there perched near the far end of the wire is a bushy-tailed squirrel, poised for something, and if he doesn't move quickly he will be shot and eaten.

Charlie raises his pistol.

"A very high-powered pellet gun," he whispers, beckoning me closer. He lifts it with his right hand now outstretched and looks down the sight.

A quick pop and nothing happens.

"I hope I didn't wound it," Charlie says, and then all at once the squirrel rolls over 180 degrees off the wire and drops, gray hair lost among the thick branches. Charlie hurries to the back of the van, opens it, and retrieves a small burlap sack. Then he scoots up the street between some trees and in just a few seconds returns with the bag now loaded with a new weight in its bottom.

"Clean shot right through the head. Through the head, goddamn it," he grins widely with thick white teeth. Doors close and he starts the engine and accelerates quickly. I know we are only two blocks from the next stop and in the burlap sack in the rear is a dead squirrel that no one else will know about.

I know now that this will be repeated, that Charlie will stop many more times to shoot a squirrel. You know these things in advance just as you know Buck will eventually go off on his own in *Call of the Wild*. You know that Tonto will always be loyal to the Lone Ranger even if that is fiction. Still, I feel now I've seen something a Jewish boy would likely never see. I will go to the yeshiva today in the Annex and tonight Charlie will clean and cook his squirrel. ▪

CHAPTER 9

Brown Bag

IT'S NOVEMBER 28TH, the Saturday after Thanksgiving, and school is a vacuum cleaner sucking every second of my life.

I am home on a frigid day. The window frost is streaked like hundreds of scars. Twinkie is still out roaming the neighborhood. I go to try to find my old friends from Chestnut Street School, Stewie Garber and Charlie Aber. Mrs. Aber says Charlie is in Garden City helping out at his dad's grocery store and no one answers at Stewie's house. The small blue ranch house at the end of Bedell Terrace by the Long Island Railroad tracks is more run down. Shingles from the roof are scattered on the lawn, which is now sprouting tall ugly weeds. I knock again and look in the rear living room window.

It is dark inside. Only the brown fabric couch remains in the living room with much larger rips than I recall, made by their cat, but now one of the front legs is also missing. The kitchen has no food on the counter.

I worry the Garbers have moved and I won't see Stewie again. There is no one like him at Yeshiva of Central Queens, really no one like him at Chestnut Street School. Rail thin and never shying away from a fracas and the only kid I knew who took larger dares than me. In truth, I hardly saw him the last two years in public school. We were in different classes and our hideout on Woodfield Road had become three homes, our peashooters long gone. I spent most of my free days the last two years working in the store.

The yeshiva is a different universe, no Stewie daredevils, no one who would wade into the middle of my fight against a group of kids two years older and go back to back with me.

Back home Stephen is in the garage, building yet another contraption. He is small and thin but he looks most like Uncle Joe, the second of Grandma Katy's five kids. He is redheaded and almost six feet tall. We haven't seen Uncle Joe in six months. Last year his wife and two daughters were in a car accident and Lana, the youngest and my age, was killed. His wife was driving and she didn't yet have a driver's license. Uncle Joe left her and lived with us for five months, didn't go to work and built things with Stephen. The two never spoke. Just hammer, saw, and nails, and then Joe suddenly left and moved back home. Stephen cried for two days.

It is late afternoon and I come into the house to go to the bathroom. Mom is at the kitchen sink scrubbing pots, her face and neck shiny and sweaty. I hear Stephen in the den and then he is in the kitchen holding a long narrow brown paper bag with a little clip on top. It is something I haven't seen before.

He is opening and closing it, attempting to figure out how it works. He pulls on a metal band across the top and then it suddenly comes off and drops to the yellow linoleum floor. Mom swings around from the sink and Stephen drops to the floor covering his head and screaming.

"What the hell did you do?" Mom yells over him. He is all curled up in a tight ball holding his hands over his head and screeching in shrill gasps.

"Shut your mouth!" she yells closer to him, and if Stephen could, he would vanish under the tiles.

"That is my vacuum cleaner bag! They are expensive and you have broken it!"

I guess the bag is for Mom's new Hoover vacuum. It is supposed to pick up any dirt but there isn't a vacuum on the planet that picks up enough dirt for her. It is kept in the broom closet.

Mom's knotted-up face is blotched red and white.

"Damn it to hell!" she yells and goes to the broom closet and reaches inside.

The thick brown belt with a wide buckle is on its hook to the far right. It has been used many times but only on me. Sometimes there is some warning like now, but there are times with no hint, and then it is worse and the beating won't stop until she is completely expended.

Never Miriam, who covers her eyes if she is around when I am beaten.

Never Stephen, who has also seen several beatings and always lies down and shrieks.

Today it is finally his turn as Mom approaches him with raised strap.

"Don't!" I yell.

She barely manages to hold her swing and for a moment is frozen and confused. She is still glaring down at Stephen, whose screams have reached a new intensity.

"I did it. I took out the bag and gave it to him," I say.

Her head shifts so slowly, the pupils of her blue eyes are barely pinpricks. She is all sweat with her mouth open and lower teeth showing.

"I gave it to him," I repeat.

Then in two steps she is near me by the fridge.

As she raises the strap even higher, I face her stiffly.

I have never turned away. I can't recall ever crying and I won't cry today. The first beating I remember was just before I was two. And they continued, but I thought they had ended when I started this new school in September. None since early June. Or was it April?

I am ten and much bigger now and very strong. No one in fifth or even sixth grade can beat me in arm wrestling.

The strap comes down like a sickle ripping at my left shoulder. Then my left arm. My mind is already floating away. I am in the waves on Rockaway Beach and the lifeguard has just whistled. Get out of the water, the undertow is too dangerous. But I watch for the next big wave to come in. I will duck under it. It will be fabulous. ∎

PART TWO

COWS AND FENCES

CHAPTER 10

Baba Kamma

MOST OF THE TIME AT HOME Dad is like Harpo Marx. Silent. The only time Dad laughs is when he reads the newspaper or watches TV, especially the Milton Berle Texaco Hour. He laughs so hard he chokes.

At the store Dad talks nonstop. He is always talking politics. Eisenhower is president almost a year now. Dad thinks he plays golf all the time except when he sits behind a White House desk twiddling his thumbs.

Dad makes a lot of jokes, most of them mocking Jews. All the Jewish storekeepers do that. It's the ugly girl in the Polish town or the dim-witted rabbi who is happy-go-lucky and whenever someone asks his advice he smiles and shrugs. The king of television is Milton Berle and everyone knows he is Jewish. Dad also loves Jack Benny and George Burns. All Jews who play parts where they seem foolish, but they aren't. They are making millions of dollars on TV. Last year Jerry Lewis and Dean Martin made the movie *The Stooge*. Martin played the straight guy and Lewis, who is Jewish, played an idiot. People at the Calderone Theater laughed almost the whole time but I didn't like it. Why is it funny that someone is stupid?

The one program I always try to see is *The Lone Ranger*. I mean who takes seriously a guy in a white hat, wearing a black mask, riding around on a white horse? But the real hero is Tonto, his Indian sidekick, who is calm and has all the good ideas.

After reading *The Last of the Mohicans*, I root for the Indians. I saw a movie about Custer's Last Stand. Really, he was stupid for underestimating Chief Sitting Bull and he deserved to lose. The Indian land was stolen and all their buffalo were killed.

I told that to Dad, who said that Senator Joseph McCarthy is worse than General George Custer. Dad says that McCarthy is running a witch hunt and the whole country is silent. Writers and scientists lose their jobs because they are accused of being Communists and it doesn't matter that there is no proof and almost all of them are Jews. "Silence kills," Dad says. "We should have learned the danger of silence."

I've moved up to fifth grade in Hebrew and that means no more shuffling back and forth from the main building to the Annex. Now I spend much of my break time playing chess with Kenny Siegel. He is so happy having a good game and doesn't seem to mind if he loses. Recently he invited me to his house for a Friday-night-to-Sunday-morning sleepover. "We can play at least five times," Kenny said.

Mom surprised me by agreeing.

Kenny doesn't know about my fighting. No one does except maybe Greenberg, but we never actually had a fight. Jews don't have guns and they don't fight. That's what people say. I think if Kenny knew he wouldn't be my friend.

By now I also spend more time with Ira Bernstein, who keeps up on politics, which no kid did in West Hempstead. I doubt they knew the name of our Governor. Mitchell Cooper is exactly my height but so much thinner and with straight black hair and a neat part on the right. He never talks against another kid.

There are eight girls in my afternoon English class taught by Mrs. Sonnenberg. One is Ellen Gordon, who is thin and dark with short hair, always in print dresses and always with a big smile. Her twin brother, Harvey, is also in our class, but Harvey is quiet and doesn't have friends.

In the mornings I am now in Rabbi Shlomo Berkowitz's Talmud class. I already missed over two months. No girls. Kenny says they do Home Economics, which means cooking kosher food. I would rather be climbing down a rope from the 86th floor of the Empire State Building.

"Okay, boychiks," Rabbi Berkowitz says, clapping loudly and pacing up front. *"Daf gimmel.* David, begin second line of today's *Mishna."* They are studying *Baba Kamma,* one of the 63 volumes of

Talmudic Jewish law. Rabbi Charny told me it's the easiest and we always start there.

Rabbi Berkowitz hesitates and quickly comes over to me and hands me his large Talmud book and points to the place.

"You missed two months," he says. "David. *Nu*, let's go."

Rabbi Berkowitz's pants are belted tightly far below his big belly, which pops a white shirt button near the bottom. No tie, worn black leather shoes, and a large black yarmulke aslant to the right, which he keeps adjusting. His black beard is thick and comes down below his neck.

"Read, read!" he demands and David struggles. The largest lettered words are in a box in the middle top of the page. This is the Mishna, with large Hebrew letters and no vowels. Rabbi Berkowitz repeats the line and it sounds a bit different than Hebrew.

He obviously sees my difficulty and says, "It's Aramaic, not Hebrew. The Babylonian Talmud was written in Aramaic. Why, boys?"

Johnny yells out, "Because the Jews were in *galut*. In Babylonia."

"Yes, and we are in *galut* now because we are not in *Eretz Yisrael*. Right?"

"We are on 104th Street in the Annex," Sammy Moskowitz says, and everyone chuckles, including the rabbi.

"It is Aramaic," he repeats looking at me, "and we can't go back two months, so you just have to do the best you can. First come up here for a second."

I cautiously walk to his desk and he grabs the corner of my shirt.

"You got *tzitzis* on?" he asks gruffly. I look down hopelessly.

"Go to the principal, boychik. Right now!"

Rabbi Charny is in and I am signaled to enter and sit down quickly.

"First day Talmud?" he asks.

"It's Aramaic, Rabbi Charny," I say.

"Of course, Aramaic. We don't change the original. I know you missed two months, but you will pick it up quickly."

I am thinking that will be impossible when he says, "So why are you here, Moishe?"

"*Tzitzis*," I say.

"Yes, *tzitzis*."

No use telling him that I meant to buy them the few times I worked at the store and forgot.

He yells out to Mrs. Fishman, "Give him a note! Yes, of course. Go back to class and wear them by Monday or you will be here again."

Howard is now reading the second line.

"What is the *Mishna* saying?" Rabbi Berkowitz demands. Kenny knows. I can see that. Ira Bernstein raises his hand.

"That it makes a difference if the cow has a history of goring."

"Yes, yes," Berkowitz says elated. "Yes. So if the owner of the cow that gored and killed a neighbor's cow knows his cow has a history of goring other cows then he bears greater responsibility. How much does he pay?"

"The full value of the gored cow?" Howard responds.

"Why not more?" Rabbi Berkowitz asks. "After all, should he not pay an extra penalty because his cow had a history of goring?"

Then we had lots of back and forth and he asked under what circumstances might the owner pay less than full price.

"Less if the owner of the gored cow had a broken fence he should have repaired," Paul Slater said.

"Good. Good. Now boychiks, let's see what follows. Mitchell, read the next line of *Mishna*."

Mitchell struggles and Rabbi Berkowitz is impatient and reads the next seven words slowly as though he loves each word and now I can understand my first words in Aramaic.

"So now we have a new question, a *mashal*," he says with a singsong inflection, stroking his beard with his right hand. "So the owner of the gored cow has a fence which is need of repair. There is a big gap and he knew about this and two months ago another cow crossed through here and gored another cow of his. Should he be paid now? Wasn't it his responsibility to fix that gap?"

I left fourth-grade Hebrew and now enter a new planet where we debate about cows and fences and recompense and the differences between public and private property and a part of me is wondering why all the fuss? Is this what Jews do? For 2,500 years? And they got chased out of Spain, debating cows and fences? Did it save them from the Holocaust?

Three hours pass and Rabbi Berkowitz is twisting and turning and pulling his beard with broken fences and untimely repairs and a cow's police record.

I remember visiting Uncle Itcha's apartment in Brooklyn when I was five and meeting Chaim, a Hasidic boy my age with long black side curls who by then knew six books of Talmud by heart, but what really disheartened me is that he knew every statistic of every current Yankee player, too. Uncle Itcha said that Chaim was going to be the Grand Rabbi someday.

Jews value learning. But if that's why I am going to this new school now, then why was I stranded in Chestnut Street School for five years? It was worse than terrible there. And now I need tzitzis and am in an annex in Queens debating about a fence? Dad wants me to go to medical school and to do that I first have to study badly behaving cows?

At the end of class Mrs. Fishman is outside waiting for me. "Rabbi Charny wants to see you, Marc."

Rabbi Charny beckons me in. "So Moishe," he says getting up from his desk and pointing to a chair on my side. "Today you started learning like a Jew. How was it?"

"Lots about cows and fences," I say.

"Exactly," he laughs. "That is the beginning. *Baba Kamma*, and from here is the journey of the mind. You think it's law about cows, right? No, it's the beginning of a discipline to learn to think independently, to ask questions, to not take simple answers at face value. You will love this class. Give it time, Moishe." ∎

CHAPTER 11

Stippled Herring

I T'S THE FIRST WEEK OF DECEMBER and mid-Chanukah, which lasts eight days, and some lucky kids get a present each day. No such luck with us. When we were little in Hebrew school they told us Chanukah is eight days because 2,000 years ago when the Maccabee brothers liberated Jerusalem and rededicated the Temple they only had enough lamp oil for one day but it lasted eight days.

I think a real miracle would be if the oil had lasted a whole year and then Chanukah would be 365 days.

A few more weeks of school and then vacation until 1954.

Charlie's van isn't heated and by the time we drop Stephen off he looks like a blue popsicle. Stephen always takes snacks to school, usually an apple and a thin peanut butter and jelly sandwich. School lunch is terrible. Everything is disguised in a thick yellow sauce. Maybe one day it's an old chicken mashed up with skin, maybe another it's leftovers from the deli owned by Schmulka Bernstein, Ira Bernstein's grandfather.

We have this Sunday off from school and I am happy to be working at the store today. It is busy and I am selling linens and bedspreads nonstop.

Schmulka Bernstein is on Rivington just one block north of Delancey between Essex and Ludlow and Dad takes me there for a deli lunch. I like chicken salami stacked up on rye with coleslaw. At the deli, Schmulka is working behind the counter. "Ira is in my class," I tell Mr. Bernstein.

He is very old and short and wears a large black yarmulke and a long white apron.

"Oh," he says, "with Rabbi Charny."

I nod.

He smiles broadly at Dad and then at me. "What's your name?" he asks me while slicing pastrami for a customer.

"Marc Straus," I say.

"That's wonderful. Here, taste this," and he extends a long fork with two big prongs. "The best pastrami in the world. Tell me what you think."

It is soft and salty with peppercorns.

"It is fabulous," I tell him truthfully.

"And you, Sam?" he says to my Dad. "Here, try a slice of fresh corned beef. We make everything ourselves."

Dad is overjoyed. On the second bite his face is a broad grin. He would never get this at home. At least when Grandma Katy is over she cooks foods he loves. With Mom it is plain broiled lamb chops or a steak from the new Sunbeam countertop broiler that makes everything taste like metal.

"Just sit down there." Mr. Bernstein points to a white Formica table. "I will bring you everything. Let me choose."

He is even shorter when he comes around. His apron is stained all over with meats, sauces, and potato salad. I have a monstrous pastrami sandwich and a double order of fresh red potato salad with little slices of onion. Then a Dr Pepper to drink.

Dad loves the corned beef and Mr. Bernstein brings him a large cup of coffee. His accent is similar to Dad's but much thicker. Soon they are kidding each other, which all Jews do on the Lower East Side. Dad is talking about Sambor. His town was in Poland but after the War was back in Ukraine. Mr. Bernstein's town was Ternopil, not far away. Dad says the girls in Sambor were far better-looking than those in Ternopil. Then Mr. Bernstein laughs and says, "The girls in Sambor were all cross-eyed. Even my pastrami is prettier than them."

Dad laughs hard and we go to the counter to pay and Mr. Bernstein waves a dirty dish towel.

"Sam, I don't charge anyone from Sambor. You already paid enough."

GOOD NEWS. GRANDMA IS STAYING with us three days. She still lives in the same apartment where she and Grandpa Max lived: 1580 51st Street in Borough Park. A walkup that is two blocks away from where we had an apartment until I was three. Grandpa Max died two years later and now Grandma Katy is alone.

We took long walks together and I showed him all the school-yards where I flipped baseball cards, the Hempstead Library, and Mr. Foster's hardware store. I showed him everything except my secret hideout. Behind thick bushes Charlie Aber, Stewie Garber, and I dug a pit that we covered with thick branches. Below was my super pea-shooter and stash of little cement pebbles. As cars came by Woodfield Road we would count how many fenders we could hit in ten tries.

All that's long gone now.

Now Grandma stays over. And she sleeps in the basement. Her long thick hair is completely white. In fact, I have never known her without white hair. And she keeps her teeth in a jar at night.

I am almost as tall as her, but her waist and forearms are twice the size of mine and she is the only one alive who can open a pickle jar from Guss's without running it under hot water or tapping the cap all around. *Whoosh* and off it goes.

I love to tease her and there is nothing I say that doesn't make her laugh. I remind Grandma she is starting to grow hair on her chin and she even laughs at that.

"Grandma, are you sure you weren't a professional wrestler?" She laughs with her face crinkled up. Right now, the wrestling champi-on is Antonino Rocca, who jumps off the top rope and gets his opponent in a supersonic death lock and wins in three quick taps.

For sure she would have beaten him and no wonder Uncle Jack, her oldest son, boxed professionally during the Depression. Uncle Jack said he was good and made as much as $500 a fight but says that my mom could have licked him easily.

Mom helped train him, which is easy for me to imagine. She did the jump ropes and sit-ups with him. I once saw her jump rope near the garage and the rope spun around faster than I could see as she crossed her hands in and out with each turn. Her concentration was like when she plays the piano. But then she almost tripped and threw the rope down and walked away.

"What about Grandma Katy?" I once asked him. Uncle Jack drew deeply on another cigar set between two front teeth with a large gap between.

"Grandma would have wiped out a whole battalion of Nazis by herself."

I was once working at the store organizing sheets and pillowcases with Uncle Hy in the basement and he mentioned that Grandma Katy was very tough in her prime. I wanted to know whether she beat any of her five children. "Just the four boys," he said, laughing loudly. "Pots and pans and anything she could get her hands on." I guess it wasn't too bad since he found it so funny.

I wanted to know what it was like for Uncle Hy fighting the Japs during the war. Uncle Hy was on a small island in the Pacific and was an anti-aircraft gunner.

Uncle Hy won't ever say much about it except that it was very bad and he sunburned easily. Then he laughed and said his best days were when a big salami would arrive that Grandma Katy sent him.

Grandma works nonstop and she and Mom never have anything to say to each other. Grandma is careful not to joke too much with me when around Mom.

I almost had a beating last year when Grandma was in the kitchen. Mom had the strap out and Grandma started to breathe in loud gasps. She turned so white I thought she would faint and then Mom stopped. I don't know what Grandma would have done if Mom had actually hit me. Grandma never saw it happen before.

Grandma Katy is a rectangle, without hips. Mom doesn't look anything like her. Aside from Grandpa Max being fat and a man, Mom looks just like him.

Grandma Katy comes by three buses about once a month and first goes shopping with Mom and then it is a whole day of cooking and Miriam is ecstatic. Aside from finding boyfriends and hanging out with Arlene Gore, her new best friend, Miriam loves eating most. Or perhaps eating comes first. The aroma from the cooking meats for the stuffed cabbage has Miriam dizzy. The *kishka* made from meats stuffed in cow intestines is Dad's favorite, and even Stephen, who barely eats, finishes everything Grandma puts on his plate. For me, I prefer plain food. I won't eat stuffed cabbage or gefilte fish. I like things laid out clearly and eat them one at a time. Sometimes the steak before the baked potato. I love seeing how happy everyone is when Grandma cooks.

Miriam went to camp this past summer and was told to lose weight and play plenty of sports. Miriam doesn't like sports and she tried to lose weight by only eating peanut butter and jelly sandwiches three times a day and as a snack at night. So, she came back having gained more than ten pounds.

Grandma still cries a lot about Grandpa Max. I have been to the cemetery with her many times, Mount Hebron, Section 12D in the front, to the right of the gates.

"I will be right on the other side, so everyone going in has to see me," she says.

"What's your hurry, Grandma?" I ask. "If you die then I will never get another fresh pickle."

She swats me with a dishrag and laughs and goes back to cleaning the dishes.

Grandma has no new clothes and she doesn't care. She has no money except the $150 Dad gives her every week and he pays her rent. Her four sons give her nothing and if Dad mentions this to Mom about her brothers there is an inevitable fight.

I am Grandma's favorite but when she comes over she cooks everything Dad loves and hovers over him and brings him seconds.

I know Dad's mother died when he was three months old and Miriam is named after her. I am named after Dad's father, whose first name was Moises. When Dad was two his father married Grandma Shviga. They had a son, Saul Straus, and shortly after that Dad's father left for the U.S. to find work. Dad didn't see his father again for 14 years until he also came to the U.S.

I heard a few stories from Mom that Dad was badly mistreated as a kid by Grandma Shviga and I think that's why Mom hates her. Mom says Shivga let Dad starve and that's why his legs are bent and his teeth all have big black pits. Grandma Shviga lives in Brooklyn alongside Prospect Park and since I am five we go to one of the Passover Seders there and Dad's two brothers and two sisters and their families come. Saul Straus, his younger brother, is now Jan Bart, a famous cantor and singer with his own radio show.

Uncle Jan is nice. He is fatter than even Grandpa Max was, and he is writing a book about how he lost 1,000 pounds, which is impossible. He explained to me that when he added up all the weight he lost it's true he lost 1,000 pounds. But he regains the weight every time.

Uncle Jan has bad diabetes and isn't supposed to eat sweets, but at the Seder he sneaks them all the time. Dad's father died of diabetes when Dad was only 21, so he didn't know his dad very long and he never talks about him.

Dad found out this year he also has diabetes and every morning he has to stick himself with a little needle and take insulin.

I heard Dr. Fallis say it's a hereditary disease, so I suppose I will also have it someday. But if Stephen gets diabetes he will never allow anyone to stick him with a needle.

Grandma Katy loves making all Dad's favorite foods, especially pickled herring. Yesterday she bought live fresh herrings from the market in Brooklyn before she took the bus. They are always white-and-gray fish about a finger-length long with heads and tails still on and I won't look when Dad puts a whole one in his mouth. This morning his plate has four fish covered with thick white cream with large slices of onions.

Then I notice one of them is different. It is a herring covered with little red specks. I can't look at that one. Maybe it is from a different sea where herrings are red.

"Don't eat that herring!" I suddenly yell to Dad. He looks at me curiously as he pops one of the gray ones whole into his mouth. "No, no, not that one! Take it away, Grandma. Take it away. Don't eat it!" I say, feeling ill and pushing my plate away.

Dad is staring at me and puts down his fork.

I don't know why this happened. He has eaten herring before. So one has speckles.

I can't stand looking at a whole cooked turkey. I won't eat chicken soup if it has little chicken legs left in.

I would never eat a herring. It would be like eating a whole worm.

Dad shouldn't be eating cream and so much of the challah bread. He was very skinny when he came to the U.S. He is chubby now and he forgets all the time he has diabetes. His father was 46 when he died of it at Mount Sinai Hospital. Uncle Ira and Uncle Jan both have bad diabetes. Dad should never have dessert. Now when I work at the store and we go for lunch I don't let him order a muffin.

I have to remind him he has diabetes and he should lose some weight. He never says anything, but then he won't eat the cake.

I am the only kid I know who doesn't like sweets. I won't even eat them at lunch in school. Mom never buys cake or ice cream except on the rare occasions I have seen her sneak a half-gallon of chocolate ice cream which she hides in the freezer and then late at night eats the entire container.

I think you can decide what you won't ever eat and stick to it. I never tasted coffee and never will. I hate the smell. If I don't like the smell of something I will never eat it. If I decide something I know how to stick to it. ▪

CHAPTER 12

Debt Collector

IT'S EARLY JANUARY, a bleak Saturday morning, overcast, freezing cold, but there is no report that snow is looming. Out the window there is no breeze but the tree branches are speckled with ice crystals. It is the tundra in *The Call of the Wild*. Dad passes by my room in his flannel pajamas and says, "You're coming with me."

Last November he opened Cottonland, his new retail store in Garden City, which I know is not doing well, and business at the main store on Grand Street is always slow in January. I heard store-owners in the neighborhood say the post-war boom is over. The Korean War has ended and Eisenhower is busy building nuclear missiles aimed at Russia.

Dad is worried. I can tell. This time it's worse. His face droops and his skin looks pasty and he says even less than usual. I think Dad is taking me to Cottonland for the first time so I can help sell things for him. I dress quickly and grab a glass of milk.

"Ready," I say expectantly.

There is no *New York Post* at the kitchen table. No cup of coffee. Dad's face is bent toward his plate of slushy eggs and toast and he takes a small bite and pushes it away. Mom says nothing. Miriam might be upstairs. Stephen ate a while ago.

In his green Dodge Coronet, Dad is as wordless as Helen Keller. Not even the radio is on and soon he is east of Garden City.

I see so little of Dad now that I rarely work Sundays, and even Saturdays he seldom goes to synagogue. Usually he would be home Saturday afternoons reading a paper in the living room, listening to a Mozart record, dozing off and snoring loudly. Now he goes to Cottonland. But this is not where he is taking me.

He drives east on Front Street toward East Meadow and south on Merrick and Bellmore. Where are we going? Now along back streets houses here are narrow clapboards with ripped wood siding, missing shingles, and no garages. Then at the end of a dead-end street he stops in front of a small ranch house with a tiny front portico and a drive up to the right with an overhang for a single car, beneath which is an Oldsmobile station wagon, fairly new.

"Come," Dad says, motioning.

Dad moves hurriedly along the driveway hunched over in his long black wool coat and no hat. I follow closely as we approach the front door, crossing a narrow lawn with a few sprigs of frozen grass.

Not a sound on this street, no kids playing, no clink of dishes from kitchens nearby. Everything feels abandoned, as though the neighborhood was built but no one lives there any longer. It seemed like a good idea once and then maybe the water was poisoned and the people all left.

The front door is white with much of the paint chipped off. It doesn't even fit properly in the frame. The bottom gap is much wider to the right. It has two big brass locks and a small windowpane to the right.

Dad knocks hard three times with his fist. His chin is curled up and his eyes narrow as pinpricks with dark baggy patches below.

Ten seconds later he knocks even harder, at least six times, almost knocking the door off its hinges. He is motionless, pulled deep into himself and not looking at me, and then he begins to pound again furiously and kicks the door bottom with his heel.

Pounding and pounding and suddenly the top bolt is thrown and the knob twists and the door pulls halfway in.

"Goddamn it, Sam!" says a man in a worn white undershirt and black boxer shorts. He has dark scraggly hair, is Dad's height, perhaps a couple of years older, with a two-day stubble.

"Just give us the goods," Dad says, very firmly.

"Come on, Sam," the man says, turning his eyes quickly left then right, and past the sliver of space between his left side and the door jamb I see part of a bed with rumpled sheets.

"Just the goods and we are gone."

"Damn it, I have company. You know how this is."

Dad says to me without taking his eyes off the man, "Get all the goods and load them in the car."

"Sam, for God sakes. Just give me an hour."

"Marc. Do it now!"

I begin to step in front of Dad and the man's face is tight and sweaty even though it is frigid out and he is in his underwear.

"Wait a goddamned minute," he says, pulling himself tightly in the doorway and reaching to partially close it as Dad jams his right foot into the breach.

"Sam, I always pay. I am just a little behind."

"Nothing, Sonny, since July. I am not in business to carry you. It's sixty-five hundred dollars."

"I will pay everything, I swear."

"In the meantime, we will take all the goods. Marc, go get them now."

I move right past Sonny as though I am a ghost vapor. His house is a single room. To the middle rear I see a queen-size bed and disheveled sheets, where a woman is rapidly trying to dress. I can't help staring for a second. Her panties are pulled up and when she reaches over to the side of the bed her large bare breasts hang down. She sees me and screeches, covering herself with two hands, and runs to the bathroom.

The front right has a decrepit brown fabric couch and a small TV on a stand. To the left is a Formica kitchen table and chairs with torn red plastic coverings. Behind that a small kitchen area with a half-size refrigerator.

Dad and Sonny are still arguing at the door.

"Give you a thousand by the end of today. Just leave everything."

Off to the left near the refrigerator is a pile of bedspreads on the floor still in their packaging. I grab four of them and trot to the door, squeeze past, and run to the street and arrange them in the back seat of the car.

Back in hurriedly for four more, these wrapped in paper and heavy string. Again and again until the rear seat is completely filled. Off in the corner of the living room I see many new towels, hand-cloths, and washcloths strewn about. I am not certain there are any matching sets but I take as many as I can.

As I exit the door Sonny pleads with Dad, "Come on, Sam. Those aren't from you."

My dad, still not looking in my direction, barks, "Take everything."

I think the lady is locked in the bathroom. Four more trips and I have filled our large trunk and there is nothing left. I go stand next to Dad and say, "That's it."

Sonny is practically hopping up and down and says half to me, "This isn't right. Goddamn it. I said I would give you a thousand today, maybe two by the end of the week."

Dad says very quietly and deliberately, "I doubt there's enough here to cover it."

"What good is it, Sam? I have nothing now to do business with and you come here and embarrass me." He darts his eyes inside.

"That's your business, Sonny," Dad answers. "Marc, get in the car."

"Come on, Sam. How do I know what you took?"

"You just have to trust me, Sonny," Dad says, as cool as the temperature outside. Then he turns half around. "I will do a complete account. Anything over and I give you a refund."

Back in the car and almost two blocks away I know that Dad will have nothing more to say. So I ask him, "Do you have to do this often?"

"No," he answers.

"I guess sixty-five hundred is a lot."

"Much too much and too long. He isn't honest."

"Dad, don't you give Uncle Shoma six thousand credit?"

He looks at me for the first time, a look like there is an alien in the passenger seat of his car. But no answer.

"I know, Dad," I go on. "I know he always owes over six thousand." I am referring to Uncle Shoma, the husband of Dad's next older sister, Anda. He has a large sloping baboon forehead and I once heard Dad tell Uncle Ira that Shoma has no business being a textile peddler. He can't sell anything. Uncle Ira won't go against Dad when it comes to extending credit. Once in the store when I was helping Shoma pick out some goods to sell door to door, Dad said to me, "First bring up everything unwrapped to the counter. I have to limit how much he takes." Adolph, the bookkeeper, hinted that Uncle Shoma never pays and Dad just writes it off.

"Are we making any other stops today?" I ask Dad.

He hesitates. "Two more."

Now my plans are changed. This afternoon I was going to see *The Robe* starring Richard Burton at the Calderone. I already know the story. Richard Burton is Marcellus, a Roman soldier tormented by guilt for helping crucify Jesus but when he touches Jesus's robe he is healed and becomes a follower, of course. But I wanted to see it anyway. It's the first widescreen color film showing in Hempstead.

I pull myself deeper into the seat. I am glad Dad took me. Dad was angry at Sonny but there have been a few times when I've seen him even angrier. Like the time last winter when a truck driver refused to bring the cartons inside the Grand Street store and that huge man with amazing thick muscles got scared when Dad reached all the way up and put his finger in the man's face. But then as soon as the man backed down and said he would bring the cartons in Dad was nice to him.

Dad usually keeps his anger hidden far away. He won't talk against his older brother, Ira, who does nothing in the store, but I can tell Dad gets upset. Uncle Hy has to fall asleep in the basement a hundred times before Dad yells and then the two of them go back and forth. And when you see Dad ten minutes later the anger is gone.

At home he is almost always quiet. He has only hit me once, two medium tush slaps. I was five and deserved it but that is another story.

Mom has a flash fuse. Usually you have no idea she is about to explode. Then she can't stop. Sometimes I think she hardly knows where she is. Like Mr. Hyde. That story is not entirely made up.

I am not like Mom. I've had a lot of fights because I've had to, and I always know exactly what I am doing. I suppose I've started a few unnecessarily. I once mistook a kid for someone else, so he got one beating he shouldn't have, but that's not so bad. It is always me Mom takes it out on and I have never told Dad. He is never home when it happens. I almost told him when I was five and was beaten badly in the living room. That's when the tip of the thin high heel of her shoe stuck in my forearm and made deep purple dents. When I was walking upstairs to lie down I calmly told Mom I was going to tell Dad this time when he got home. She pleaded and pleaded with me not to. She said she hits me because she expects more of me. I couldn't understand that, but I told her I wouldn't tell but I would never forget.

I never told Dad and sometimes wish I had.

But I know if he knew he would leave her, and then where would Miriam, Stephen, and I go? ◾

CHAPTER 13

Holdup

SCHOOL HAS NOT REOPENED as yet so I am at the store today. Roman Cotton Goods is almost empty. January is always slow but on this frostbitten Sunday almost no one has come in. At 5:45 p.m. it is coal black outside. Cars going by are hazy shimmers through the thin layer of frost on the front windows.

The good news is that *Playboy* has published its first issue with a naked woman in the centerfold and someone already placed the picture of Marilyn Monroe on the wall in our filthy upstairs bathroom. It's probably the reason that bathroom gets used so much now.

My sales are less than $300 and I spend time reorganizing the price lists. They are out of date again. Uncle Hy and Bert, one of Dad's salesmen, think they know all the prices by heart but they don't. Some items we no longer carry, a few new ones are not listed, and prices have gone up for sheets and pillowcases.

Recently Stephen was forced to come in and for the entire day he stood near the front register and didn't utter five words. Dad was disappointed, but he won't make Stephen come again. Miriam occasionally comes in to help in the office. She loves counting money.

Dad came to the U.S. at age 15 and got a 16-hour-a-day job organizing the stock in a five-and-dime store on Delancey Street. Within four years he was managing Uncle Manny's textile store on Grand Street and the year I was born he opened Roman Cotton Goods with his older brother, Ira. There are over a thousand different items in the store and I make price lists in code that I tack up in different locations for the salespeople.

Normally Sunday is the busiest day but in this cold few venture outside, and I guess most people already bought all their Christmas gifts last month.

Not only is this store slow but Dad's new store, Cottonland, is losing a lot of money. Dad is worried. When Izzy, one of Dad's other salesmen, left Roman Cotton Goods and took another job in New Jersey, Dad didn't replace him. Our school tuition is expensive.

Diagonally across from our shop on Grand and Eldridge Streets is a six-story apartment building where Patricia lives with her mother and younger sister. I met her a few months ago while walking to Hester Street to pick up a challah for Mom. She is out now in this cold, sitting on her front stoop with one lighted bulb above. I open the front door of the store and wave hello. She waves back. It is a bad night to sit outside in the cold.

Patty is Italian, with dark hair, a narrow face, a big smile, and round dark eyes under thick eyebrows. Her grandmother often visits and is always dressed in black, with thick nylon stockings and thick black shoes.

Her grandmother doesn't like me. She once asked me if I am "Jew," and I nodded yes. But Patty's mom likes me. She says she sees my dad all the time, he works hard, and we must live in a big house.

Herman is working in the store today. He's a second cousin of Dad's, 34 and very thin and dark-complected. Herman is usually out of work and more recently has been in drug rehab clinics, and Dad will give him work every now and then, but in reality Herman can't do much more than sweep. There are always yellow dry scabs on his face and red and purple splotches on his arms. He also smells like he has not showered in two weeks. I don't know where he sleeps.

After making certain that everything is put away in the basement I go upstairs. It's 5:55 p.m. and I expect we will close up and leave in a few minutes. No one else is on the first floor. Uncle Hy, Bert, and Adolph have left. I sit in the two-desk office just past the curtains near the back.

Adolph's bookkeeping register is here. The chairs have had the same worn gray fabric as long as I have been coming here.

I hear someone approaching and I reach for my coat. A young man with thick sandy blond hair covering his ears appears in the doorway. He looks in, carefully surveying everything, and notices me.

"Excuse me," I say, not recognizing him. "We are closing."

"Get in the back," he says, one foot now planted in the office.

His skin is very white with old deep pockmarks across his entire face. He must have had bad acne. He is wearing a worn thick tan-green army coat, tan pants, and no gloves or hat.

"In the back now," he commands, much louder.

"I don't know who you are, but we are closing," I respond.

He takes one more step into the office and raises his left hand, in which he is holding a small paper bag. He reaches inside the bag with his right hand and pulls out a black pistol, which he aims right at my head.

"Are you going now?" he asks, his lips drawn into slivers.

"Why didn't you say so before?" I respond, quickly getting up.

I know it's stupid but it feels like a movie and this isn't real. Maybe it's a joke. Dad has customers who frequently pull pranks.

The man is really tense. His eyes narrow and dart right to left quickly.

"It's a holdup," he says, motioning me to the back. I pass him carefully, turn left, and see Dad, Herman, and Uncle Ira in the far aisle, with two other men pointing guns at them.

None of them wear masks. Like the blond man, the other two also look about 25 to 30 years old. The short one with a flat nose sounds like he is Hispanic.

I've heard about holdups before, mostly in grocery stores. A part of me knows this is dangerous and I should be really scared, but I know how to push fear away and this still feels like it's only a movie.

Dad turns to Uncle Ira. "We are closed. Why did you unlock again?"

The third guy, the tallest, in a thin black wool coat, yells, "Shut your mouth!" and pushes his gun toward Dad at face level, his gun hand shaking badly.

Dad criticizes Uncle Ira again and the blond man who came into the office with me says, "No one will get hurt if you give us the money. The cash from the safe."

He is in charge and the little guy focuses on Herman and Uncle Ira.

Now I understand. Uncle Ira let one guy in who then pulled a gun and the other two followed.

The leader steps closer to Dad and says more quietly, "Don't be stupid. Just open the safe and we leave."

Uncle Ira is sweating across his entire forehead and doesn't move a muscle. Herman is staring at a spot on the floor.

Dad says, "You guys think you are smart. You cased us? But the boss left over an hour ago."

The blond man cranks his head side to side and says, "You just lose some money. You people have plenty. Just do it or you will lose much more today."

I am trying hard to study his face so it will be easy to identify him later.

Dad calmly repeats, "We are just the paid help and don't have the combination."

Of course Dad is lying. Dad never likes a threat. But this is not a trucker refusing to bring our cartons inside. This is three guys with real guns.

But once Dad makes up his mind there is no turning around.

Then the man with the shaky gun runs up against Herman and shoves his pistol against Herman's right temple. "Open it now," he screams at Dad, "or I will blow his head away."

Herman's hands and body are quivering and his face looks folded up while his eyes stay lowered.

Dad says calmly, "It won't do any good. We don't have the combination and if you kill him you get no money and the electric chair."

The leader tells the shaky guy, "Just back off. Move away, John." Then to Dad very quietly, "You are not a smart man. I haven't threatened your boy as yet."

Suddenly Uncle Ira says, "I can open it."

Dad glowers at Uncle Ira. The leader points at Dad, Herman, and me and says, "You three to the basement." And to me again, "You are going to tie them up."

Downstairs he asks for rope. I tell him we only have long strips of thin nylon used to wrap curtains.

"Okay," he says hurriedly. "Tie them up tightly. Now."

I nod my head in agreement. "Come on, faster," he demands, "and now back to back."

Then he does a terrible job tying me and says to the three of us, "Stay here fifteen minutes. Anyone comes upstairs, I shoot them." Then he bolts upstairs.

In under a minute Dad and I are both free. Dad's face is dark, with his lower lip pulled up. His black eyes are liquid and narrowed. I have seen this twice before.

Dad shouts to Herman and me, "Stay here!"

"Where are you going?" I demand. "He warned us not to go upstairs."

"I am going," he says.

"No," I say. "If you go then so do I."

"You will stay right here!" he shouts. "Do as I say!" And he quickly leaves.

Herman is sitting in the same place not trying to loosen the tie. He picked the worst day to work in the store.

I have to force myself not to run upstairs. I know Dad. I guess I'm not surprised. He will chase the robbers and they will either throw back the money or shoot him.

Finally, I can't hold out and after three minutes I run upstairs. Uncle Ira is sitting in the office and barely looks up. "Where is he?" I demand.

"He ran after them. I called the police."

Uncle Ira's face looks like he was out in a snow blizzard without a coat and just came in. Then he says mostly to himself, "Just like Poland."

I run up Eldridge Street past Broome as fast as I can. On Delancey I look east and west. Nothing. Then back and into the store. Two police cars are in front with lights whirling and inside the store two big cops are speaking with Uncle Ira.

I am in the back office when Dad returns. Herman is gone. The senior cop has a badge that says D. McDougal and he tells Dad that he is a damn fool chasing armed men. Dad says he almost caught them. He was a half block behind but they made it into the subway and got away.

I can picture it. Dad running like a deer and three men with guns being chased by an unarmed small dark Jew. They were afraid for their lives, as they should have been, and all they could do was run and run.

Uncle Ira once told me, "The Polish boys in Sambor were told to beat us and we were not allowed to fight back. Sometimes they came with dogs. Your father has deep bite marks on his legs. He was a shrimp but my God could he run, and pity the boys who attacked him. I was sure a couple of times if he didn't kill them he would be killed."

At the police station Sergeant McDougal brings over thick books of mug shots and places them on the dirty gray metal desk. Close up, he has a very thick neck and puffy face with small red lines down his nose. "Look carefully," he says to me, turning to the first page. "You say you are certain you can identify them."

"The leader," I explain. "Late twenties and blond."

It is a thick book with 20 small pictures on a page, each with a name and number, all Negro men. Then more Negro men young and old. They look bored and like they have posed for mug shots many times. Some have beards and some are fat and a few are really old. But most are young, perhaps even 18.

"He is white. White," I say after many more pages.

"Just keep looking, kid," he says, walking to a counter and retrieving a container of hot coffee.

By the end of the book there is still not a white face. I ask, "Don't you have any white criminals?"

"Here, try this." He shoves a new volume in front of me.

Then several more books and my guy isn't in them. Many of the white men have broken teeth and lots of tattoos.

After three hours and more than a thousand pictures the image in my head is blurred.

Around 9:30 p.m. we are back in Dad's Dodge headed to West Hempstead. We cross the Manhattan Bridge in silence. My feet and shoulders suddenly begin to shake and then everything inside is roiling around like clothing in a washing machine. Dad sits up ramrod straight, his chin tucked in, and stares ahead stonily, his face glistening in the night.

I can't remember ever being scared before and now I shiver so hard I think it might never stop. ▪

CHAPTER 14

Cottonland

FEBRUARY. SCHOOL IS AS DULL as watching acorns grow. Mrs. Sonnenberg gives me private assignments every week. Talmud is much easier.

And not a single fight in school or the Borough of Queens, New York.

The hardest thing for me is not being able to work at Roman. But I am still trying to convince Dad to let me help every Saturday at Cottonland.

COTTONLAND. Big blue neon letters on a background of white plastic. The sign measures some six by twelve feet, supported by thick aluminum poles. It is seen by thousands a day as they drive east or west along Jericho Turnpike in Garden City. The 12,000-square-foot store had been in the planning for two years and opened before last Thanksgiving.

Dad was excited about Cottonland. His store on Grand Street caters to wholesale customers. Sundays are the exception, when retail customers come to buy linen goods for at least 40 percent less than at Macy's and Gimbels. Now it was time for a retail store that specialized in linens and offered a wide variety at a discount compared to the big retailers. The population was booming in Long Island and he thought it would be easier for shoppers to buy locally instead of trekking to Herald Square in New York City to shop. Open several nights until 9:00 p.m., it sells bedspreads, towels, and sheets set out in beautiful racks and wide rows. He added drapery, hardware, garbage pails, potholders, and even sets of knives and forks. He first thought to call it Linens Plus and finally settled on Cottonland.

Dad knew that this concept would work. He would get rich like some of his friends who were manufacturers or owned a lot of real estate. Someday he would have Cottonland stores across the country.

Dad felt obliged to include as a partner his older brother, Uncle Ira, who hated every aspect of the business, and this led to endless arguments between Dad and Mom. Mom said that Dad does all the work and Ira gets half the money. And Uncle Ira has only one child and we have three. Mom thought that with two tuitions to pay Dad should at least take more money.

Mom is right. Uncle Ira won't move away from the cash register even if there is no business, but he always insists the money be split evenly. Dad doesn't like it, but he will never get rid of his older brother.

Dad hired Mr. Kirshner to run the store and also gave him some ownership and the title of president. He is 15 years older than Dad, mostly bald, several inches taller, with very pale skin, and he is considerably overweight. He always wears a neat white shirt, bowtie, and suspenders.

The store is spacious and bright with wide aisles and new fluorescent light fixtures. Racks and racks of towels with prices marked in bold colors. Fieldcrest Bath Towels: Retail $2.75–NOW $1.75.

The Christmas rush began at Thanksgiving. Dad took a full-page advertisement in *Newsday* and that Friday and Saturday after Thanksgiving the store was crowded and Dad said we sold over $2,000 worth of goods in a single day.

I really wanted to help but Dad explained the beauty of the concept is that you don't really need a salesman. Everything is clearly marked and there is no bargaining. You only need a few people on the floor to tell customers where items are and watch that people don't steal, which he said is common in department stores.

Dad was there at least two days a week and soon he was complaining that Mr. Kirshner was in the back office too much, that he wasn't rotating inventory enough.

Within weeks, business dropped off and the store did poorly over Christmas. No one could explain this. The prices were good. People must have seen the full-page ads, which cost so much to place, but they didn't respond.

And then there was worse trouble. The town of Garden City cited Dad for not having a permit for the sign outside. I went with Dad to see his friend Ben Bartel, a lawyer who heads real estate for a big New York company. Mr. Bartel said that if Dad wasn't Jewish, if his name was McConnell, the town would give him no trouble, but now the cost of fighting them is too high. He told Dad he should have started in Brooklyn or Queens.

That was only the beginning. Then Macy's and a couple of the other big department stores mounted a campaign to stop Dad from carrying his major brands. They didn't like that Dad was undercutting them with lower retail prices at Cottonland. Bates and Wamsutta pulled out and even threatened to cut off his Grand Street store. I didn't understand why. Roman Cotton Goods is mostly wholesale. But apparently Cottonland was a thorn in the side of Macy's and the other big stores. It was a large specialty retail store that was giving them a black eye by lowering prices so much, and if it was not stopped now there could soon be others like it across the U.S.

Finally, Dad eliminated several name brands at Cottonland so as not to jeopardize Roman. Now the towels and sheets at Cottonland are from companies I've never heard of.

I accompany Dad to Cottonland on a Saturday morning in mid-February. Adolph is in the back office reviewing the accounts. Mr. Kirshner is away on vacation.

"This is not working, Sam," Adolph explains in his clipped German accent. "The ads in the Newsday are not yielding a return and I don't think we can maintain the salaries."

By now Dad is working seven days a week and many late nights. In a week, on February 25th, he will turn 40, and it seems as though he has already aged ten years in one.

"Kirshner makes fifty thousand a year," Dad responds. "That's a huge salary and maybe it's time to cut him. The rest of the staff combined is only eighty thousand."

"Who would you get in his place?" Adolph wants to know.

"I don't know but he holds us back. He is lazy and makes bad decisions."

"Sam, don't forget you have a contract you guaranteed for three years."

"It doesn't say he can be lazy and waste money. I can't pay someone like that."

"Did you speak with Mr. Bartel?" Adolph asks.

Ben Bartel lives on Ocean Avenue in Brooklyn in a four-bedroom apartment. He is one of three people Dad looks up to; the others are Lucky Maze, his accountant, and his Uncle Mendel Rothman.

Ben Bartel provides advice on almost everything and always says to me, "Marc, when you are ready, tell me what college you want to attend." I think of him as the Jewish fixer.

I accompany Dad to see Ben at home. We are sitting at his dining room table. Ben listens for a long time and then says to Dad, "I have to show this to a contract lawyer, Sam. It is not easy. Why did you sign this sweetheart deal without showing me?"

"Kirshner was difficult to get," Dad explains. "He has experience in wholesale and retail, and Herby Rothman—"

Ben interrupts, "Sam, stop using relatives, for God sakes. Your cousin Herby did not include the necessary loopholes. I know he is Mendel's kid but the man who uses a cousin to do contracts...."

Not counting Mom, no one except Ben Bartel can speak to my Dad this way. Dad is stuck with slow sales, a bloated payroll, and a company president who is sinking him.

"What is his equity, Sam?" Ben asks.

"Twenty percent," Dad answers.

"Ah ha. Then maybe we do a big capital call and drive him to the trenches."

"But Ira won't go for a capital call."

"You have always saddled yourself with your brother Ira and this time just tell him there is no choice. Look, Sam, this idea is ahead of its time. Close and cut your losses and do it by yourself in a couple of years."

The store continues its downslide and Mr. Kirshner is still there. I hear Dad tell Mom one night he is already $20,000 in arrears and Ira is complaining all the time. A shouting match follows.

Dad looks exhausted all the time. I don't know much about the business because I commute to Yeshiva in Queens and there are classes most Sundays. The little time that Dad is home there is constant war between him and Mom.

One night it is worse than usual. Mom and Dad are downstairs in the den and fighting loudly. Stephen is sound asleep. Miriam comes down from her attic room to the second-floor landing and nervously motions me to come out of my room. She is in her nighty with a frilly pink ribbon at the bottom. She looks petrified. She is three years older but when she is this scared she runs to find me. She grabs my hand and I can feel the shiver running through her.

Dad yells, "You have a goddamned lazy brother who sleeps in the basement half the time. I have to carry dead weight." I am not sure how Dad knows since I never squealed on Uncle Hy. Uncle Hy is the older brother closest in age to Mom and I think she already knows he doesn't work hard.

Mom goes on endlessly about Uncle Ira. "He is a sponge. He does no work and stands behind the cash register and gets half the money and he has only one child to feed, not three. And you went ahead and gave him equity in Cottonland as well. How stupid can you be?"

That's the worst thing you can say to Dad and he won't leave a fight like this without saying something about Mom's younger brother, Bob. "He is a lousy drunk and cheat."

Uncle Bob is Mom's favorite. She helped take care of him when they were growing up and Uncle Bob always calls her "Sis."

Once Dad gets onto Uncle Bob the war has escalated to atomic bombs.

They shout over each until Dad yells, "Just shut your damn mouth!" And he walks away, which makes Mom much angrier.

We hear Dad near the bottom of the stairs, so Miriam hurriedly goes up to her attic room. I duck back into my rear bedroom and close the door partway. It is 10:15 p.m. and Dad is trudging up slower than a toad. I see him at the top of the stairs and he turns right to the bathroom. His whole face is red and sweaty.

Dad and Mom's bedroom and the guest bedroom where I used to be before I moved in with Stephen are to the front of the house.

I must have fallen asleep because I didn't see him leave the bathroom or see Mom come up. Friday morning Stephen and I are up for school and Dad has not come downstairs.

"He is not feeling well," Mom volunteers. I have only seen Dad miss one day of work in his life, ever. That evening he is still in bed and the next morning Miriam huddles with me upstairs in her room.

"What's going on?" she asks fearfully. I shake my head.

"You know," she says. "You can figure this out."

But I don't know and Miriam won't let up.

"Is he dying?"

Miriam has a way of coming to the worst conclusion, even though she only reads books with love and nice endings.

"Why can't you find out?" she insists.

I go down to the kitchen and ask Mom, "Is Dad sick?"

I expect an explosion, but she answers, "Just temporarily."

The next morning is Saturday and we have no school. Dr. Fallis comes in at 9:30. Stephen is about to holler thinking he will get an injection, but I quiet him. "He is here to see Dad," and then Stephen goes downstairs to play in the garage. I lurk near the open door to Dad and Mom's bedroom. Mom is in there and her look shoots daggers at me with a clear message to leave.

She won't yell at me with Dr. Fallis here and I want to know what is going on, so I pop my head in. The room is dark with the blinds closed. The double bed is now against the wall between the bedroom and guest room. I didn't remember that it had been moved from the other side of the room. Dad is lying back on two pillows with his eyes closed. Dr. Fallis takes his stethoscope and listens to Dad's chest and wants Dad to sit up to listen to his lungs but Dad doesn't cooperate, so Mom hoists him like a sack. Then she sees me and says nothing.

Dad's chest has thin hairs with some gray now and sweat covers it down to his belly, which looks inflated like the inner tube of a football. Dr. Fallis hammers Dad for reflexes and tries to look into Dad's eyes and says he can't see anything without dilating them.

"No fever, Dora," he says. "Heart and lungs okay. Has he eaten anything since Wednesday?"

Mom shakes her head no and says, "I managed to get in some fluids but he knocked over the glass this morning."

I step a bit closer. There is no use trying to make me leave. Dad doesn't even move a single muscle, like he is paralyzed. And he isn't eating or drinking so he must have a terrible disease and I worry that Dr. Fallis can't make the diagnosis. I am thinking to tell them we need to take him right away to a specialist when Dr. Fallis says, "We could admit him to the hospital and give IV fluids. We can't allow him to be severely dehydrated." He hesitates. "Shall I put you in the hospital, Sam?" he asks, close to Dad's face. There is no response and Dr. Fallis says, "I think I have to do this," but then slowly Dad shakes his head right and left, letting Dr. Fallis know he won't go.

Dr. Fallis says to Mom, "I think we should give him a shot," and she agrees, but that idea seems very painful to her. Perhaps the shot will have terrible side effects. I am allergic to penicillin and they say if I take it I could die.

Dr. Fallis goes downstairs to prepare his syringe and comes up with it on a tray. Mom helps turn Dad over, then he gets a large injection in his butt and doesn't flinch. More than even me I think that Dad doesn't feel pain. I would have bitten down on something if it were really bad, like the cowboys do when they remove bullets with no anesthesia.

Then Dr. Fallis says to Mom and me, "Let's give him some rest. Dora, make sure he gets plenty of fluids and call me if you have to. I will be here in the morning."

I have to fend off Miriam and I don't have many answers. Knowing her, I had better not say that I think maybe Dad will die. Why else would he be in bed and not eating? He has early diabetes but now it could be out of control. His father died at age 46 of diabetes and Dad doesn't watch his diet. But Dr. Fallis tested Dad's sugar with a finger stick and said it wasn't bad.

Maybe Dad can't walk. President Roosevelt was paralyzed from the waist down from polio and tried to keep it a secret. I want to stay with Dad. I want to ask him to tell me what is wrong. When I work at the store I am with Dad all day and know almost everything he has to say. I know all his opinions about politics and unions. I know how he chooses which curtains to buy for the new season.

I might have to cut school for a few days and go to the store. Without Dad there, Roman will also lose money.

A few hours later when Mom goes outside, I quietly open Dad's door and peek in. He is still and deep under the sheets and blankets. He didn't die in the Holocaust like almost all his friends did. He got out and came to New York and is a fighter.

But he is very sick and I don't think Dr. Fallis knows what to do.

Almost four hours later Mom brings in some tea and fresh chicken soup and I wait and wait until finally I see that Mom takes the tray out and Dad has eaten some of it. I hear Mom telling Ben Bartel over the phone that Dad's stomach is very bad from worry and maybe they have to operate because of ulcers.

Dr. Fallis visits every day but I am off to school before he comes. The next Saturday it is the same and Dad has still not come out of his room. Grandma Katy is over now and her food should make Dad much better. I have not seen her so upset since Grandpa Max died. When I sneak in I see that Dad is eating even less.

Monday April 12th. It is about five weeks that Dad has been in bed. Next week I have a holiday from school because it is Passover.

This is a small benefit of being in the yeshiva. I am in my room getting ready to go when I hear Dad's door open and through my doorway I see him walking down the hall to the bathroom. He has lost so much weight that the skin on his face is hanging down. His mustache is long and uneven with lots of white now. Even his skinny legs are thinner.

He gives me a quick glance and passes me. I guess the disease must have ended. Soon he is downstairs at the breakfast table as though nothing happened. He eats two poached eggs. Miriam looks at Dad tearfully and she almost can't eat, which for her is a first.

Mom tries to hurry up Stephen, who is taking his time with his Cream of Wheat. Dad stands and tucks in his shirt. It is still too early for him to go to work. He knows I checked in his room every day. I know he will eventually tell me what happened when I go to the store with him again. I am going to do that all summer after school ends.

"The second night of Passover we are going to Shviga's house," Mom says coolly. Dad's stepmother. He nods okay.

"I am going to see Ben's lawyer, Feldberg, early this morning," Dad announces clearly. Mom says nothing. "I will close Cottonland and screw Kirshner. He will have to fight to get anything more out of me."

Mom removes the dirty dishes. Dad has finished every morsel of food. He has never sworn before, not even in the store, as Uncle Ira and Uncle Hy always do. Now he has made his decision and I doubt that Mr. Kirshner is ready for my Dad when he goes to war. ▪

CHAPTER 15

Passover

PASSOVER IS LATE in the season this year. The first Seder is April 18th and at our house. Grandma Katy has been over cooking for four days, but besides our immediate family and Grandma the only guests are Milton and Adele Small and their two daughters close to Miriam's age and another man I've never met.

Dad leads the service with as much gusto as I can ever recall. He takes time doing the prayer over the wine.

I love his Hebrew accent, which emphasizes first syllables, and his Os sounding like Oys. For the four questions it's Stephen's turn and everyone sings loudly along with him.

I guess Dad's problems with Cottonland are behind him now, though when I was recently in the store Uncle Hy told me it wasn't going to be easy. Apparently, Dad started a textile mill around 1949 and the plant straddled the border of South Carolina and Georgia. The result was difficulty with different state laws and unions and payoffs and the plant went bankrupt.

Uncle Hy said Dad had no obligation to repay creditors, but he did so out of his own pocket over three years and no one was stiffed.

I had never heard this before. So Cottonland was his second try at another business and now too I am sure Dad is going to pay back everyone owed money.

On Grand Street Dad's word is better than a contract. Every company and merchant knows that and when he wants money for Israel he goes up and down the streets of the neighborhood and tells each business owner what they are contributing and they do.

It is so good to see Dad this happy tonight and when he sings I try to be just as loud as he is, which isn't easy.

Dad is seated in the middle of the table and as the oldest son I am on his right. What I have not understood since the service began is why another man is seated at the head of the table, in the largest chair and on a beautiful cushion. That is supposed to be Dad's seat. And then during prayers Dad gets up and personally refills this man's glass. You would think it was Felix Frankfurter or David Ben-Gurion over for dinner. But his name is Isaac Dvorkin and he is likely about 50, ten years older than Dad. His jacket and pants are badly worn, and no one says what work he does but it can't pay much.

Mr. Dvorkin knows all the songs and sings very quietly. I try not to stare but he has three long scars on his face and neck as if he was cut deeply and with a dull blade.

When he gets ready to leave, Mom gives Mr. Dvorkin leftovers: a big box of cake made without flour, extra roast beef slices in tin foil, and a full bottle of wine.

"Who is he?" I ask Mom, who is deep in dishwater at the sink.

She looks at me and then back to scrubbing.

"Was he from Dad's town?" The accents are similar.

She shakes her head no.

Usually I don't press, but I ask, "Is he a cousin of Dad's who was in a concentration camp?"

Mom throws down the dishrag in annoyance and Grandma is signaling me to make my getaway before there's more trouble, but I persist.

Mom wipes her soapy hands and says, "He is a great hero."

I am really surprised. No one said anything.

"Mr. Dvorkin?"

"He has a hard time making money now and your dad helps him out as do some others."

"Why?" I want to know.

"To your dad and many others he might be one of a kind and you can't go by his being poor now."

"What did he do? Why is he a hero?"

Grandma is back and forth cleaning up the dining room table.

"During the war," she explains, "Mr. Dvorkin was second-in-command in his region of the Polish Resistance. He came from a town about forty miles from where Dad was born."

"There were Jews in the Resistance?" I ask. I never read that. I thought the Poles hated the Jews almost as much as the Nazis did.

"He would have been the leader if not for being Jewish and only the top leader knew. In fact, few even knew his identity."

"Why?"

"He was too important, and if anyone was caught and tortured it was necessary not to give up Mr. Dvorkin. Those who knew him thought his name was Pavel something, a Polish man from Krakow. He kept up that disguise for almost six years."

"What did he do?" I press again.

Mom looks at me with steely blue eyes and presses her hands together. "He was in charge of assassinating Gestapo."

I feel a part of my stomach knot.

"He killed Gestapo?"

"The Germans didn't know his identity. But when they came to a small village to roust out all the Jews, many of the Gestapo left in a box. He was like a ghost."

"How many did he kill?" I ask breathlessly. I have read several books on the Holocaust but never anything like this. They're about edicts. About Hitler taking over the government and then Jews wearing armbands and businesses being destroyed. About the Final Solution.

"It is said he personally killed around five hundred."

It is hard to take all this in. I imagine he swooped in from the forest. Maybe he was a sharpshooter.

"With Pavel, or shall we say Mr. Dvorkin still alive, the Gestapo agents were scared to be in that territory."

No wonder Dad treated him like a king. "I wish I knew this when Mr. Dvorkin was here," I tell her.

"He has no interest in discussing it. It's best to say nothing. Your dad says that whenever Mr. Dvorkin killed a number of Gestapo agents in a town, the Germans often then came in and killed every Jewish man, woman, and child in retribution, and sometimes even Poles. There was a huge price to pay for these assassinations and I think he lives with this every minute. I think it's why he can't even work."

"But he is a huge hero," I say.

"A hero who will likely never be in a single history book."

More and more I read history books and I know we never get the whole story. It depends who took notes, who survived.

"Then maybe we should make sure we write about this," I say.

Mom half-smiles while Grandma moves more assuredly in the background.

"Maybe," Mom says. "But we have to respect Mr. Dvorkin. I don't think he would be happy about it."

I am lying in bed awake a long time, Stephen long since asleep.

To Dad Mr. Dvorkin is a great hero and the story will remain untold, but perhaps I can tell it someday and fix its history.

Even in Yeshiva they don't teach about the Holocaust. Partly I think Jews are embarrassed. Some writers say we didn't have to give in so easily and march to our death. Mr. Dvorkin is Superman, a hero who is now poor. A hero who few know about and maybe that's the true way to be a hero. ■

CHAPTER 16

Spelling Bee

"*CARNIVORE*," MRS. SONNENBERG pronounces precisely, and Ann Cohen spells, "C-A-R-N-A-V-O-R-E."

"Wrong," Mrs. Sonnenberg says. She spells it correctly and Ann sits down. Only four left in our class, two of whom will go to the finals in the main auditorium, and the winner will go to the regionals and then possibly the nationals. It is down to Ira Bernstein, Paul Slater, Ruth Kallor, and me.

Ruth is the surprise, a large blond girl, taller than me, who would have beaten almost any boy in ringolevio, a rougher game of tag, had she chosen to do so. Her only good friend is Ann Cohen and the two are like glue, Ann just as tall, very slim and dark-haired. Neither has much interest in school and whenever Mrs. Sonnenberg calls on Ruth she fidgets and mumbles. But here she is in the final four, having already gotten five words correct.

Everyone expects me to win but on the fourth word, *facilitate*, I quickly make a stupid error on the second I, but before I finish Mrs. Sonnenberg immediately interrupts and says, "I am sorry, that is not the next word. Let's begin with the next one."

I know she changed the word for me and I feel embarrassed. Everyone knows I am her favorite, but this isn't fair. I knew the word. I tried to see it in my head when I was spelling it but I got it wrong.

A couple of weeks ago Mrs. Sonnenberg told me she wanted me to prepare hard for the spelling bee. "I think you can represent our school in the nationals," she said. "Your reading is advanced even for high school." By then she had been meeting with me weekly and discussing books I had read.

She gave me a spelling primer to study. "I have been doing this for sixteen years," she said. "Here is a list of the words students have gotten wrong in the finals."

I was quickly bored. Maybe she is wrong and I am just not a good speller.

But today she interrupted me when I was making an error and my classmates knew it and I don't want to win this way but I say nothing. Finally, Paul and Ira each make a mistake, and when Ruth gets her word correct, she and I win. Ruth's final two words were the most difficult and I have this uneasy feeling that Mrs. Sonnenberg was making it tougher on her. She isn't a good student and likely Mrs. Sonnenberg didn't want her to win, assuming that Ruth would quickly be eliminated. But no, she spelled both words correctly: *syllogism* and *hemorrhage*. Those are two terrible words. How many kids could possibly know that hemorrhage has two Rs and what about that nasty second H?

Ruth deserved to win, and Ira should have as well but Ruth and I will compete in the school finals. It is the end of April and light when we return home. I want to do anything but study spelling.

I worked in the Grand Street store one day while we were on school holiday. Dad is back to joking with customers and arguing with Uncle Hy. He closed Cottonland and I think sales at Roman Cotton have started to improve.

Dad is also elated because the Army has made charges against Senator McCarthy and now the committee McCarthy chairs is investigating him. Dad admires Edward R. Murrow for speaking out against McCarthy on TV. And baseball season is underway. The Yankees have great pitching this year and Mickey and Yogi are batting three and four. In the National League the Dodgers are really solid with Roy Campanella behind the plate, who is the second-best catcher in baseball. Yogi is first.

The auditorium of the main school is completely full. The spelling bee is for students in fifth through eighth grades and 16 of us are seated on the stage with a podium middle front. Ruth is really nervous. She hates being called upon in class and now I know that she is very shy. Walking onto the stage she is sweating. Her large yellow dress has a wet circle in the rear and she wants to take a seat as far away as possible from the audience but everyone has assigned seats and Ruth and I are in the first row.

The audience is quieted as Mrs. Ginsberg, a sour seventh-grade English teacher, explains the rules. Her reputation is she is the strictest teacher in the school.

"I will say the word and the students may ask me to repeat it if they choose," she says. "They can ask for the definition. Otherwise they must begin to spell the word. Before they get to the end they can correct the spelling. Once they are finished I will indicate whether they are correct or not. If they misspell the word, they must leave the stage and sit in the audience."

Her voice is high-pitched and tinny, like an old church bell, and she speaks as though she might be British, reminding me of Winston Churchill. But Churchill is much slower and more deliberate and he elongates the ends of many words: Nowww my friendsss....

"We need perfect quiet," Mrs. Ginsberg continues. "No noise. No clapping. No interruption whatsoever. This is very serious. These are our sixteen best spellers and the winner will go to the regionals next week in Washington, DC."

The other teachers are all in the audience. Rabbi Charny is standing in the rear to my right.

Mrs. Ginsberg begins and calls on us in alphabetical order. "Jonathan Adelstein."

Jonathan is at the podium and she says, "*Vulgar*," which he gets easily. I suppose some would think there's an E rather than an A. Ruth Kallor is fourth and I am not certain she will make it to the podium as she is quivering so badly.

Mrs. Ginsberg says, "Okay, Miss Kallor. We will wait a few seconds. Just settle in."

I know that saying that never helps. There is nothing that can calm Ruth down, and when Mrs. Ginsberg says, "Are you ready?" Ruth barely nods her head.

She gets a very tough word and asks Mrs. Ginsberg to repeat it and then as slowly as a train starting to pull out of a station she begins, and between each letter the pause is several seconds and Mrs. Ginsberg is getting angry. Finally Ruth finishes and looks down at the floor.

"Correct," Mrs. Ginsberg says, and a huge sigh goes up in the entire audience, as though everyone was holding their breath like just before King Kong falls from the top of the Empire State Building. He is holding on, holding on, wounded with so many bullets.

I am next to last, my usual fate as almost everything is alphabetical.

"Marc Straus," she announces, and I see my classmates together in the middle rows to my right.

"*Avillity*," she says, and I don't understand the word. I have never seen this. I can recall almost everything I read and I wonder if this is fair.

"Repeat it, please?" I ask. I didn't want to ask. I know the meaning of all of them in the study book. But I never heard of this one.

She repeats it. "*Avillity*."

I wait. I am embarrassed to ask her to repeat it again. I could ask for the definition but I begin. "A-V-I-L." Then I wait.

"Please continue," she prompts.

"L-I-T-Y."

A groan goes up and she says, "Incorrect. It is A-B-I-L-I-T-Y."

I walk down the left stairs and into the audience. I thought she said V and not B and then I said two Ls and not one.

I don't know why she didn't correct me when I said V, realizing I had not heard her correctly. But it is too late. I lost on the very first word.

I sit down in a chair in the row with my classmates. No one says anything. I won't look at Mrs. Sonnenberg. I disappointed all of them and I should never have been here. I didn't deserve to be in the spelling bee but it is fate. I lost because I couldn't understand her. Her sound confused me. Even when she repeated it I thought it was V.

I might be the best reader in the entire school but that doesn't mean I am a good speller. It is different. I know every baseball statistic of every major league player. I never forget numbers. Not a single price in the store—the same as Dad. But Ruth Kallor, who is a mediocre student, is a much better speller than me and now I am really rooting for her.

There are three students left and Ruth is given another terribly hard word and looks frozen onstage. She is staring right at me now and I begin to mouth the letters and she frowns and looks away quickly.

"Any help from the audience and the student is eliminated," Mrs. Ginsberg says loudly. Johnny Applebaum shoots an elbow into my ribs and I lower my head. Ruth spells it correctly and finally two rounds later a seventh grader is eliminated.

It is Ruth now and an eighth grader who won last year. Now the audience cheers as Mrs. Ginsberg warns them. Two more words for each and then Ruth is asked a word and I see it is hopeless. She doesn't understand it and the spelling is difficult. Incredibly, she approaches the end without an error and I am so nervous I have difficulty remaining in my seat. And then she makes an error in the next to last letter.

"That is incorrect," Mrs. Ginsberg says. "Mr. Shornstein. It is your turn. If you can spell it correctly, you win."

Ronald Shornstein, tall and thin and confident, spells it carefully and correctly and wins, and Ruth Kallor walks down the steps head lowered. Her lower lip is rumpled up. She is almost in tears and as she approaches our row I stand up and cheer and all of our class does the same.

"Yay, Ruth!" we chant. "Yay, Ruth!" in unison, and a small smile crosses her face. ▪

CHAPTER 17

Dodge Coronet

DAD IS RAILING AGAIN, jabbing his right index finger at the windshield of the Dodge Coronet, and all around him cars are honking loudly. The front nose of the green Dodge is pointed at the center white line dividing a two-lane road and no one can pass him on the right or the left, especially since he is also weaving and pumping the gas pedal in fits and starts.

"They picked a Jewish judge," he has said a hundred times since the Rosenbergs were executed. "They knew he would have to hand out a tougher penalty."

He still believes they were innocent and that Ethel Rosenberg's brother David Greenglass lied at the trial. Uncle Manny has suggested that in the late 1930s Dad was a communist, but Mom says he wasn't; he just liked to hang out with girls who were loose. It's probably true. When Stalin died last year, Dad was elated.

Dad says again mostly for my benefit that Felix Frankfurter is only the third Jew to serve on the Supreme Court. His dad was also an immigrant linen merchant on the Lower East Side.

For Dad and his shopkeeper friends this is the standard. You can be a poor immigrant from Eastern Europe and your son can make it to Harvard Law and beyond.

Dad continues to let the windshield know all his disagreements, and drivers of cars that finally manage to get past him raise their right middle fingers and curse. The women use more imaginative language.

Sometimes Dad decides something and he just does it. Or he doesn't decide and does it anyway. Like one day in March he bought this car. He passed by the dealer and went in and now he has a new green '54 Dodge Coronet with air conditioning. The new car has PowerFlite, 152 horsepower, automatic overdrive, and no clutch pedal, which makes it really fast—all wasted on him. He never speeds and miraculously he has never had an accident. His car must have invisible letters outside that light up and flash as cars come near: Beware—This Driver is a Maniac.

New York City cab drivers are petrified of him. They cut off almost anyone and then stop to let a passenger off, completely blocking traffic. But none of them cuts off Dad since you never know what he will do—turn right when you think he's turning left or stop where there's no red light.

If that new windshield had memory it would learn a lot about politics. Dad must know the names of every president and prime minister in the world and every U.S. senator and each is judged first by their attitude toward Israel and Jews.

"You can't be supportive of Jews and be against Israel," Dad says, which makes sense.

Just nine years ago the Holocaust ended and then many of the Jews who survived the concentration camps lived in temporary camps. I read that Britain did not want them emigrating to Palestine. But they did, and David Ben-Gurion, a short stout man with a shock of white hair around a bald dome, is Prime Minister of Israel. He is the voice of the new Jew, Dad says many times, not deferential to the Brits or the French. But then, Dad points out, who would be intimidated by the French? The Germans overran them in less than three weeks.

Right now Dad's big concerns are mostly Jews and anti-Semitism: Senator Joseph McCarthy, Secretary of State John Foster Dulles, and Secretary of Defense Charles E. Wilson had all pushed for the Rosenbergs' deaths.

Dad probably thought West Hempstead was a perfect suburb for three redheaded Jewish kids. Then he sent Stephen and me to a Jewish school in Queens but not because he had a clue about our neighborhood. Since we go to a Jewish school, why not move to a Jewish neighborhood and he would have a short commute as well to the store? I tried to tell him that recently but he was busy talking about Israel. "Colonel Nasser took over Egypt. Arabs always need dictators."

We are only a few miles from the store now. The sky is cloudless and the temperature has warmed. Dad is back to the Rosenbergs and McCarthy.

I guess there are always bullies but in the case of Germany they had guns and poison gas. In Dad's town in Poland, which is now back in Ukraine, the local people killed the remaining 2,000 Jews all on their own in early 1943, right around when I was born.

They made them undress before killing them and dig a huge ditch for their own graves. They shot them all. Even babies.

It is the Ukrainians Dad hates the most. He lived there. So he knows.

"Roosevelt knew from the beginning. So did Churchill. They did nothing and here they rushed to execute two Jews." At home Dad says almost nothing about politics and as a result Miriam and Stephen will never know this side of him. I am not even sure Mom knows many of his opinions.

It is a warm day, the middle of May. Soon the end of my first year at Yeshiva.

Thick smoke rises in gray plumes from factories in Brooklyn. We are nearing the Manhattan Bridge and I ask Dad why Herbert Lehman, our first Jewish U.S. senator from New York, doesn't speak out against McCarthy. Dad's face accordions in, then he says Lehman did speak out early against McCarthy, but he didn't do enough in the war.

I want to hear more but Dad shuts down and changes the subject.

But I think I understand. Lehmann was very rich, from the German Jewish family that started Lehman Brothers, the banking house. He became the first Jewish Governor of New York when Roosevelt was elected President. The relief agencies he headed hit roadblocks everywhere, and they didn't try to stop the killing, just help Jews who survived. Lehman could have done far more.

Rabbi Schwartz at Temple Beth Israel and all Dad's friends and every Jew who speaks about Roosevelt loved him, which I don't understand since Hitler killed all the Jews while Roosevelt was President. I once asked Uncle Hy about this and he said Jews are hypocrites. Roosevelt turned away a ship hoping to dock in Miami in 1939 with more than 900 Jewish refugees aboard and when it was forced to return to Europe and other countries would take in only some of them, almost a third ended up in Auschwitz.

I was upset when I learned about this. But it's hard to get a straight story about exactly what happened. I am in a Jewish yeshiva and no one has ever mentioned the Holocaust. Once I saw Dad looking at a book that had pictures of piles of dead bodies and he shut it immediately when I came near.

"Did you know that Edmund Hillary is the first man to climb to the top of Mount Everest?" I ask Dad.

Dad mumbles back, "No one gives credit to the Sherpa who took him up there."

By now I know everyone on Dad's team and who the opposition is. Like the New York Yankees against the Brooklyn Dodgers. He hates Senator Kennedy's father, Joe, who was a Nazi sympathizer, and worse yet is Charles Lindbergh for whom our street is named. And top of the batting order for the opposing side is Joseph McCarthy.

Being on Dad's team means you are for Israel and for workers having a good wage and his team includes Senator Hubert Humphrey from Minnesota and Robert F. Wagner, Jr., Mayor of New York City. There are over two million Jews in the city but Dad says what's here is like yard goods. It's only a remnant.

He was in Sambor as a boy. His older stepsister, Aunt Essie, told me Dad wasn't permitted to attend public school after age 11.

Dad has pitted teeth from starvation. He is thinking of getting all his teeth capped but that is $10,000, three times the price of the new Coronet. ■

CHAPTER 18

Belly of the Beast

SWEAT SLIPS OFF her long nail-bitten fingers like miniature diamonds. Mom's gray and blue housedress with large front buttons is soaked through under her arms and along her neck. Her thick raw hands are kneading stuffing she makes with bread, mushrooms, onions, and thin slivers of meat. Two fists dip into the wide glass bowl and squeeze the thick contents, compressing so hard it seems she could rupture anything; she could as easily break open a live cow just with her hands or serve as the executioner for the French Revolution who would have no need for a guillotine.

Rarely now does she play our Steinway baby grand piano; she is unable to tolerate her increasing errors. I loved listening to Chopin, which she played with a fiery propulsion that I am certain no one before has equaled.

Miriam is upstairs with Arlene Aber, Charlie's older sister. They are singing loudly and even from up in the attic room it is deafening as the floor knocks to the rhythm of "Sh-Boom Sh-Boom...." For two months, earlier this year, all I ever heard was "Oh! My Papa," by Eddie Fisher.

Boring. And then "Three Coins in the Fountain" by the Four Aces and on and on. I am always surprised that Mom never says anything. She knows this music is drivel and sometimes I think Miriam is simply off her radar and Mom doesn't care. She might as well be dancing in an attic in some house three miles away.

Miriam's hair is much more strawberry-colored now. I liked it with two braids but now, just turned 14, she tries to mimic the hairstyle of Doris Day, a short bob with the sides turned forward. I say why not that wavy thing falling across her right eye like Marilyn Monroe, whose naked picture is still in the upper rear bathroom of Dad's store.

No, it's Doris Day, probably because she has another Top Ten song.

I am 11 soon. School ends in less than two weeks, a long year commuting from West Hempstead to Queens. I think that if the Spanish Inquisition had stopped trying to convert Jews and instead made them travel four hours a day to an Orthodox Jewish school, there would have been less of a problem convincing them to convert.

No one has said definitely whether Stephen and I are going again next year. He is seven and a half now and still puny-sized.

Miriam is starting at the local high school in September, where all her friends will be. Lucky for her she doesn't have our commute that no doubt she would hate. At religious school the girls wear plain long skirts and long-sleeved blouses and no jewelry on their wrists, and Miriam loves jewelry. If the girls at Yeshiva know the latest song hits they are keeping that to themselves.

I am looking forward to no school and being out with my friends, but now I don't keep up with the kids in the neighborhood anymore. No one comes by and Stewie moved away a while ago.

I went to playgrounds as far away as Merrick to flip baseball cards, to build up my stash of mints, of players long retired. But since starting Yeshiva I have not done this once.

I often used to bike to the library in Hempstead to exchange books but have done that infrequently this year.

Today I have no ambition to go anywhere. Summer is edging near. It's humid and I need a break. I could go see a Yankees game if Uncle Jack will take me to the stadium. I have been to the Polo Grounds twice with him to see the New York Giants, his favorite baseball team. I have even lost a lot of interest in baseball. Sometimes I don't even know the standings of the teams.

I could have been working at Dad's store but today he isn't there so I am off as well. He went to North Carolina to visit a textile mill.

I go by the kitchen again and that mix turning in Mom's hands has given in to her power. Now she has a huge turkey with its abdomen split open and she is packing the mixture into the belly. Miriam must be gone. No music from upstairs. Stephen is in the garage as always with enough wood and nails to build the Taj Mahal. He might do that someday.

There is a trickle of a breeze through the small window over the kitchen sink that faces the driveway. I want to look away from this bird. It has become a subject of jokes that I am unable to look at a dead animal that we will later eat. Not even a fish. I won't ever go with Grandma Katy again to Pitkin Avenue where she picks out a live carp that she will turn into gefilte fish. Or where Mom points to a live salmon and then they chop off big fillets while it still wiggles.

We are not vegetarian. I would not want to give up roast beef, but it doesn't mean I have to see the cow before it's slaughtered and skinned and hung from a huge hook in a meat market.

This turkey is a beast. It's massive and I don't like to think about what it looked like before they slit its neck, before they picked off the feathers.

It must weigh well over 20 pounds. It's heavier than the briefcase I carry back and forth to school every day.

It has so much body for feet that are so little and a tiny head. Bred to be eaten. That's it. It's the only purpose. It would not otherwise have been alive.

And now where there were intestines and a gizzard and a liver there is a thick gluey yellow-white substance jammed into every possible crevice, unnaturally. It was enough to kill this big bird but now the bird seems shamed. Mom wants this mixture to soak through the muscle so that it takes up the flavors of onions, carrots, and spice.

I cringe inside but this time I can't help looking. My parents are hoping that Stephen and I become doctors. Surgeons, to be exact, and will that be possible? Cutting a person open and cutting out some diseased intestines or lungs? But I suppose at least there you are trying to help, to eliminate an illness, but everyone knows that patients also die during surgery.

Mom's back is to me, flat and taut, arms reaching around and packing the beast, her neck extended, arm muscles rippled, no looseness behind her upper arms as most women have. She is steel and birds are just birds.

I have looked away for some reason. Perhaps I will go see if one of my former friends is in. Even Humphrey Plant across the street, who is and is not a friend. He's a year younger and I've known him since we moved here eight years ago when I was three.

I remember that. A summer just like this and the basement

filled with hundreds of empty beer bottles and old newspapers and magazines.

Memories often stay in me as though they might be now.

I turn back to the window. I think I hear something. Probably a bee banging against the screen.

Mom is facing me. Her arms slightly out and bent as though she doesn't want to touch her dress with those hands red and greasy with flesh, her fingers scored open in several places.

She is staring silently in my direction but it is as though she is seeing past and through me, as though I am a mirage.

I know what this means. I had thought that perhaps by going to this distant religious school this aspect of my life might change. But hope is never the same as reality and if I hope too much then the reality is worse.

Beatings sometimes have a prelude like some musical pieces, like opera. Usually but not always it begins with a quiet moment where it seems that time is extended and drawn out with a violin bow. Sometimes it is directly related to a specific event: I broke a pitcher or the lavender toilet-tank top. But only sometimes. If I had a choice, as if I ever had a choice, I would prefer the predictable. When the rage starts without an event, without warning, it will be much worse. It will last longer.

I wish that I had really thought about this more, that I had made an exact plan in case this ever occurred again. Because now I am strong. I can easily get away, get out the door, and not return for hours.

Maybe next time. In this moment with the bird turned over and its guts replaced with Mom-made stuffing, it feels as if everything is inevitable.

Maybe next time I will concentrate and if I do, it might be the last time.

This is going to be really severe. The leather strap is in the closed closet just a few feet behind and to her right. That would also be more predictable.

This will be worse. The hands that worked the beast.

Knuckles and gritty palms.

It has never been Miriam. Never Stephen. That I will not permit.

The air stops. There is no bee. No music. Time compresses to a nugget and into a Black Hole. ▪

CHAPTER 19

Grandma Katy

I DON'T REMEMBER VERY MUCH about Grandma Katy from the time when Grandpa Max was alive. I can see her making pickles in a wooden barrel in the basement, adding thick cloves, bay leaves, and onions.

She was sixty and I was five when Grandpa Max suddenly died.

In Brooklyn we lived two blocks from Grandpa and Grandma and after we moved when I was three they came to visit about every two months. For their whole visit Grandma cooked and Grandpa spent time with me.

I don't remember Grandma and Grandpa ever talking to one another as other adults do about work or money or their children. With Mom and Dad you know their every opinion and most of the time they don't agree. Maybe at Grandpa and Grandma's age they were finished with their disagreements. Or maybe they argued somewhere else.

But I don't think so because Grandma misses Grandpa every day and he died more than five years ago. She cries instantly when Grandpa is mentioned and I can tell when she is thinking about him. Her eyes droop. She is quiet and forgets what she was supposed to do. I might poke her and she will look at me but wants to still be somewhere else in her mind.

Grandpa once told me the worst thing for a parent is to lose a child. For more than a year when Uncle Hy was fighting in the Pacific, they weren't sure if he was alive. But Uncle Hy came home and it was Grandpa who died.

I go with Grandma to the cemetery whenever we can convince Mom to drive us and as soon as Grandma comes near Grandpa's headstone she wails, "*Max!*" for five or ten minutes while Mom stays at a distance angrily waiting. She won't go near the headstone until Grandma is done.

Then Mom stands quietly and finds a nice clean rock nearby and places it on top of the headstone. She is also crying but she keeps it deep inside. I once asked her why she puts a rock there and she said so he would know she was here.

I couldn't understand why a little rock on top of his stone would make a difference but since then I always look for a stone that is different and place mine there as well.

Stephen doesn't remember Grandpa and Miriam has never gone with us to the cemetery.

Now Grandma Katy stays over about once a month. She and Mom say little to each other except where the extra flour is or the large glass bowl. I don't think Mom really likes Grandma. She doesn't ever ask Grandma if she needs something like a dress or a new refrigerator.

Grandma spends all her time cooking and the thing you have to learn about eating when she is here is that she will take your plate away before you can finish. I like to eat everything one at a time in order. First string beans, then my baked potato, and last the large slice of roast beef. But if I am not careful Grandma has my plate and I am only halfway through.

When I see her sneak up behind me I hold my plate tightly with both hands and she laughs really hard. No problem with Miriam who is usually done in seconds.

Stephen is going to stay skinny because he dawdles with his food and if we waited for him to finish it could be breakfast the next day. I doubt he has ever had the chance to finish one stuffed cabbage, but then again they are the size of submarine missiles and if you believe Uncle Bob they are more lethal. Grandma never eats with us and except for holidays Mom eats dinner by herself around 5:00 p.m.

IT IS THE FIRST FRIDAY NIGHT in June and the weather turns really warm. It was my birthday last Wednesday and Grandma and Miriam are the only ones who remembered. Grandma bought me another pair of flannel pajamas, this time green with little white circles all over. They remind me of strep throat, green pus with white spots.

Miriam said she was going to buy me a record. I don't have a record player, I reminded her, and I am not allowed to use the Victrola in the living room. I was thinking I could really use a pair of leather handball gloves but I didn't want her asking questions about where I play. So she bought me a birthday card that had a picture of a redheaded boy on the front and said inside "For the best brother."

We are seated for dinner and Dad is already slurping his chicken soup while reading the *New York Post*. Usually at home he doesn't comment but he grunts and says the Supreme Court has finally done the right thing. The Brown v. Board of Education case. They banned segregation in public schools. He is happy now that it looks like the Senate is going to censure Senator McCarthy.

I walk around to have a look at the pages. Everyone knows that in most places Negroes go to separate schools. That's about to change. Dad makes the blessing over the wine and bread and sings the Friday night prayer and then it is off to the races.

THIS SATURDAY AFTERNOON is like summer. I am supposed to mow the lawn, which Miriam will never do. She is at Arlene Gore's. Dad is back to Temple Beth Israel for a meeting and Stephen is probably in the garage building his spaceship to Mars. I am on a new book and I decide to go down to the kitchen for a glass of water. I can smell Grandma's new sour pickles curing in the wooden barrel in the basement and she is stewing meat in the kitchen. Something really pungent is in the frying pan. It is *gribenes* for my baked potato. Grandma takes pieces of chicken skin and cuts them up and adds onions, garlic, and butter, and then fries them.

At the bottom of the stairs I hear Mom scrubbing the kitchen linoleum with hard even strokes. She uses a large bristle brush and she is always on her hands and knees with a pail of soapy water and box of detergent nearby.

She has a meeting later this afternoon with her Hadassah group. I hope for their sake they raised enough money for the hospital in Jerusalem.

I go by Mom quietly, careful not to step in the soapy water on the floor. Grandma is at the sink kneading dough for challah with her bare hands. She never uses a machine. She is in her gray housedress, her thick white hair pulled up in a bun, her wide neck wet with sweat.

She hands me a clean glass and I fill it at the faucet and then pretend to steal some stuffing in a large bowl and she swats me with a towel and laughs noiselessly.

Twinkie is out roaming the neighborhood. I see Stephen just inside the garage hammering away. He will do this all afternoon.

The grass is perfect now. Between Mom and me, crabgrass has no chance. In the rear of the yard the pine tree's needles glisten from the humidity and the free-standing hammock is back out underneath. Dad and I are the only ones who use it.

Mr. Mitchell is working near his garage. Last weekend his daughter Diane was visiting him from New Jersey with her five-year-old daughter, Betty-Ann. Diane used to lend me books when I was five and then she got married and left.

Mom is still scrubbing and Grandma is in and out of the dining room, which surprises me. No one goes there except for Mom, unless we have a special dinner. Since Dad closed Cottonland two months ago we have had no company over. He is back full-time at his store in New York City.

Grandma is in the dining room again. She turns to come back into the kitchen, sees me and smiles. She has deep sparkly brown eyes, a large flat nose and a wide mouth.

"Hey, Grandma," I say. "I hope you cook something good for a change."

I see the dishtowel appear readied to swat me. I shake my fist at her.

"Watch out, Grandma," I say laughing. "I am almost as tall as you."

"Out of the way," she orders me in Yiddish, as I am half blocking the entrance to the kitchen.

Then she puts her finger to her lips to keep me quiet as Mom is still scrubbing the floor, now closer to the stove on the right.

"Grandma, maybe we can take a bus to Mount Hebron tomorrow."

She nods her head yes.

Without looking up Mom says, "There is no way we are going tomorrow."

Grandma is very glum and tearful and I say, "Okay, Grandma, I will take the bus with you. I want to visit Grandpa Max."

Mom yells, "You are not going!"

Grandma is planted just inside the threshold to the kitchen. Her face has stiffened, and thick tears are in the corners of her eyes.

Mom is up and headed towards the den and swings back around. The knuckles on her right hand are red and cracked.

"No," she says. "Every time I take you there you shriek like a witch! It's embarrassing."

"I can take her there. I know how," I tell Mom.

She glares at me. Her whole dress is soaked from sweat.

"Do you understand the meaning of no?" she yells at Grandma.

Grandma nods her head up and down and mumbles, "Max, what did I do?"

Mom is white-faced and her long narrow nostrils pinch in more deeply.

"We go to the cemetery and you scream like a crazy banshee, and then the screaming stops on a dime. You are a phony."

Usually in Mom's storms I get calm but now my skin has crawlies going up and down.

Mom takes another step toward Grandma and I step in the way. She aims her right index finger past me to Grandma and says, "You are a stupid old woman."

"Stop!" I suddenly yell at her. "You can't talk to Grandma like that."

Mom's mouth becomes a small O and she yells even more loudly.

"Step out of the way or you will be very sorry!"

Grandma is trembling. I guess she knows what Mom means. Soon Mom will be at the broom closet to retrieve the leather belt.

I don't even blink. The fear has left me and everything slows down. I am curious seeing Mom so close up yelling in my face with the sound almost gone. Maybe I didn't notice before but Mom's lower teeth are really uneven and they are more stained from cigarettes than I realized.

"I tell you for the last time to move!" I hear her say as if from under a blanket.

Behind me I can feel Grandma shaking harder. She doesn't know what to do. Mom has beaten me so many times since I was very little but she has never hit Grandma and I don't know if she might do it.

"I am not moving," I say, quietly looking up at Mom, who is only about six inches taller than me now. I have grown and am thick and strong.

Mom's mouth is quivering.

Staring right into her harsh blue eyes I say evenly, "You can't speak to Grandma like that."

"You know nothing," she says.

"I won't allow it," I tell her and somehow I know things have turned and I won't be hit, but one way or another I am not sure it matters to me.

"You know nothing," she repeats. "You don't know anything about my childhood."

"I know one thing for sure," I say. "She is your mother and you are teaching us that it's okay to speak to a parent this way."

"This is different," she says more sorrowfully. "My children won't do this."

"Yes, we will," I say.

"No," she insists. "This is different."

"No, it's not," I say much more firmly. "I will remind you when you are old."

"My children are different," she pleads. Mom's face begins to get some color back. That moment when she is lost in some other place is receding.

I can hear Stephen hammering. I might go outside now and lie down in the hammock in the deep shade. ■

CHAPTER 20

Mitchell Cooper

MITCHELL COOPER LIVES in an apartment building in Kew Gardens on the third floor of a six-story walkup with narrow dark hallways and dark-brown stone floors. He and his family are at the end of the hall on the right. This is the third time I am sleeping over. Mitchell has never slept at our house, nor has Kenny Siegel. The reason is that Mom doesn't want anyone else to clean up after and that includes making a bed and washing out the bathroom sink and toilets. But then Miriam has sleepovers. Maybe girls don't have to pee.

I have never explained the real reason to my friends. I say that Mom leaves the house too early and comes home too late. She is busy running Hadassah at Temple Beth Israel. That is true but Mitchell's mom works long hours selling cosmetics in a department store and his father sells car insurance and is out most nights meeting customers.

But Mrs. Siegel and Mrs. Cooper never complain that the sleepovers are always in one direction. Every time I come they are happy to see me, especially Mrs. Cooper.

"Maybe you can help Mitchell," she says hopefully, "so he can do better in school. He doesn't do any homework."

I say okay and then Mitchell and I go out to play in a nearby park. He is embarrassed that his mother says this to me. His huge ears get really red and stick out like raspberry-colored ice cream scoops.

He can't get away from his ears but he could do his schoolwork.

"Why should I?" Mitchell says flatly to end the matter as we get ready for a game of handball.

When I stay with Kenny we play chess around the clock and hardly speak. Mitchell likes to talk a lot and what I really like about him is he has such joy about almost everything except school studies. "Isn't that great?" he says constantly. It could be the way a dog catches a ball in his mouth in the park.

That's where we usually head. It's a small park with one baseball field and a few handball courts. Out here handball is played with a genuine small hard black ball and if you are not used to it your hands soon kill.

"Okay let's see who gets closer to the back line," I say. That decides who serves first.

"I mean you don't study ever," Mitchell says, hitting his shot way short of the line. I hit mine a few feet behind his and I am up first.

"Yeah well, I read a lot," I tell him stepping toward the left and deciding on my opening serve.

"I read," Mitchell says, moving right and left, knowing that if he is too far to one side my serve will be out of his reach.

I hit the ball with half power on the top half of the wall and it comes down in a high arc. There is little chance to return it if you wait till it lands because then the bounce will be so high that when it comes down it's almost in the court behind.

Mitchell knows he has to hit this on the fly coming down and if you do it right you generally win the point.

He misses the ball completely and curls his mouth up and heads back to the baseline to await the next serve.

"You read those stupid comic books," I say, taking his mom's side.

"Not stupid," he responds.

I am about to say something else when he butts in, "Just serve the ball and none of those trick shots."

I get really low, drop the ball, and hit it with my right hand. The black ball zooms low and fast, bounces off the wall, and hits just in front of the rear right baseline but Mitchell never gets within three feet of it. He doesn't know how much practice I have had during this year.

"What are you going to learn from another *Superman* comic?" I want to know.

"Whether he'll find the Kryptonite bomb before Lex Luthor blows up Metropolis," Mitchell says.

"So what?" I say. "It's fake."

"Ha. Big Shot," he laughs. "You served out. My turn now. Get ready for my super killer."

Not even Kenny knows that when I am not in Talmud class I am usually outside playing handball with older kids in a local school-yard near the Annex. Mitchell sometimes asks me where I go. I tell him I am just hanging out near the gym. But he knows it isn't true because then I would be found out. I am always surprised I get away with playing hooky so much.

"Three–six," Mitchell says. "I am catching up and you are going to lose."

At 15, I win. It isn't as if Mitchell doesn't expect it. But he never gets sore.

We are setting up for the next game when Carlos, a tall thin kid with stringy black hair, comes over. I have seen him play a few times. He is the best handball player here. He moves more quickly than you think.

"Hey guys, want to play for some bread?" he asks, speaking to us for the first time. Mitchell knows that it is for me to respond and I say, "Mitchell, you are up. Your serve."

"Me and Juke will give you ten points head start," he says, jutting his jaw at us. "Anyway, you have no choice. I challenge for the court."

The other kid is shorter and square and probably a year or two older than us. Out here if you don't accept a challenge you forfeit the court.

"Ten points!" Carlos repeats with a snicker.

Mitchell is frozen.

"Serve," I command. I don't have to give up the court until our game ends.

"Shit. Just as I thought. Jew boys can't play."

I haven't faced any anti-Semitism around here until now and I haven't had a good fight in almost a year, but I am thinking it's going to be much better when I whip him in handball. But the problem is Mitchell. I know they will mostly serve to him and there is no chance we can win unless we have good strategy. In doubles half of winning is knowing exactly what your partner will do.

I pull Mitchell aside and say, "Do you want to win this?"

"Sure," he says, but he doesn't mean it.

"We can win," I tell him. "He called us Jewish losers."

"We are Jewish," Mitchell says innocently.

"Hey dickheads," the same kid yells toward us. "What's it gonna be? Are we playing or do ya wanna quit before we start?"

"Mitchell," I implore quietly. "We will win. Just this time follow instructions and if I tell you go left do it without asking."

I win to serve first and quietly tell Mitchell, "Stand just outside right near the service line and as soon as the ball passes you, jump inside two steps."

"That kid is going to hit me with the ball in the butt," Mitchell protests, looking fearfully at Carlos. "It hurts a lot."

"What's it gonna be, dickheads?" Carlos sneers, placing himself just before the back line toward the right. He knows very well the ball is coming to him.

I lean low. Smack to the right near the right rear corner, almost hitting the line, and miraculously Mitchell steps in just where I told him. Carlos wants to win the point. If he hits Mitchell in the ass it's a do-over and Carlos wants to show off. As I serve I quickly move in closer and three steps to the right. If Carlos hits beyond my left reach it will be out. Straight ahead he hits Mitchell. The only open space for Carlos to hit the ball is the middle, and from the far-right side where he is, it will come back exactly at me.

I don't even turn around. I see the ball rocketing to the wall, a low shot, which careens just toward my left. A great shot, and as it is about to zoom by I just put out my left hand and softly drop it into the left corner where the bounce takes it back only a foot. Carlos's partner, Juke, is still standing near the back wall frozen.

"One–nothing," I say loudly, moving into position again.

Carlos screams to his buddy, "Juke, you shithead! You can't let him drop it in front of you!"

Juke shrugs and they are back in position. What Carlos left out of course is that it was his return that enabled me to do a drop shot that they would never have reached even if Juke was playing at half court. Now I know just what to do. I tell Mitchell to stand further back near the baseline. Juke moves up as I go into a low crouch. I knew he would without looking back. He doesn't want to be berated by Carlos for another drop shot.

I rise a bit and let the ball bounce higher and up it goes in a beautiful arc and comes down behind Juke. Carlos hopelessly runs to get it from the far right but he has as much chance as a pitcher has to strike out Willie Mays three times in a row.

"Two–nothing," I say slowly. Now they don't know where to stand and Carlos is yelling and Mitchell has a wide grin.

I want to end this as quickly as possible. I keep serving until they can get me out.

At seven–zero we give up the ball and they get five. It's too close. Mitchell makes out on his serve, then I am up and I move right, not far from where Mitchell stands out of bounds. Then I smash the ball on a sharp angle to Juke. Just past the baseline it is already headed to the next court and Juke isn't close. Carlos yells to switch sides and Juke hopelessly moves to the right side. Bang, right past him, and then right at his stomach, and he has no chance.

"Eleven–five, Carlos," I say matter-of-factly.

"Sure, you too scared to serve to me. Ha, hotshot? Chickenshit."

Bang, back to Juke some more, and it's 14–5. One more and we win.

I am thinking about what to do. If I win this serve we win the court and Carlos has to sit one out. Lots of kids are crowded nearby watching us take apart the best player. This is much better than winning a fight.

I move far left and take two steps back. I crouch and slam the ball to Carlos, high and to his left. His only chance is a good shoulder shot with his left hand.

He quickly moves in position and swings, and the ball loops far up to the left and misses the wall.

I walk over to Mitchell and say, "Great game, pal."

I don't give the final count and don't look at Carlos but go to shake Juke's hand.

"Yeah, good game," he says sullenly. I had watched Carlos. He isn't as strong on his left side and his best chance would have been to hit the ball low. By allowing it to bounce and hitting it higher up, he lost force and direction.

I guess I wanted to win by serving to Carlos. Otherwise victory wouldn't have been the same. This way he had no one else to blame. Great athletes know their own weaknesses. They either fix them or the opposing side will always take advantage. Mickey Mantle is a switch hitter, but everyone can see he is slightly better from the right.

Carlos starts to walk away and then turns, thinking to say something, and I glare at him. Our eyes are locked that way for a few seconds and then Mitchell tugs on me.

"Are we playing again?" Mitchell asks cautiously.

"Nah," I say. "Let's go back now."

Mitchell is happy as we enter his mother's tiny kitchen. Mrs. Cooper says we are having dinner in 30 minutes, when her husband gets home.

I know they always eat together and they don't have much money. Dad is usually home too late to eat with us except on Saturday night. Mrs. Cooper dresses nicely for dinner. She has on lots of perfume. It smells a little like the cloves Grandma Katy puts in the pickle barrel. It is really strong and stings my nose.

Mom doesn't wear perfume. She usually eats before us in a cotton housedress. Dinner is getting the food out, hurrying us up, and getting the dishes done, and then doing it all over again when Dad comes in.

Dad is a much slower eater than me because he usually has his paper to read. Mom is cleaning in the kitchen and she and Dad don't speak. He is tired and she wants him to finish.

Mr. Cooper comes in wearing a nice wool jacket and thin tie.

"Hi Marc," he waves, going to the sink to wash his hands. "Good to see you. You boys have fun?"

"We won big at handball," Mitchell volunteers.

"That's great," Mr. Cooper says.

"We beat the best kids in the park," Mitchell adds.

"How is school, boys?" Mr. Cooper continues as he sits down and puts the white linen napkin in his lap.

"Good, Mr. Cooper," I say eagerly.

"You start, darling," Mrs. Cooper says to her husband. "Green beans, potatoes, veal, your favorites." She smiles.

Near the end of dinner Mrs. Cooper comes back smiling widely and carrying a small chocolate cake with several lit candles. I don't realize at first it's for me.

She says, "It's for your eleventh birthday this week." Mitchell is grinning as hard as if the cake were for him.

She places the cake in front of me and Mr. Cooper says, "First make a wish." ▪

PART THREE

COMEBACK KID

CHAPTER 21

Iron Lung

A T LEAST THE YANKEES are doing well though Cleveland is stronger this year with four great starting pitchers. Bob Feller is fourth in their pitching rotation. He's nearing the end. His fastball used to be almost 100 miles an hour and you had to have supersonic eyes to see that.

Since school ended, I have worked almost every day in Dad's store and I want to keep working there all summer but in less than two weeks I go to Camp Massad, a sleepaway camp in Tannersville, Pennsylvania. It is a religious camp and none of my friends go there. Jack Heller's kids all go but they attend Yeshiva of Flatbush in Brooklyn.

Dad has known Jack Heller since they were boys in Ukraine. Jack has a jewelry business and owns a large building in the Financial District.

Now it's going to be Jewish camp with rich kids and all they will do for the entire summer is argue. Baseball and tennis but no football or handball.

We visited the Hellers last week and Mrs. Heller said she has picked me for her daughter, Arlene, who is a year younger than me and is as dark-haired as any girl I have ever seen.

Susan, who is my age and overweight, said, "They have amazing food. I have pancakes and omelets for breakfast."

Arlene chimed in, "And we have to speak in Hebrew."

Jack Heller slapped Dad on the back. "Get ready to pay through the nose, Sam, and you have plenty of room." He was referring to Dad's nose, of course, which is among the largest anyone has seen and I imagine he was teased a lot as a kid. But neither my sister, Miriam, nor I have large noses, though I suspect when Stephen gets older his will be twice the size of mine.

Camp Massad is coming, and even though Dad's business has picked up since Cottonland closed I am worried about the expense.

Harold is back working in Dad's store. He worked for dad for years and left to open his own store in Brooklyn that didn't succeed. He said the rents have doubled on 13th Avenue.

He is totally bald, not even one hair, and short with soft arms and legs, and big all around. Not just his belly but even his legs and arms and neck. He has a tenor voice like Richard Tucker.

"You leave me nothing to do," he said to me laughing the other day. "You are so grown up now and selling full-time."

"I was selling full-time last time you worked here," I remind him.

In the car home I tell Dad that I don't want to go to camp. I want to work in the store all summer as usual.

Dad is tired and I can help. He makes sure Grandma Katy has money. Without him Uncle Ira and Uncle Hy wouldn't have a job. He gives to the synagogue and Jewish causes. He pays a lot of money for tuition and I tell him again not to waste his money on camp. I have too much to do in the store.

He glances quickly at me and looks ahead again. Not even the radio on. I think he never had anyone to count on, not his Dad, who left when he was two, and not his stepmother.

He was on his own and working full-time so young.

The lines around Dad's eyes are much deeper and his hair has thinned in front. His diabetes has worsened and I think the new pills are making him sick. He has lost another ten pounds and the skin on his neck is droopy.

"I will work every day all summer," I offer.

Dad says quietly, "You and Stephen are going to camp." I don't know what their plans are for Miriam.

For Dad and his family and friends who came from the same towns in Ukraine there is no compromising on education. Camp Massad is part of his idea of education. If you have less money, then you don't buy a car. You take a less expensive vacation or no vacation.

The sky is beginning to dim now and a huge cloud hangs overhead like a gray lampshade.

"I never had a chance to go to camp," he says and stops speaking with his mouth half open.

Dad never talks about his childhood. Jack Heller once said to me, "Your Dad could kick that soccer ball right between the legs of those dumb Poles. He ran like a man on fire. And those girls loved that huge nose."

I could imagine Dad running that fast. I remember when he helped me learn to ride my 20-inch blue Schwinn. The training wheels were taken off and I asked him to hold the back seat and run alongside until I could do it without help. It took me a few tries and Dad was getting all sweaty and was going to quit but I asked him to hold on once more. Then I pedaled as hard as I could from the front of our house all the way to Woodfield Road and I never outraced Dad. His leather shoes cracked against the cement sidewalk like firecrackers. Jack Heller is right. Dad might be the fastest runner ever. Walking with him on the Lower East Side is like jogging. I can never keep up.

It looks like Stephen and I are going to Camp Massad.

I wave to Humphrey Plant across the street. He is a year younger, but it seems every day he grows taller than me.

"Where is Lorraine?" I ask. She is his younger sister.

"The swim club," he answers.

The Plants aren't Jewish. Their swim club doesn't allow Jews.

We go to a Conservative Temple. Stephen and I go to an Orthodox school, and now an Orthodox camp. Susie Heller told me that the camp is Modern Orthodox, at least, which means boys and girls sing and dance together.

We eat in unkosher restaurants but our house remains strictly kosher. It makes no sense. Jews are confused.

A few more Jews have moved to our neighborhood and Dad said some of them want to start a new synagogue. I heard the joke a thousand times about two Jews stranded on an island with three synagogues. They started one synagogue together and when they had a disagreement they both left and started another one on their own.

THIS SATURDAY DAD IS ASLEEP in the living room and the only place not steaming hot is our basement. So I go down there to finish *Great Expectations*, which is a good name for a book. Mrs. Mahoney at the Hempstead Library sees me much less often so she holds books aside for me. Last time, she suggested Thomas Hardy's final novel, *Jude the Obscure*, but I've already read it. Jude Fawley is like Dad's older brother, Ira. Jude dreams of becoming a scholar at Christminster but ultimately isn't accepted because of his impoverished background. Perhaps Uncle Ira was meant to be a professor but like Dad he had little education. Uncle Ira is lucky to work in the store and make money, but he hates being there and stays behind the cash register without moving. I think the worst thing would be to grow up and not be able to do work you like.

Months ago, Mrs. Mahoney gave me *The Old Man and the Sea*, which is my very favorite. It is a short book that tells the story of an old fisherman who goes to sea in a small boat every day for months without catching a fish. You think the book is going to be dull but it isn't. All the time you hope that the old fisherman, Santiago, will catch a great fish and it is only on the 85th day that he hooks a great marlin and then the fish pulls him out to sea for two days and nights. Santiago's favorite baseball player is Joe DiMaggio, who in real life married Marilyn Monroe in January. When we were unloading several cases of towels Uncle Hy said, "Now DiMaggio has hit a grand slam. He hits the ball right up the middle."

Santiago finally wins his fight with the 18-foot marlin but pulls into the docks with only the skeleton, sharks having devoured the carcass. But it doesn't matter. Santiago thinks that no one is worthy of eating the great marlin. Santiago had courage he didn't know he had. He never gave up and even though he came back with only the skeleton of the marlin everyone realized from its size that he had accomplished the impossible.

Mrs. Mahoney shows me some other books. I am the only one there that day except for an old woman in a pink hat with a red ribbon on the side. It is so humid the books smell of glue.

"I saved *For Whom the Bell Tolls*," she says pointing to a book, "since you loved the recent Hemingway."

"I read it last year," I remind her.

"Oh yes, I forgot. I really should keep a list. I am thinking of Faulkner or perhaps," and she smiles widely, "a Somerset Maugham. Perfect book in the heat. And maybe a spy novel for a change." Her eyes twinkle as she reaches below the desk. "And a new biography of Abraham Lincoln."

At home Mom and I start a new jigsaw puzzle, this one with 1,500 pieces. It looks almost impossible. A picture from a painting of a prairie with a girl sitting in a field turned away. It says *Christina's World* by Andrew Wyeth.

Mom and I are puzzle double-team champs. We easily won at Temple Beth Israel, but we haven't done any in over a year. I do all the borders and she focuses on one color or character. When we do puzzles I think our brains must be overheated. We can work at it three hours without saying a word.

I head back to the basement after lunch with my book but even down here the red floor tiles are sweating. I go upstairs thinking I might take a nap. I never do that but I feel so tired and I have read the same page three times. Mom is in the kitchen and from the scraping sounds I know she is washing large pots.

I usually don't sweat much but my blue and white polo shirt is soaked through.

"Where are you going?" Mom yells from the kitchen.

"Upstairs," I answer quietly with the steamy air deep in my lungs. I will try to read a few more pages. Too bad Dad won't let us turn on the Philco air conditioner in his room. He doesn't like paying the Long Island Lighting Company.

I lie back on the deep brown Piping Rock bedspread. This is our bestseller, $10.50 for the twin. I pull my pillow higher against the headboard. It is early afternoon and outside I can hear Mr. Mitchell hammering in his garage.

I lift my head, bleary-eyed. A few strands of light arc in from the window near Stephen's bed. It must be late afternoon and I try to see the clock on the bureau. It's 4:14 I think, but the thinner second hand is blurred. It is moving too quickly.

I must have slept over three hours in the middle of the day, which has never happened, probably not even when I was too small to remember. I sit up to the side of the bed. The bedspread is soaked, and the book is open to the same page.

I think I will pee and go downstairs and get some cold water. In the hallway the carpet threads burn against my bare feet. I don't have to pee, and I start downstairs and on the first step my right foot buckles under. I barely grab the rail in time to keep from falling. I step again with my left holding the rail more tightly and I am unable to get my leg to stay in place. It wants to cave in. I sit back down on the landing and begin again. Right leg, but it is too weak to hold me up.

I can't stand back up. Perhaps I slept too long, and I am not used to that. I try to stand again but I can't even get halfway up.

"Mom," I say nervously. I don't know if she is in the kitchen. I don't know if anyone is home. Where is Stephen? Probably building an unmanned spaceship in the garage.

"Mom!" more loudly as I lean back, trying not to slide down the stairs.

"Mom!" I try to yell.

"What is it?" she shouts from the kitchen or the den. I can't tell with the sound being absorbed by the heat.

"Mom!"

She is at the bottom of the staircase to the right and I can't see her.

"What is it, damn it?" she asks. "Come down if you want to speak."

"I can't," I plead.

"What? Just come downstairs and quit yelling."

"I can't stand up. My legs are buckling."

Mom has appeared instantly. She is wearing a green flowered cotton housedress soaked through under both armpits. Even her eyes are sweaty.

"What are you saying?"

"I can't stand up," I repeat.

Mom's bright red hair is all shiny. She leans in closely, her face the color of bleach.

"Let me see you try," she says. I grip the rail with my right hand and try to pull myself up again but I can't get more than a few inches up and collapse down. She reaches over and puts her palm on my forehead.

"You have a fever," she says nervously. She reaches under my arms and tugs me up like a ragdoll. She practically lifts me off the ground as my legs are dragging. I do have a fever and I am dizzy. It is like when I have bad sore throats, but right now my throat isn't sore. She lays me down on my bed, swings my feet up, and gets a cold-water compress to put on my forehead.

She is back with a thermometer under my tongue. I am thankful she didn't take my temperature in the tush.

"One hundred point four, but you feel much hotter. I am getting Dr. Fallis here immediately."

She is downstairs and I think I might take another nap. Probably my legs are weak from the heat and I might be better with some orange juice. Recently Dad had a weak spell from his diabetes and had to drink a large glass of orange juice and then was much better.

Maybe I have diabetes. All the men in Dad's family have that. You take pills and eat less sugar and stick your finger with a lancet every day. I don't like the idea of that, but I am going to get diabetes sooner or later and if it's something else then Grandma Katy will come over and make me chicken soup.

Mom is on the phone a long time I think with Dr. Fallis. I fall asleep and the next thing I hear Dr. Fallis downstairs speaking with Mom. You can't mistake his deep gravel voice from constant smoking.

"I don't know, Dora," he is saying. "We would have to get him to a neurologist."

Mom says something, and he says, "It is Saturday."

"I don't give a damn!" she says loudly and Dr. Fallis had better duck for cover.

"Okay, let's just have a look and not be panicked."

But Mom is already panicked and this is something I haven't seen since I was eight and broke my arm in three places and a bone was almost sticking out. Usually she is as cool as Gary Cooper in *High Noon*.

Dr. Fallis has a big thick stethoscope against my chest, his face near mine with smoking breath, and he says, "Breathe in slowly deeply." Then he reaches under my wet shirt and says, "Breathe in and out when I tell you." He has Mom help me sit up and he puts his index finger in front of each eye, closing the other, and says, "Look straight ahead and say yes when you see my finger wiggle."

"Yes, yes, yes."

Then he scratches the bottom of my feet with a needle, which feels terrible. My big toes jerk up, and he shakes his head.

"A Babinski sign, Dora, but I am not sure."

I remember a girl in third grade named Babinsky, Yvette Babinsky, so maybe she is related to the person who named the sign.

He asks me to push my right leg and then the left leg straight out and then up and down against his hand. "As hard as you can," he says, and I try to knock him over. Then maybe he will go home. But I can't lift my legs.

"Yes, Dora, it probably is. There is a good neurologist in Garden City. Monday take him there. I will get him seen first thing."

"What about the vaccine?" she asks. "It came out in April."

"We discussed it," he says carefully. "That's a trial. It is not available yet, and won't be for a while. It is not perfected."

"Why not take a chance now?" she insists.

"We can't get it, but if we could if he is already infected it might be too dangerous."

She begins to speak and Dr. Fallis interrupts, something no one does with Mom.

"Look, Dora, the truth is I am not sure. There is no exact test, as you know. Maybe yes. Likely yes. I have seen dozens of cases in the last three years alone."

"God, I was thinking we should rent a bungalow for the summer in the Catskills. Few people and clean air. Mary Brenner's daughter died!"

"I know. She was my patient. Please don't panic. We don't know and Monday Dr. Fielding will give us better information."

"What can you do right now? Something to slow this down!"

"Nothing that is safe. Gamma globulin injections might retard the disease, but Dr. Fielding will have to make that decision. Even that drug is not without issues. Many have significant reactions to the injections, even anaphylactic shock."

The room is squeezing in and out like an accordion playing very slowly and Dr. Fallis finally says, "I think we should discuss this in the kitchen."

In the kitchen I hear him say polio. I know what that is.

DAD WAS AT THE STORE and when he came home I must have been asleep. I awake, and he is standing silently right next to my bed just staring ahead blankly. His face is as gray as his new whiskers. I know he is scared. He gets like that and freezes up. I was playing doubles in handball with him once and I suddenly got such a bad stomach cramp and fell to the ground. Dad just froze in place and another man came over to question me. Mom handles all the times I break a bone.

On Monday Mr. Mitchell and Mom each take me under an arm and help me to the car. "I can go with you, Dora," Jim Mitchell offers. He is always wearing a nicely pressed light shirt but today it is too hot for a tie.

"Thank you so much, Jim," Mom says. "We'll make it."

Mr. Mitchell has a big frown but won't go against Mom. My temperature is down to 99.5 and I'm not sweating as badly but my legs still can't hold me up. If it is polio I don't want to be in an iron lung. Some kids stay in that until they die. It is useless. It is better to be run over by a car or hit by a train. Then you don't have to be in a metal tube that is breathing for you and I don't even know how they pee.

When I was five, Janie, a girl my age on the next block on Lindberg Street, was put in an iron lung and she died anyway. I saw pictures of it, a round metal tube you can hardly fit a body into. Janie even had to eat in there and I can't imagine how.

In World War II they put Jews in gas chambers the size of a room and they died in 20 minutes. Or they shot them and threw them into a ditch.

Mom helps me into the office in Garden City and they wheel me into an exam room immediately. I think the patients in the waiting room are happy they take me right away since maybe what I have is catching, but Dr. Fallis didn't seem worried.

Dr. Fielding has a plaque on his wall that says he did his neurology studies at Columbia-Presbyterian. He is tall and a few years older than Dad. His hair is thick with sprinkles of gray. His teeth are large and very white. He helps get me up onto an exam table covered with a clean white sheet.

Then he looks at notes Dr. Fallis sent him and says, "I have to do a little exam. Nothing will hurt." From a large leather bag he takes out a small hammer with a rubber tip and bangs against my knees and arms and watches for reflexes to pop. Then the pin against the bottom of my feet, and testing my strength just as Dr. Fallis did, and more eye tests.

"We can't be absolutely certain, Mrs. Straus," he says to Mom. "But given experience we are best off assuming that it is."

"Do I have polio?" I ask him.

Dr. Fielding turns to me and looks to Mom, who nods her head as if giving him permission to answer me. "I am not certain. It is possible. What most people don't realize is that many people get it mildly, and it is likely that in most cases it is so mild they don't even know."

"Then how do you know if they don't feel anything?" I want to know.

"That is a great question. From blood studies. Many people have the antibody—" Mom is about to cut him off when he says, "Please, Mrs. Straus. This is relevant." And then half to her he continues, "Antibodies were isolated in serum from patients who had clear symptoms of polio and tests also showed antibodies in people with no symptoms."

"What can we do now?" Mom asks firmly.

There is gamma globulin serum available, which might retard or even stop the disease."

"Will it help my son?"

"It is best given before there are symptoms but there is evidence that it decreases the progression to paralysis. But there are issues."

Mom waits with narrowed lips and he goes on.

"We don't have that much experience with it and it is very expensive and in limited supply. Two hundred dollars, Mrs. Straus, for a single injection, and most doctors are recommending a repeat dose in five weeks."

"And?"

"There can be reactions to the injection, even deaths, and it is best given first in a test dose with an antihistamine. Some doctors pre-inject cortisone, but I oppose that because we don't know the effect of cortisone on the polio virus."

"If I go to another neurologist in New York City?"

"By all means, please do. Right now, most neurologists recommend giving gamma globulin. Unless of course this isn't polio and then we take the risk unnecessarily. We can wait a few weeks and see."

"But by then it is possible the disease will have gotten much worse," Mom says.

"Yes, of course, but—"

"No buts. Can we start now?"

"I won't have it before Wednesday."

"We will be back on Wednesday. What can we do in the meantime? Any diet?"

"Keep him on bed rest. Buy a portable urinal so he doesn't have to get out of bed to urinate. Keep his activity to the minimum."

Stephen has been moved to the front guest room and he cried a couple of times because he can't stay with me. I told him to build a rocket ship so we can fly around the planet and he laughed. He won't like going to camp by himself. It's a mistake.

Miriam might be finished growing. Her pigtails are long gone. When I come back to the house she is so upset she can't speak, which is a first for her. Mom says Miriam can't come into my room until I am better.

Grandma Katy comes over and this is like a vacation. I get my meals in bed, lots of chicken soup, and I can read all day. The only difficult part is peeing in a thin metal container. I need help to get to the bathroom to do number two. Now I am reading *Gunga Din*. He had a more difficult time than me.

Mostly I think I will get better. I heard that if you are going to be in an iron lung it happens pretty quickly but so far I have no trouble breathing. My legs are really weak but they haven't gotten worse in the past two days.

Wednesday I am in the exam room and Dr. Fielding is turned away working at a table. When he turns back to me he has a massive glass syringe with a long thick needle on the end filled with yellow fluid. He squirts a few drops to check there are no air bubbles.

"I am sorry, Marc, but this has to go into your butt. There is too much so I have to do both sides. It is going to hurt a lot. You have to put up with it. First a little test dose and we wait five minutes and if there is no reaction then we do the whole amount." He waits a few seconds, the syringe and needle aloft like a machete.

I don't want Mom in the room but it is not possible now to get her out.

"Okay," I say quietly and turn over on my left side. I can take any punch, even from an eighth grader. I can block my mind so I don't even feel it. Then my arms pump into their abdomen in piston-like strokes just like Sugar Ray does. I can make pain disappear into the air and what is a syringe with some yellow fluid? Maybe it will help me or maybe I will get a reaction and die.

Then a quick sting of the needle and I flinch when it goes deeper into my muscle. Okay, it will be over. It always is. Then my butt is scorching hot. The liquid is on fire and burns me so badly I quiver. I won't yell or cry but I never felt anything like this.

"A little more," Dr. Fielding says, "and then we wait and give you the full dose in five minutes."

That is only a small amount, he has made clear. In five minutes it will be longer and terrible. I know what it is to get ready for a storm. In five minutes I will be drifting out in the ocean like the old man on the sea, alone, holding that massive fish for two days with the line wrapped around my body. ▪

CHAPTER 22

Under the Door

*D*OLOROUS. I THINK I GOT that word from a Tennessee Williams play. Mrs. Mahoney at the Hempstead Library knows I am stuck in bed and sends me books. In a previous note she said it is time I read some plays and first it was one by Ibsen and then Williams. Chekhov's *The Cherry Orchard* is boring. No one seems to be speaking about the same subject. *A Streetcar Named Desire* is more interesting. The movie starred Marlon Brando as the nasty Stanley Kowalski. Now he's in a new film called *On the Waterfront*. I wish I could see it, but I can't go out until the doctor says it's okay.

Dolorous. Maybe it is Blanche DuBois who said that with a thick Southern accent. When you are reading you have to imagine what characters sound like. It is one thing to read lots of books when I don't have to. It's hard to concentrate on the book when you are reading it because there is nothing else to do.

I get my second gamma globulin shot and I think if the Romans had it they could have skipped crucifixions.

They test me in the doctor's office. Dr. Fielding taps all my reflexes again and says my toe went the right way when he scratched my foot with the needle and I can plan on getting out of bed in two weeks.

Mom wants to know if there is a chance I could attend camp the last week and a half and he says I can but no strenuous activity. Swimming would be healthy.

The dictionary says *dolor* means mental suffering. Mental suffering is lying in bed for six weeks and only getting out to go to the bathroom.

You never think about how you spend your time until you are so limited. I hardly ever planned much ahead. If I felt like going to the library I would. I might go to a schoolyard to flip baseball cards, or play football or baseball at the Chestnut Street schoolyard, although I have rarely done that in the past year.

I am stuck in bed. I can sit up. I can walk to the bathroom but then what? It's so boring sometimes I might not even like rereading a great book like *Robinson Crusoe*. He was marooned and all alone, but he could explore the entire island. He could build a better tree house and figure out how to catch fish.

I don't have options but I am going to get better.

One of the things that really annoys me is how adults treat me now. Uncle Mottel, Dad's uncle, comes over with a present. A blue and white polo shirt. I think it's the first time he's been to our home. I have several new shirts now but nowhere to go. I have four new puzzles, but they are much too easy. Uncle Hy bought me a first baseman's baseball mitt, the only present I like. Everyone is visiting because I am sick, otherwise they would never come over, but I needed a new mitt and when I get out of bed I will use it.

Then it is Uncle Ira and Dad's oldest sister, Isabel. She brings me a new portable TV from her store. The store is in Merrick and called Roman Furniture. Anyone in Dad's family with a store uses the name Roman, though we are from Ukraine. Mom says I can only watch one hour of television a day so I wait for *Candid Camera* and Milton Berle. But lately I sneak in some afternoon baseball games. This is the first time I have ever seen a baseball game on TV in the middle of the week. I bet after I get well the TV will disappear. At least the Yankees have a good shot at the pennant, and if they win it, I expect they will play the Giants in the World Series, but that is two months away.

The yeshiva doesn't have a baseball team. Just basketball and the team is so bad that a midget could be a starter. At Chestnut Street I played first base for the Hawks in Little League and wore out my Hank Arft trapper mitt. But I haven't played in almost a year.

Mom says Mrs. Sonnenberg has called several more times to see how I am doing. Even Rabbi Charny called a few times. Mrs. McIntyre down the street came in with a coloring book. Does she know how old I am? And she made a sign of the cross and said she is praying for me.

Mr. Mitchell next door looked really worried. "Hurry up and get better," he said. "Come out and I will teach you to tune up a car."

I like that idea. I would like it better if he taught me to drive and I told him so. He laughed hard and said, "Not without your mom's permission."

None of my school friends have visited. I think their parents are afraid they'll catch polio. I wouldn't mind playing chess with Kenny. Now I have to play both sides of the board. That isn't easy since I know what the other side is planning to do.

I am likely to go to Camp Massad in the Poconos in the middle of August, with almost all Orthodox Jewish kids. Just the last week and a half, which makes no sense. I won't know anyone in my bunk. Everyone will already have their friends. If there is a baseball team, they'll already have their first baseman and I am not allowed to play baseball anyway.

My favorite book I read this month is a play, *Death of a Salesman*, and I know exactly what Arthur Miller is saying about Willy Loman, who is in sales but can't sell. That is Uncle Ira and Uncle Shoma.

Because I am stuck in bed I hear all the records Miriam plays upstairs on her new 45 RPM record player. For weeks it was "Shake, Rattle and Roll" endlessly. I heard it so many times I could puke. Now it's "Rock Around the Clock" by Bill Haley and His Comets, and when Arlene Gore is over they dance the jitterbug. I can't stand it.

Stephen is still in the front guest bedroom and I hope Mom will let him back in our room soon. Miriam sneaks in to see me but stays at the doorway. She wants to tell me all the new "juicy" gossip. Her hairdo has changed yet again, and she is always on the phone talking about boys and which girls are nasty. I don't know why she cares but that's how girls are. Dad constantly complains the AT&T telephone bill is too high. Miriam can't wait to start West Hempstead High School in September.

She and Arlene are dancing upstairs this afternoon and it's hard enough to read without their screeching and shuffling.

No use complaining. I am invisible.

"Arlene is sleeping over," Miriam yells down to Mom two stories below, but I am sure that Mom could hear her even if she were in a subterranean bunker. More dancing and they will be giggling in the attic room until late at night.

If I wasn't sick, I think I would go up there and take the record player and stomp on it.

Miriam and Arlene bounce down the stairs. It is only 5:00 p.m.

"We are taking a shower together," Miriam announces gleefully. "Don't come in."

I don't know why she would say that. The door locks. It's just that maybe I will have to pee and they will stay in there for hours.

They are laughing and giggling and even though it is still so light out they have their nighties with them.

Arlene is also 14 and a few inches shorter than Miriam, who isn't very tall. Arlene is slight with small breasts and Miriam is so proud that hers are pretty big now. Once she pranced around in a new pink bra with lace edges saying to me, "Don't I have perfect boobs?"

I was thinking that perfect is Marilyn Monroe in the *Playboy* centerfold. She is lying almost sideways so you can see the side of her tush but not her crotch. "The magazines don't show crotches yet," Uncle Hy said, "but I can get you a picture."

I have only seen Mom's, as red as her head, like a thorny triangle. That's where men put their penis to have a baby.

Arlene and Miriam are dancing in the bathroom. I don't understand why they want to shower together. Maybe to check their boob sizes.

Then the shower is on and I remember that the door to the bathroom doesn't touch the floor at the bottom. There is almost an inch of space and I wonder if I look under if I will see anything. I only get out of bed to go to the bathroom and then I think that this is the same thing. I am only going as far as the bathroom door.

I walk slowly towards the hallway, my pajamas soaked from sweat. My legs are much stronger and just near the bathroom I listen to hear if Mom is in the kitchen. The floor is being scrubbed. I try to find a good position to lie down and look under the door. It seems to work best if my legs hang out over the stairs. I press the left side of my face into the thick gray carpet and can get my left eye where the opening is under the door. The toilet and sink are to the right and straight ahead toward the rear is the shower with a small window behind. They are still singing and I am hopeful. I can see the bottom of the windowsill but no matter how much I try to press down I can't see much higher.

They just keep singing and screeching and I think they will never come out and my face is burning from the carpet. I am worried Mom will come up and I won't be able to get up quickly enough.

I want them to hurry. It is taking too long and I should give up.

And then the shower stops and I see the shower door open. I am hoping it isn't Miriam. I don't want to spy on my sister.

They still don't come out and then naked feet and legs emerge and she is turned around. I can see halfway up the tush. I am not sure who it is and I wait while she towels off her feet.

Then she turns around. A thick patch of black hair that I can see just to its top. It is Arlene. She stands there doing nothing for a few seconds, maybe admiring herself as girls do. I don't understand why men like to look at this. It's just kinky hair that's pretty short.

She moves away and I hear the shower and another leg emerges and I quickly raise my head. I have difficulty getting up, having been in this position so long.

But then I push myself up and stand straight. I close the door to my room and stand near my bed and I lift my right leg up high and then my left. My biceps have thinned out a lot but I plan to do lots of push-ups and sit-ups. As soon as I am able I am going to get stronger than I ever was. ▪

CHAPTER 23

Twinkie

AFTER SIX WEEKS IN BED I am allowed to go for a short walk. The doctor says I should try but go slowly. Next week I have to go to camp, which is ridiculous with less than two weeks left. I come downstairs and out the side door wearing shorts on this breezy early August day. Twinkie is there almost spinning in circles with her short tail going back and forth more quickly than I've ever seen. It is as though she knew I would be there. I know dogs have an amazing sense of smell but usually at this hour she is busy roaming the neighborhood.

I haven't seen her since I got sick. Mom almost gave in when I was totally bedridden and thought about Twinkie staying in my room. But no luck, Twinkie still slept in front of the kitchen sink and if I called down to her she came to the bottom of the staircase and barked.

My legs are a little wobbly, so I take a chair from the garage and slowly sit down and stand up ten times. I wait and do it again.

I motion to Twinkie that we are going to take a walk and she is so excited she almost pees.

I will get strong again. As soon as I am able I am going to ride my bike even farther, maybe all the way to Westbury where Kenny lives.

You can never let people think you are weak. Israel understands that. The surrounding Arab countries are afraid to attack this little neighboring state that they hate. Israel's strength is the best defense against a war ever starting.

"Twinkie," I say. "Let's walk around the corner to the Kassovers. I was told that is as far as I should go," and like a dart she turns right and trots a few feet ahead of me always checking where I am.

"No cat today," I tell her when I see one five houses up. For Twinkie that's like putting blood in front of a great white shark and saying no biting today.

She ignores the cat but the cat knows it is best to run for her life and find a tall tree.

We turn right on Woodfield Road. I know Twinkie crosses streets by herself and she knows how to look out for traffic but we stay on our side. Francis Rodman sees me and waves hello. I haven't seen her since the end of school. Her face tells me she knows I have been sick and she is hesitant to come near me. Everyone knows about polio.

Woodfield Road looks different and smells different. I don't know why. Then I think it might be because I always zoomed by on my bike and didn't notice as many things. Or I was walking home as quickly as possible from the Lakeview train station.

Across the street in front of a small white ranch house are three wide flower pots, each holding flowers of a different color. I don't know much about flowers.

A car comes by that must be a new model. It's a Chevy Bel Air in a powder blue color with a white top. The headlights are big chrome circles.

Right on Spruce. At the Kassovers, I knock on the side door and Twinkie parks herself next to me. After a few seconds Mrs. Kassover opens the screen door and says, "I am so, so happy to see you. This is a treat. Will you come in? I can make your favorite snack."

She has two kids older than me and always likes to make me a salami sandwich, which I rarely get at home.

"No," I say. "I just walked this far today, and Mom says then I should come home."

"Dora tells me you are out of bed and getting stronger and stronger. I am so pleased to hear that."

"Maybe tomorrow I will walk to Hempstead," I say, and Mrs. Kassover laughs loudly.

"What a minute," she says. "At least let me give Twinkie a snack."

I like that idea and she returns with a thick brown wafer and I tell Twinkie not to jump.

"I think she was by our yard a couple of days ago," Mrs. Kassover says. "Watch out. There is a neighbor across the street over there who hates dogs on her property. I think she hurt a couple of dogs who wandered in."

I don't ask her how the lady hurt the dogs. It worries me, but Twinkie is smart and she won't take handouts from a stranger.

Back home I tell Twinkie to run around and come back in a couple of hours.

I don't even own a leash. She has a flea collar and a dog tag just in case she is really lost, which has never happened.

She needs freedom and I really doubt that she has ever actually killed a cat. They are fast enough to find a tree.

YESTERDAY I WALKED as far as three blocks. This morning I am up and out right after breakfast. It is cloudless and the tar in the street is hot. I take Plymouth Street to Spruce, then right to Hempstead Avenue and just before the corner pass Sal's tiny barbershop and then Joe's Drug Store on the corner. A part of me doesn't expect to see them even though it's been only two months.

I haven't had a haircut since I was in bed and now if I comb my hair correctly I could look like Elvis, who just turned 19. But Elvis has black hair.

Two doors down I stop in the Library Annex, which I've long since stopped coming to. I was five when the librarian first gave me books to read but the Hempstead Library is ten times larger and Mrs. Mahoney seems to know just what to recommend.

A young woman, perhaps a college student, is sitting alone behind the small desk to the left and no one else is here. I remember now the smell of this room, the old floor and worn books and dust that is everywhere.

She doesn't even bother to look up.

It was here I first read a full-length book about the great Babe Ruth and started on the Freddy the Pig series by Walter R. Brooks.

I have almost forgotten about all the free time I used to have. About all the times I was off to schoolyards trying to win baseball cards. My trips to the Hempstead Library. Commuting to Queens has sliced that all away. And then polio. When you are stuck in bed all day for six weeks walking one block feels as good as climbing Mount Everest.

Today Hempstead Avenue is the most beautiful I have ever seen it. I love the way they stack shampoo bottles in the window of Mary's Beauty Salon. The colorful gumballs in the machine outside Mackie's dance around waiting for a kid with an extra nickel. I love knowing every street and store in West Hempstead.

I am like Twinkie.

I go past the small grocery where Mom keeps an account, then a few more blocks to the outer fence of Chestnut Street School Park. Back behind those huge trees I found so many peanuts in the kindergarteners' peanut hunt that they thought at first I might have cheated. Miriam made me give her some to eat before I turned them in because she said I was going to win anyway.

I will never be at that school again. In September I begin sixth grade, my second year at YCQ in Queens, and it will be Talmud three hours every morning and English with Mrs. Rosenberg, new to the school.

My legs are getting much stronger and I don't think either one of them is shorter. Grandma Katy says I have grown at least an inch since June and likely that is true since I am now taller than she is.

I am back at the house near the garage.

Stephen is in Camp Massad and I miss seeing him here and I wonder how he is doing without me nearby.

Then Mom is outside by the back door looking around and sees me and comes my way. I don't like this look. I didn't walk very far and she is going to punish me by sending me to bed; I already did that for two months. She won't hit me as long as I am recovering from polio.

"There's a problem," she says, stopping about four feet away.

I already know that. I can see that. I hope nothing happened to Stephen in camp. Maybe it's something terrible. It's Dad, or Miriam, or Grandma Katy. There is no sense in asking since she will let me know soon enough.

"It is Twinkie," she says and my heart stops. Twinkie must have been hit by a car. I saw a dog killed on Woodfield Road when I was five.

I remain as still as I can. Twinkie is the greatest dog on earth and if she is dead I will never own another dog.

"She is inside in the kitchen but very ill."

I don't understand. She wasn't hit by a car so why would she suddenly be ill?

Mom continues, "Poisoned. Poisoned by someone who obviously doesn't like a dog going through their yard."

"Who did it!" I yell.

"I am not sure," Mom says. "We can't prove it. But it is poison and she is throwing up blood."

I run to the kitchen. Twinkie is lying on her side and lifts her head. There is a fresh pool of blood near her mouth and she seems so tired that she can hardly keep her eyes open.

"We have to get her to the vet!" I yell at Mom.

"I called him," she says, "and he told me that a dog can't survive something like this."

"I will carry her to Hempstead if you don't take us in the car right now!"

Mom knows I will do exactly that. I am like her. There is a moment when there is no turning either of us away.

"I would take her," she pleads. "She can't survive this. Believe me."

"She will survive and we are going now. Now!"

"You know I shouldn't admit this," Mom says plaintively. "I actually like her. Like her very much. This dog is goddamned brilliant. Smarter than many people I know." She grins meekly.

"We are taking her now. I am picking her up and either you drive us or I go myself."

"You can't do this. This is only your third day out of bed."

I say to Twinkie, "We have to go now to the vet. Get up."

She tries to get on her feet and then I reach down and pick her up and hold her close against my chest. Mom gives in and we get in the car.

The vet starts IV fluids. He tells me not to expect her to be alive in the morning.

I tell him she will be fine. Give her dog blood if she needs it.

Back home. Even though I am allowed now to eat at the kitchen table, Mom brings me up a meal on a tray: a well-done baked potato and butter and a thick slice of medium-rare roast beef. I put the tray aside. Now I will plan carefully. The woman across the street from Mrs. Kassover who poisoned Twinkie will be sorry. Sorrier than she could ever imagine. I will work on my plan until it is perfect, and she will know my wrath. ▪

CHAPTER 24

Camp Massad

TWINKIE IS RECOVERING QUICKLY as I knew she would and I made Mom promise to walk her on a leash while I am at camp. She had to agree or I wouldn't have gone.

The first thing I do at Camp Massad is check on Stephen. When I approach him, he is jabbering away with another kid his age. Maybe Stephen really likes it here. I tap him on the shoulder and I am surprised that he doesn't seem exactly eager to see me.

Stephen has been at camp since the season started. He is in the youngest boys' bunk and I am with 11- and 12-year-olds in Bunk 13, which sits second on the left side of the boys' quad, a small wooden building with screened windows and 14 beds crammed inside.

Of course I see no point in being here but I intend to do as much swimming as possible and regain all my strength.

My bed is a thin metal frame with a mattress lacking most of its stuffing. They probably hadn't figured I would be in camp, so they squeezed me near the screen door and everyone coming in and going out bangs the door into my bed.

Across from me is Charlie Benjamin, the counselor. Midway along the back wall is a portico to the clothes cubbies and the rear bathroom with its two stall showers.

All of the boys in my bunk go to a yeshiva. Five are at Yeshiva of Flatbush, two from Ramaz in New York City, and two from St. Louis.

When you show up to a new school as I did almost a year ago you quickly learn who is in which clique, who are the best students, the teachers' favorites, the most popular, and the least liked. Yeshiva isn't about athletics; we have no teams except basketball and that is only taken seriously in high school. But here in Camp Massad I know within the first day that sports are an important marker of popularity.

Charlie Benjamin is 19 years old and spends half the day as assistant waterfront director. During swim period at the lake he is lying on his back on the far part of the pier wearing just a small blue nylon bathing suit. Now and then he turns over and does 50 quick push-ups, then turns back over and does 50 sit-ups. What his actual job is isn't clear. Judging by the way the girls look at him I understand why he got this job. This is the first time I have seen a Jewish boy with thick arm muscles and a rippled abdomen. He is deeply and evenly tanned, which will never be possible for me.

Our swim group includes boys and girls age ten to twelve. The oldest girls twitter like chickens looking at Charlie sunning himself. They pretend not to notice the exact outline of a bulge in his bathing suit. But Judy Goldhaber, whose breasts are just beginning to grow, is fixed in place like a marble sculpture with her right hand covering her mouth. I think that eventually she might faint if her counselor doesn't forcibly pull her away.

I am a strong swimmer able to go under the waves at Rockaway Beach, but now when I try to swim one lap between the docks I have a hard time and have to stop. Before I was sick I bet I could have done this 20 times. But Dr. Fielding promised that my weakness is just because I was in bed so long. I am going to be even stronger soon. I plan to swim more than 20 laps by the time camp ends and do more push-ups than Charlie.

Baseball is after lunch and I am not certain how anyone has the energy to play after the massive meal of hotdogs, hamburgers, and fries where you take as much as you want and Freddie Summerstein from St. Louis eats at least eight hotdogs and three ears of corn.

The baseball field's infield grass has so many knobs that any ball hit to the shortstop is likely to career away. At any rate the kids are terrible and the winning team is determined more by who makes the fewest errors than who hits the best.

I had hoped to play first base as I did for the Hawks in Little League, but that position is firmly occupied by the biggest boy in the bunk, David Berger. Everything he does is slow and large and deliberate, and he makes few errors, but for all his size he has limited range. I guess he thinks that it's only his job to catch the balls thrown right to him. As a batter they put him in cleanup because of his size but he isn't strong.

You know immediately that Berger is the scholar of the bunk. He speaks like a record turning at half speed and his answers are given in a nasal tone like he is the head judge in a court trial. Everyone says that David is the star student in elementary school in Yeshiva of Flatbush.

At first the baseball counselor sends me to right field. That's the least important position, where you can do the least harm. I have never played outfield and have a difficult time judging fly balls. Melvin Adelman, also in Yeshiva of Flatbush, is shortstop, and he is good. When baseball is played this badly one good shortstop, a good center fielder, and an okay first baseman may be enough to win even with limited hitting. Carmi Horowitz from another yeshiva in Brooklyn tells me that Melvin is also the fastest runner and the star basketball player.

Dr. Fielding said I am not supposed to overdo any activities and clearly all the counselors have been warned but I insist on taking my turn at bat. It's not really strenuous.

We play softball instead of real baseball at camp and softball is new to me. A large ball pitched underhand in a high arc looks like a white watermelon descending from heaven.

It should be a cinch to hit but I swing and miss three times in succession and am out. I feel embarrassed, but no one seems to care; half of the kids strike out.

Out in right field nothing comes to me except the balls that go through the legs of the second baseman. On my third at bat I try to wait until the ball is almost on top of the plate and instead of swinging up at the high arced ball I try to smack it parallel with the ground and I hit a stinging liner between shortstop and third and trot to first base. Just with that hit I see the kids have all taken notice. Tomorrow I plan to hit a home run along the left foul line, which has a really short fence.

Dinner is lamb chops, baked carrots, and mashed potatoes and here you can eat enough for a small African village and it seems that many kids do. Solly Greenstein is reaching to the middle for a large well-done lamp chop and Melvin stabs it first with his fork and laughs. Solly says nothing and I know how it works now.

Tonight is Israeli dancing. An instructor lines up the boys and girls to do steps together, which involves holding hands and lots of hopping. This is something I have never seen, but here they prefer to do everything as they do in Israel and near the end they sing Israeli songs and then "Hatikvah," the national anthem, and even though I go to a yeshiva now I have never sung it. I don't even know what it means. I can read Hebrew well but in YCQ we really didn't speak it. Talmud is Aramaic.

The kids from Flatbush already speak Hebrew almost as well as English, and in Massad there are periods of the day when we must converse only in Hebrew. The director of the camp comes by at the end of the dancing and singing. Shlomo Shulsinger is a slight balding man about age 50, wearing tan shorts and a short sleeve blue shirt as most Israelis do. He reminds us, as I suppose he has done a hundred times before I got here, that this is the first and most important modern Hebrew camp in the U.S. The head of the camp is Rabbi David Eliach, who at about age 30 is already a principal at the Yeshiva of Flatbush. Eliach is very thin with stooped shoulders and has an accent from Europe different than Dad's.

He comes over to introduce himself.

"I am happy to see that you are here now," he says in Hebrew, or at least that's what I think he says. He sees my confusion and proceeds in English. "Yes, I know, you have had a difficult summer and now hopefully almost two weeks here to enjoy and fully recover."

I like the way he looks at me directly. "I know Rabbi Charny from your yeshiva," he goes on in English. "A great scholar. He speaks highly of you. Here we focus on *Ivrit*—Hebrew—and two hours a day we have Jewish studies."

I nod. I went to the classes. Today one hour was Jewish history about modern Israel since statehood six years ago. The other class is language. I had hoped of course that camp would be all sports.

Back at the bunk Charlie tells us it's lights out exactly at 10:00 p.m. and he reminds me that the bugle blows to awaken us at 6:30 a.m. After commuting all year to school it would be nice to sleep until 8:00 but Carmi tells me that by 7:00 we have to be at the main hall for *shacharit*, morning prayers, which take 30 minutes, and then it's breakfast.

David Berger is sitting up in his corner bed reading a Hebrew text with small print, looking as though he is preparing to give his rabbi's sermon on Saturday. The boys file into the bathroom, brush their teeth, and file out. Freddie comes out wearing short floral pajama bottoms and a blue and red top, and just as he is about to hop into bed Mark Spilkowitz, three beds to his right, starts laughing ferociously and pointing to the bottoms.

Freddie is really fat and in this pajama top he looks like he has two big breasts. I can see that he has gone through this before and how things are lined up. He tries to duck under the bed sheet to disappear when Mark says loudly and with a wide smirk, "Freddie the Pig, Freddie the Pig."

Freddie doesn't turn around and says nothing, but he is shaking from crying soundlessly. David's face is locked into his book and Melvin is busy talking to the kid next to him. Some of the boys laugh, especially Carmi, though no one else repeats this insult.

The book series I most loved when I was in kindergarten was Freddy the Pig by Walter R. Brooks. I got every new one that came out. Freddy was a pig living on the Bean Farm and he was the head of the animals. He was an intellectual and a poet. But perhaps Mark doesn't remember or he is not referring to the book.

My stomach turns sour watching Freddie get picked on. I hate bullies. They only pick on kids, like Stephen, who can't defend themselves. I don't understand why no one says anything to stop it. I thought it might end there but Mark stands up and says loudly, "Come on, Piggy, let's see that inny." A few boys laugh along and Mark repeats this several times and now Freddie's sobs are easily heard.

Mark is tall and very thin with wide thick black eyebrows and black eyes. I don't remember that he even played baseball but now in Bunk 13 he is clearly a leader. Several boys guffaw loudly and finally Mark throws up his hands in disgust and plops down on his bed.

Charlie has stepped out so I don't know if Mark would have done this were he here. I suppose that Mark was making fun of Freddie's penis, which does seem lost in the fat folds of his abdomen.

The next morning breakfast is a feast where we are offered soft, medium, or hard-boiled eggs and we hold up our fingers to say how many. Three hard-boiled I indicate, and kids are eating volumes of pancakes, bread, cake, and cartons of milk.

Today it's swimming and baseball again and in the afternoon two hours of Hebrew discussions. Here at least we are not given homework or textbooks. The first hour is a discussion of Israel's War for Independence in 1948 and the leader is a counselor named Amnon Haramati, who fought in the war. He has a lean angular face and a deep crater on the right side of his face that Carmi tells me is from a bullet wound.

Back at the bunk at 5:30 we shower and change and get ready for dinner, after which will be Israeli dancing again with the girls. Several of my bunkmates are horsing around and snap towels at each other's bare butts. As I walk to get some clothes from my cubby I accidently knock into Melvin Adelman and just past him I turn to say sorry when a fist crashes into my abdomen. My knees buckle quickly and I hear him laughing and saying something like, "Next time watch where you are going, Strausie."

I struggle up to my feet and try to set myself to fight as he cackles at me and most of the boys are laughing along. He backs off a step into a fighter's pose and dances right and left extending his right fist.

"Come on, Strausie. Rumor is you think you can fight." Then a sharp jab to my chest and I am almost down again.

I have been in many fights but none since I began at Yeshiva almost a year ago. I can't stop the tears welling in my eyes and that has never happened.

"Are you going to cry like a baby?" he asks.

I think I really have to fight now but I feel as though I can't do it. I am not afraid of being hurt. I am weak and afraid of being embarrassed.

Just then the bunk door flies open and Charlie jumps in and yells to everyone to back away. Melvin laughs and Charlie says, "Back off, big shot. I told everyone that Marc was sick this summer and is here just recuperating and it takes a real moron to hit him."

Adelman still has a smirk and moves toward his bed.

I am wobbly and have a hard time trying to stand erect. This is only my second day in Camp and a little more than a week to the end and it is horrible. It was a mistake to come.

I can't recall ever losing a fight except when I was eight and Miriam asked me to hit an 11-year-old girl in her class. Before I could land a punch, it felt like a refrigerator crushed my upper chest. It was her fist. And now I have lost this one without throwing a single punch. I know if I continued it would have been worse.

I lie down on my bed and no one says anything. Melvin is already joking around with Carmi and Stanley Raskas.

I am surprised there is fighting here. There is none in my yeshiva and I can't even imagine where Melvin would have heard about my history.

In Yeshiva things are mostly determined by how smart you are and it helps to be good-looking. That must be the same everywhere.

After a year without a fight I was beginning to think it's better that way. And sometimes I started to think maybe I don't like fighting even though I did it so much. I don't like hitting another kid.

I thought I was in most fights because Stephen was being picked on or kids were mocking me. Now I think I started a few I should have avoided. Maybe I hurt a kid who didn't deserve it. My best friends in class—Kenny, Ira, Mitchell, Paul—they would never like me if I was beating kids up.

But if you have to fight, doubts get in your way. Doubts mean you might hesitate and then you will get hurt.

There is no excuse when you lose. It doesn't matter to anyone if you had polio and were stuck in bed for six weeks. When you lose there is shame and I plan that starting tomorrow I will build myself up. I will fight Melvin again no matter the outcome. ■

CHAPTER 25

Freddie the Pig

"FREDDIE THE PIG. Freddie the Pig."
Mark Spilkowitz is standing on his bed bare-chested in black briefs chanting, "Freddie the Pig, Freddie the Pig," and clapping in time.

"Come on, boys," he implores. "Everyone join in." Then he springs to the floor in front of his metal bed and does jumping jacks and as his arms go up and down he repeats the refrain, exhorting everyone one by one, and finally Jonathan Figman and then Carmi Horowitz join in.

I don't know whether this taunting of Freddie has gone on since camp began. I have only been here three days. I know Freddie is a loner, a very white doughy overweight boy with thick sandy hair who participates in no sports. So far I have never seen him go swimming.

Freddie lies back and puts his head under his pillow. David Berger, our in-house professor, appears to be deep into a book as though there is nothing going on and Mark is only one bed away from him. Stanley, who like Freddie is from St. Louis, busies himself putting away some items in his cubby and Melvin Adelman is joking about something with Michael Davidson.

Mark says, "Come on, girls, stop being sissies," as he jumps higher with his penis noticeably popping up and down each time. "Yeah, see this," he says, grabbing his crotch. "This is a real one. Not a shrunken inny."

Two more boys join in and after a while Mark is breathless and stops.

"Ah, fuck it," he says. "I'm tired."

His black hair is matted down over his neck from sweat. He is darkly tanned and almost a head taller than me with very narrow lips and slender hips and legs. He slowly saunters over to Freddie's bed and raps hard on the frame and yells, "Come out, come out, Mr. Freddie, and show us that little worm of yours." He turns around twice looking for support and says, "Puny penis, puny penis."

There is widespread laughter now and Mark howls like a coyote. "Oooh wee! No wee wee!" Suddenly turning to me he lisps, "And what are you staring at, Strausie?"

I don't answer.

"Hey Mel," he yells to Adelman. "I think Strausie wants to fight you again."

Melvin ignores him and most of the boys now are trying as hard as possible to appear busy.

"Well Strausie, do you like his puny penis?"

"Is that the best you can do, Spilkowitz?" I ask.

I had no clue that I would say anything but my mouth continues as though it is not controlled by brain.

"Are you no more gifted than to call someone a pig? And puny penis? That's really rich."

Spilkowitz leans in my direction and glowers with a much reddened face.

"Hey Straus, didn't you learn your lesson with Mel?"

Mel Adelman, who had whipped me with one blindsided punch, is turned around and paying close attention. Even David Berger has lifted his eyes from his book.

"I don't see Mel taunting Freddie," I say. "It's just you and you are trying to get everyone to join in your nasty stupid game."

"Then maybe I have to teach you a lesson," he cackles looking around for support. "Whip your ass and shut that carrot head for good."

This is no time to get involved but I can't help myself. "All you have is a big mouth," I respond, "and you are nothing more than a bully."

"Ha. Ha," he says, spinning around again to gauge the group. Everyone is now riveted on us. Even Freddie has peeked out from under the covers, his face drenched in tears.

"You need help, Spilkowitz. It's not enough to embarrass him by yourself. And you, Carmi, shame on you that you joined in. It's not like you, or any of you. And you, Mr. David Scholar Berger. You keep your face in your book and by ignoring this you are aiding it. What good is all that Torah study when this is right in front of you and you are silent?"

There is silence, sticky and thick. Nothing moves. Even the flies are stilled.

"Well, well," Spilkowitz says, "I guess I have to teach you a lesson myself."

"I look forward to that," I answer, which seems to surprise the boys. They saw Mel knock the wind out of me with one punch. But they could not possibly know what I was like before my legs buckled under me almost three months ago.

"This will be great fun," Mark laughs.

"You are going to be sadly surprised," I say.

Suddenly Carmi blurts out, "You two can't fight now. Charlie is supposed to be here in a minute."

"Too bad, Strausie," Spilkowitz says. "You dodged a fist in your face tonight."

"You are a coward," I answer crisply. "You are lucky to avoid this fight."

"Bullshit," he says. "I can't wait. Tomorrow I will shut your mouth and then you and Freddie can whine together."

"Not tomorrow," I insist. "Tonight! Tonight, Spilkowitz. We wait for Charlie to be asleep and then we step outside and have it on."

In my head deep down I know this is me speaking from my old self, a life that has almost vanished, but now I am so angry that my long illness these past months seems irrelevant.

I don't know why Melvin punched me. I don't think kids fight here. In my few days at camp I have learned that fighting will get you kicked out of camp. I think it's one thing for Mark to tease Freddie mercilessly, but he never expected a fight. And then he shot off his mouth.

"Tonight?" he says with slight hesitation.

"Tonight! I challenge you to a fight at midnight exactly. I challenge you."

"No problem."

"I want to know out loud in front of everyone whether you accept the challenge and we will fight at midnight. Yes or no!"

Mark seems unsure now and everyone can feel it. He grits his teeth, feeling the reaction in the room, lowers his head and says, "Sure, I accept. No problem."

"How do I know you will be awake?" I chide.

"Hey, no problem," he laughs. "Me awake? I can't wait."

"Solly," I direct. "Set that alarm for eleven fifty-five so Charlie can't hear it?"

"Sure," he says eagerly.

Carmi adds, "I will set mine as well."

Then there is silence, not one boy speaking to another but the air is dense with boy thoughts buzzing about. Each tries to find something to do. Mark goes back to his bed cackling and starts reading a magazine.

Charlie is in and the lights are out at 10:00 p.m.

I know no one in the bunk will fall asleep but a cloud drifts over me and I am dreaming. I am back in West Hempstead on a sunny Sunday early afternoon. I come toward the garage to get my blue Schwinn and I hear a choking sound. Then I see Stephen cowered in the left rear corner hunched over and sobbing. I touch him on the shoulder and he pulls away. As I lean in closer I see a red raised wound on his left cheek and cuts on his neck.

I feel rage. "Who did this?" I yell. He doesn't respond. Then Mom is standing in the entrance of the garage, her cheeks are drawn in tightly and her blue pupils are tiny dots. She is holding a wet white dishrag encircled by nail-bitten fingers.

I feel myself lunging and know that this moment I will smash her face in half. I will rip away her hands and then suddenly I realize she is not the one who has beaten Stephen and I start shaking so hard I awaken.

This dream has repeated itself many times and it always wakes me up.

I always know the time, even in my sleep, and always awaken exactly one minute before any alarm goes off. The clock near Solly says 11:54 p.m.

I am fully awake now and rested. Here am I, five minutes from a fight I really don't want. Likely I will lose. But I know once it starts I will keep going as long as I breathe.

Still I need a plan, a strategy. Spilkowitz is lean and wiry. His arm reach is so much longer than mine. I will have to get inside in a hurry. But I haven't even paid attention to whether he is right- or left-handed.

This might be a big mistake and if I lose the fight I will be further humiliated and the taunting of Freddie will just continue.

I begin to dress: shorts, T-shirt, socks, and sneakers. The cool air feels refreshing through the screens.

11:58 p.m. I stand up. It is very dark but I can see across to Mark's bed and he remains under the covers. I see Carmi lift his head and Solly and then Stanley. Everyone is up and tense with expectation.

I try to stand tall in place and calm myself. Very soon there will be no fear.

Midnight exactly and Mark remains deep under the blanket.

The alarm tinkles near Solly and he quickly shuts it off. We all look to see if Charlie has stirred.

12:02 a.m. Nothing. Everyone is up except Charlie and Mark. Freddie is sitting up in bed kneading his fingers.

12:05 and I ask Stanley to awaken Mark. Stanley doesn't want to be involved and Carmi volunteers, Carmi who had joined in the taunting.

I nod to him and he goes over and shakes the bottom of Mark's bed.

There is no movement.

I nod more firmly. Carmi shakes Mark's lower legs and Mark seems to bury his head deeper under his pillow.

Carmi shrugs as though there is nothing further to do when I say quietly, "Once more and really shake him."

Carmi waits a bit. It is 12:14 a.m. Almost everyone is sitting up including Mel.

"Do it," I order.

Carmi shakes Mark much harder. He finally groans and pushes Carmi's hand away and digs himself deeper in the bed.

"I am waiting for you, you chickenshit," I say loud enough for everyone to hear and risking waking Charlie.

I say this once more then begin to take my clothing off and get back into my pajamas.

I am lucky. I am glad Mark chickened out and I know what will happen in the morning. No one will say anything. I will not mention it either.

And Freddie will not be teased again. ■

CHAPTER 26

Color War

BONNIE BREITMAN has a personality matching her name, all cheery-eyed and optimistic.

"I think I will be on Blue," she says, knowingly. Bonnie lives in northern New Jersey and goes to school near the George Washington Bridge. "I can almost see it from my house," she brags, and I don't wish to point out that almost is the same as not.

She is referring to Color War, Blue and White teams, the colors of the Israeli flag. As a three-year veteran of this camp she knows Color War will begin sometime during the second or third week of August and for her the expectation is overwhelming. Nearly everyone who has been here before is speculating as to how it will start, which is always a surprise.

"One year clowns came in to dinner and threw handfuls of pamphlets around the room listing every camper on the Blue or White team," Carmi said.

I also heard that it had once been announced over the camp loudspeaker. I guess at a time they were trying to save money.

Even more than which color team they will be on, almost every camper worries about who their teammates will be. Each bunk is divided in half and the rivalry is intense. Everyone already knows who the best athletes are and for three days there are hundreds of competitions. There are even singing and dancing contests and bonus points for sportsmanship. During dinner the end-of-the-day tally is announced.

I am not just new this season, I am new this week. I started doing sit-ups and push-ups. I row as much as I can to build up my legs and chest. It is already clear that I am not competitive in running. It's not just my recent polio. I would have won in fighting. But then I found out even with this I am not ready. And they would never have fighting as a contest. Certainly not in a Jewish camp.

Neither am I a fast swimmer. I think my slow speed is due to my small feet. You need those large flipper-like feet to push the water.

Anyway, it really doesn't matter.

"They are going to start tomorrow at bugle call," Freddie says knowingly at breakfast. But I expect that Color War will be terrible for him. He is the worst in the bunk in any sport and no one will let him compete.

The next two days are too intense as everyone expects Color War to begin at any moment and we know it can't be put off much longer because it has to wrap up before we leave.

Mark Spilkowitz has had nothing to say to me since the evening of the Freddie incident but now at lunch he smirks and says, "It's going to start in an hour. A plane flying overhead." Several bunk-mates immediately press him for more details but he refuses to say.

Mark has lost most of his credibility since he chickened out with me and no one is taking him seriously. Everyone says that the time and manner of starting Color War is more secretive than when the Zionist underground blew up British headquarters in the King David Hotel in 1946.

But I know that Mark is telling the truth. I don't know how he found out, but I expect that within about an hour he will be vindicated. I quickly glance at him and he knows that I know.

At 1:35 p.m. I am standing in the center of the boys' quad awaiting the plane, which I expect will be soon.

The blue sky in the Poconos is different. It is more transparent with a blending of sharp orange and yellow. Perhaps the small mountains make a difference. From the outskirts of the camp one sees a mountainside with ski trails that look like thick spider webs etched in it. The deep-water lakes shimmer back hunter greens.

I like it. You don't know how clogged the air is in New York until you see this sky and breathe in this summer air.

They are already preparing dinner and from the kitchen I can smell fresh corn still in the husks, and they are baking something with sweet chocolate.

I could be working in the store on Grand Street again, organizing sheets and towels in the dank basement. Now it's camp and I guess I should make the most of it.

Suddenly I hear a rumbling in the sky, but nothing is visible. Quickly Mark comes into mind. The plane coming for Color War. And then just ahead and to the right a small crop duster drops its left wing and slopes lower over the girls' section.

At first no one seems to notice but then there is a growing awareness that planes don't fly this low over camp. Could it be? Are they announcing Color War?

The plane comes around the boys' section, climbs then circles back towards the girls' section. There can be no doubt now.

The flyers flutter down by the hundreds and kids are frantically grabbing them and shrieking for joy. That's just it. They have to be happy whichever team they are on. From this second, they want as much as anything to win.

There's Bonnie Breitman again. "I hope you are on my team," she yells so joyfully to me.

"I don't know," I answer truthfully.

"Read it! Open it!" she implores. "I am Blue! I am Blue!"

Here is the pamphlet with each camper's name and team.

All things being equal, I would like to be on Bonnie's team.

"Okay," I say. "Let's see." ▪

CHAPTER 27

Blue Team

N O SURPRISE, MELVIN ADELMAN is head of our team for our bunk, but more than that he is also a section head for the boys ages ten to twelve. It's better to have the best athlete on your team as a leader but I doubt he will choose me to participate in anything.

Freddie comes up behind me and slaps my shoulder. I am glad that Freddie is on my team and that Mark is on White. There has to be something that Freddie can compete in. David Meyers is also on Blue and like Freddie he won't compete in a sport, but I expect David will lead the singing group or organize a show.

David has been here every summer since age eight and behind his back so many campers make fun of his screechy voice and mannerisms. He is really loud and sprays spittle when he speaks. But I like David. I know that like me he reads a lot, in his case current plays, which I know almost nothing about. He knows every show on Broadway and the actors. I won't be surprised if I see him on TV someday accepting an Academy Award.

Today at 3:00 p.m. the early swim events begin and I am one of the contestants in the 50-yard event. I will lose of course. Everyone knows who will win. Jerry Markowitz.

David has been chosen to organize a skit to be performed the last night. He is ecstatic and asks me to be in it. I can sing pretty well. But I tell David I can't sing or act and he should ask Freddie.

I am competing in tennis tomorrow morning then rowing in the afternoon. I guess Melvin knows what's going on. The most anticipated events are running, when the entire camp is present, and our star will be Melvin. My best hope is getting a few points in rowing and that will be it.

It seems that the whole camp is at the lake and every kid is wearing a blue or white ribbon. There are separate flags and separate places to stand and cheer and Bonnie Breitman almost chokes me when she grabs me and says we have the best team. We are going to win.

I am in the third boys' swimming race and in the first two the younger kids on Blue did poorly. I think Bonnie is going to faint. Here we are at the beginning and we are behind eight points and you would think it's curtains for us. But in my group we will win at least first and third and I will come in fourth or fifth and get nothing.

I lean over, head down, hands almost touching my toes the way Johnny Weissmuller did when he swam in the Olympics. This is the 50-yard freestyle and it's two lengths between the docks and even if I can go out quickly enough I am terrible at the turns.

Boom. I am churning my arms in overhead windmills and not even picking my head up for one breath until I reach the opposite dock. I don't even look around to see how anyone else is doing. What's the difference? I curve around quickly and go back and it is as if it's not even me swimming. My arms are like turbines spinning around and suddenly I touch.

Left and right and there is Jerry and now Michael Berenson and Robbie Carmel. I don't know what happened. Jerry is near me and gives me a huge thumbs up. Did I get third?

On the dock Melvin comes over and slaps me hard. "Nice going, Marc."

Then the scores are posted. Jerry first, me second, and Michael third on White.

Jerry says, "That's the fastest I ever swam and I only beat you by a fingertip." Of course, I am thinking it would have been nicer if I'd won by a fingertip but I got my team four points and everyone is cheering more for me than for Jerry. He was expected to win but I am the surprise.

In the team 200-yard medley I am now one of the four on Blue and we win.

All the time I was stuck in bed at home I didn't want to think about whether my weakness would be permanent, whether I would wind up in a wheelchair like President Roosevelt. I am excited that I won a couple of points for my Blue team but what I now know makes me feel really excited. I am going to have my full strength back and I am going to practice a lot so I can be stronger than ever. I want my stomach muscles to ripple like Charlie's do but I am not sure I want to wear such a tiny bathing suit.

At dinner it is announced that Blue has 258 points and White has 242.

I win two tennis sets using my heavy Tony Trabert wooden racket with an octagonal grip. Now I play for the finals tomorrow. Perhaps because I am surprising everyone they let me play first base for our team and I hit two singles and a double but we lose 14–12.

David Meyers has written new songs for the stage events tomorrow night and he says, "You must, you must be in the play." Not a chance.

At dinner Blue is ahead 788–726 and there are those who are saying that by now White will never catch up.

The third day in the morning I am against five other rowboats and just as we begin Joey Machlis swerves 90 degrees right and crashes into me. It takes me several seconds to get out of the tangle and soon I am 20 feet behind the other four. It takes even more time to come up to speed and I decide to push the heavy wood oars in deep and pull with my back and legs. Deep and long and an even hard return. Again and again I increase my stroke and I am near the fourth rower and then the third.

It is a long distance to the opposite side. I probably have no chance but I row as never before and Mitchell Sanger seems angry as I pass him for second. Only 30 feet to go and I am half a length behind Arnold Millstein and he is pulling fast and hard and I am coming alongside and then the whistle.

I lose by two feet. I am thinking to punch Machlis in the face. I am certain he was told to bump me. I walk by and he smirks and lucky for him that my teammates are clapping me on the back and there is the ever-present Bonnie jumping up and down for joy.

I should have won. Everyone knows that but there is no disqualifying the kid who bumped me and came in last. In fact, he didn't even finish the race.

I should be angry, but I am not anymore. I am getting stronger. Dr. Fielding said that most people recover completely from polio but mostly I didn't believe him at first.

Tonight we are ahead 150 points and the senior camp director announces that the 50 points awarded to the team with the best Jewish spirit goes to White. So now it's a 100-point difference. What is Jewish spirit and how is it decided? Bonnie looks as if we did something wrong and didn't have the right attitude.

Melvin easily wins the 100-yard dash and our team is increasing its lead.

The day is gray and my younger brother, Stephen, is running for the White. I am excited he will be in the upcoming 200-meter event and I go up to him. He doesn't know whether he is permitted to speak to someone on the opposing team. I say, "Stephen, you can do this." He is nervous and pale and doesn't like competing, especially in front of the entire camp.

I have the feeling he doesn't want me rooting for him. He wants to be on his own. He turns to speak to a kid his age.

Then it's Stephen's race. He is out really fast and finishes second and seems shocked. People are hugging him and he still looks stunned.

I try to give him a thumbs up but he doesn't turn my way.

After about another hour they announce the upcoming 400-yard races and Melvin comes up to me and says, "Bobby Schatz is sick. I am putting you in."

"Oh no you're not," I respond. "No way. I can't run this."

"It doesn't matter how you do," he says. "We will take first and second but we are disqualified without a fourth on the team. Do this for the team."

We line up and I sense something at play. The way the White group is looking at each other, they have a strategy. There is no chance they will beat Melvin unless they mean to bump him or keep him boxed in.

Off we go and immediately I understand their plan. Their lead runner is Nathan Aronstein and he holds back near the end of the tight pack and they are setting a very slow pace with Peter Blumberg up front. They hope to go so slow that Nathan has the kick at the end to beat Melvin.

Suddenly I take off. I kick out and pass everyone and am ten yards ahead and I am opening up this incredible distance as we pass the 100-yard marker. They are panicky behind me and I run harder than I have ever run before and I have this momentary thought that I am faster having recovered from polio. I will win and break a camp record.

I feel great and now Nathan and his other three are scrambling as quickly as possible to catch me and among them only Nathan gets close.

A quick look back and Melvin is running evenly in fifth place.

Now I am at the halfway marker and everyone in camp is on their feet and screaming. Only Nathan stays close to me and I want to run even faster.

Then as we are nearing the three-quarter marker all the air leaves my body. My right side cramps up and the pain increases so quickly I feel like I will collapse. It is worse and worse and Nathan senses it and pulls alongside and grins quickly.

"Big shot," he laughs.

I think I can't go another step and then I am alongside deep bushes to my right and at a place not visible for the crowd.

Suddenly I duck into the bushes and fall down. I am down on the ground struggling for breath and laughing so hard I am coughing. I pull myself up and walk to where I can see the race nearing the end. Melvin has the great kick at the end after all and Nathan is totally winded and comes in fourth.

Later I appear with the group and no one comments that I disappeared during the race. Melvin looks over at me. He understands.

I don't care that I couldn't finish. I am not disappointed, I am elated. I had tucked the fear of having polio so far away and now realize I was scared. This is the fastest I ever ran and soon I will be back on my bike and go from West Hempstead all the way to Queens hoping for good hills.

At night Blue is very far ahead and David Meyers of course wins for his stage productions. They give White all kinds of extra points and Bonnie is fretting that we will lose.

At the end of the evening we all come back to the dining hall and the Director announces the winner and Bonnie claps and cheers and in two days we leave for home.

Tonight I will escape the bunk. I am leading a raid against the girls' section. I have planned it carefully. The camp leaders and counselors know to expect raids and more hell tonight and tomorrow night. They warned us that no one will slip out for a raid.

We will get there and come back.

The next morning on the flagpole near the dining room a number of girls' panties and some bras are hanging, one unusually large and pink. ▪

CHAPTER 28

The Fence

LEON PERLMUTTER AND I agreed to play tennis this morning. It's after Color War and two days until camp ends. It is around 11:00 a.m., a hot and hopeless day, and I go to the courts an hour early to practice. At the ball field battalions of grasshoppers have taken over. Only a maintenance man wearing worn brown slacks and a brown button-down shirt is nearby. The two asphalt tennis courts, near the camp exit, are in serious need of patching. On the right court a part of the surface has cracked open like two split lips puckered out. Balls hit there careen out of play, but there are no do-overs. You play with what you have.

My wooden tennis racquet has a 4 5/8-inch grip which is perfect for a great ape but Dad no doubt bought the one the salesman said I would grow into. Yes, if I plan on being eight feet tall. But in a way I like it. I have a strong right arm and this racquet requires a strong grip.

The courts are enclosed by a Cyclone fence with thick wires in a diamond pattern. A squeaky door with rusted hinges opens on the left side facing up toward the camp buildings. The back side running along the road is shadiest as the fence there is lined by a row of bushes and high weeds.

I enter and circle the court kicking away some pebbles. I walk along the fence to the deepest shade and bend over to put my ball can down. Halfway down, my face is suddenly gripped with searing pain. I try to jerk up and the left side of my face is stuck on the fence. I pull and pull and the more I do the worse the pain is. I try to remain still to assess the situation. When I lean in closer to the fence the pain is fractionally less. I move my left fingers up slowly against my face and it is wet and sticky. I can't see my fingers since my head is jammed against the fence but I taste them and it is blood running down my face and neck and under my shirt.

I am getting panicky. It's my eye. I am stuck and have ripped something open but I can't pull off the fence and see what it is. I begin to yell as loud as I can for help. I stop then yell some more. The pain is almost intolerable. I then try to remain still and wait, not wanting to tear anything further.

No one comes and I yell some more and it goes on this way as much as 15 minutes and by now my chest is soaked with blood.

I know I have to get help but I am afraid of pulling away. It is my left eye. I can't open it. And I know that maybe I am already blind but without help I have no choice.

I pull back hard and the pain might be the worst I have ever experienced, like the claw of a rake ripping under my face. Nothing happens and then with full force I jerk back and my face seems to explode and I am away.

Back about two feet from the fence I am wobbly. I begin to focus with my right eye and see that stitched into the fence about three feet up is a line of jagged barbed wire that holds the fence to a post and the knot of the barbed wire has two prongs facing into the court.

I ripped my eye with this and I can't open it and even trying is too painful.

I pull my T-shirt over my head and then grip a corner and press it against my eye to staunch the blood flow. Soon I pull it away and it is soaked in blood. I press another corner against my eye as firmly as possible and head to the infirmary.

The road up to the campground is long and steep and today it feels insurmountable. A few steps onto the grounds, a girl about 14 years old sees me and suddenly grabs her mouth and gags and turns away. A few more kids and everyone turns away gripped by fear and no one offers to help.

I turn right towards the main office, which is a tiny cabin. I push open the office door and try to focus. The assistant to the director is turned away.

"Mrs. Bernstein." She doesn't turn around at first, busy with lots of papers. "Is Mr. Shulsinger here?" I ask more loudly.

No, she shakes her head.

"I need help, now," I insist.

Mrs. Bernstein swings around angrily and freezes.

"Oh my God," she says, grabbing her mouth.

"I need help!" I repeat.

"Oh my God," she repeats and stutters. "Shlomo is in New York and the nurse has a day off. Oh my God, let me think."

"Do you have a mirror?" I ask, and now I think I almost can't stand but I refuse to sit down.

"No, we don't."

"A mirror!"

"We don't. Believe me."

"A mirror!"

"Let me try to call someone," she says reaching for the phone.

"Where is a mirror?" Now I realize she doesn't want me to see myself.

She is dialing and relents. "There behind Shlomo's door."

The corner of my shirt is plastered against my eye and I am fearful of pulling it off but I need to see.

My entire eyelid is ripped through and hanging in two flaps. I can't see how bad the damage is to my eyeball. I can't see anything through the hanging pieces of lid and blood.

"The nurse says we have to get you to the hospital in East Stroudsburg." Then Mrs. Bernstein is frantically speaking to someone and I am not listening for a moment.

"The soonest they can send an ambulance is an hour."

"Then put me in a car," I say.

"I can't. I can't. We have rules and I need to ask Shlomo."

I have trouble pushing the pain away but need to think clearly. If my eye is damaged my only chance is to see a skilled doctor and there won't be anyone around here. "Dial my Dad. He is in the store."

"What? Just sit down. Wait for the ambulance."

"Dial two-one-two, Canal six, oh-three-one-three."

"Please, please. Sit down in Shlomo's office. I will get you orange juice."

"Dial this now. It's my father."

She turns the rotary and then it rings. Someone picks up.

"This is Camp Massad calling for Mr. Straus."

"For Sam Straus," I order.

"Sam Straus," she repeats.

I wait a few seconds and then she hands the phone to me.

"What is it?" my dad is repeating. "What's wrong?"

I don't think that Dad is as good as Mom in emergencies, but I need him now. Mom gets too emotional. Dad has the cooler head and he will know how to find the best doctor.

"Dad, this is Marc." I take a breath. "I had an accident. I tore my left eyelid and probably my eye on a rusty barbed wire."

I can feel he is taking this in.

"They can't get me an ambulance for an hour and won't drive me to the hospital."

"How is that possible?"

"But I don't want to go there. You have to find a doctor for me."

"Let me speak with her."

I put Mrs. Bernstein on the phone and then she is saying yes and yes, really bad and bloody. She says we can't take him by car to New York. It is an insurance issue.

She hands the phone back to me.

Dad is very quiet and speaks evenly. "I will deal with those bastards later," he says. I know that tone and I know he will. "Take a train to Penn Station and when you arrive I will be there and get you to a specialist. The best in New York. I will call back in five minutes and let you know which train. Now put her back on."

Mrs. Bernstein listens and nods and says yes and hangs up and runs into the next room and retrieves a large glass of orange juice. I drink a second glass and refuse more.

The phone rings and she answers and nods and says yes some more and then she hands the phone to me. "Go to the bus station," Dad says. "They will drive you. The bus leaves at four-thirty from Stroudsburg."

Dad's quiet instructions calm me.

"I know you can do this," he says. "It is really hard but there is nothing you can't do when you set your mind to it. They will pay dearly for this," he says, very firmly. "We will be there when you come in at eight-twenty. Get some money."

Mrs. Bernstein is on the phone again. I go sit in Shlusinger's office holding the rag to my face. Dad calls a couple times to check on me. I sit there for hours.

THE GREYHOUND BUS is about two-thirds full. No one sits next to me. No one will even sit across the aisle. I know now how lepers must feel. I got a new white washcloth before I left camp. The blood has soaked partially through and I hold it tightly against my eye the whole time. A senior counselor drove me to the bus station and she didn't even wait with me.

A lady in front of me is snoring loudly and the bus fills with the smell of farts. The time drags so slowly it hardly moves. If I look at my watch it is worse. The bus makes stop after stop. It starts getting dark. I have never had pain that lasted this long and the pain is even worse than when it began.

We pass Parsippany, New Jersey, and after what seems like days we are through West Orange. And then finally we pull into the terminal.

I come through the door and Dad and Mom are standing nearby. Mom looks terrible and unable to move. It's Dad in charge.

"I have a car service here," he says. "We are going directly to New York Eye and Ear. The surgeon is waiting there. He is the best."

We go through the small emergency room to check in and a woman is asking me to explain what my injury is. Dad tells her that Dr. Rosenthal is waiting and just call him. She asks which Dr. Rosenthal, the son or the father. Dad tells her the father and call him now.

An orderly puts me in a chair and wheels me into an area with cubicles closed off by pink curtains. They make me hop onto a gurney.

"We are going to draw blood," he says. "We'll be back in a second."

"Can I have a pain killer?" I ask.

"Not until Dr. Rosenthal orders it," he answers, walking away.

I wait. Dad looks like white paste was rubbed over his face. Mom doesn't take her eyes off me. I think she is trying to go backward in time and make this go away, but that won't happen.

Dr. Rosenthal is very tall and thick with a full head of gray hair. He says with a friendly smile, "I'll have you upstairs in a few minutes. I have some questions but first I have to see under that cloth." He motions for Mom and Dad to leave.

As he removes it the pain grips me right down to my stomach.

"I am going to give you a pain killer, Marc. That should really help. It's ridiculous you traveled this way. What the hell were they thinking?"

I am now wondering the same thing, but I am anxious to know what he sees.

He has a light on his head now with a lens to see my eye close-up.

"Tell me," I say.

"You have ripped your eyelid completely apart. It is ragged and a mess."

"My eyesight?" I ask.

He looks some more and now with a little piece of eyelid he has probably moved aside I see light but the image is a blur.

"A deep scratch into the eye," Dr. Rosenthal says quietly. "I have to see when we operate."

"Let's do it now," I tell him.

"That's a really bad idea," he responds. "It's late. The full staff isn't here. I need to start you on an antibiotic and get you a tetanus shot. That wire was rusty."

Before I can say anything, he quickly adds, "I will get you a big shot of pain killer and then you will feel much better. I know you haven't had anything to eat but we can't feed you now since we will operate early in the morning."

"Okay," I tell him.

"You are really brave," he says.

I LIFT UP MY HEAD. I am in a room with two large windows to my right. I squint hard and see a clock on the wall. It is 4:10 p.m. and the sun is just above the large apartment building across the street.

I hear Mom. Then she is at my side.

"Why didn't I go to surgery? Why didn't they do it yet? Dr. Rosenthal promised first thing in the morning. Call them!"

I have never known Mom to be so quiet.

"Where is Dad? Tell him to get it done now!"

A small smile comes across Mom's face.

"It's not funny!" I yell.

"Come," she says. "I will bring you a mirror."

"Forget the mirror and—"

A nurse comes in and I repeat the same thing.

The nurse puts a large mirror in front of me, an old one with a large handle.

"Here, have a look," she says gently.

I don't understand this but try to focus on the mirror. It's even a little blurry with my right eye. Then I see myself looking. My face is clean and now I see a thick white gauze bandage across my entire forehead crossing over the top of my head. Looking more closely and following the bandage, I see that it completely covers my left eye.

"What is this? I ask. "Why can't I have surgery? Why is it delayed?"

"You had the surgery," Mom says. "It was a long operation. It took nearly seven hours."

I am trying to do a little calculation.

"So I just woke up from surgery then," I say, realizing that I didn't remember anything since being downstairs after nine o'clock last night.

Mom comes closer. "It was yesterday," she says, and I still don't understand. "You have slept one and a half days. You slept from the time you got the pain shot until now, almost two days."

Dr. Rosenthal comes in two hours later. He knows what I want to know.

"The eyelid will be fine," he explains. "I took a lot of time so I could do fine under-layers first. I think the scar will hardly be noticeable in time."

I wait.

"We will have a patch on the eye for about two weeks. There is a local antibiotic and special cream on it. We won't know for sure until we remove it. The gash on your eye was significant but I think there's a decent chance you will be okay."

I AM ALONE NOW. Mom and Dad have left. They didn't bring Miriam or Stephen.

First the polio and then after more than two months in bed I was sent to camp for a short time to help me recuperate and I was feeling so much stronger, but now this. If I never went to camp, I wouldn't be lying here in this hospital. But by now I know you don't get to choose.

I have no pain. I am still thinking about sleeping from the time I got the shot until this afternoon. It was all the pain I had for so long that made me sleep like that, Dr. Rosenthal said.

I was actually starting to like camp. Not everything but most of the kids are really nice. It is interesting with kids from all different places. And then it ends this way. Maybe I will go back next summer for the entire two months.

Two weeks with a patch and I have to wait. That's it. There is nothing else to do so I lie very still. Hope makes no difference. I know that. ▪

CHAPTER 29

Bathtub

SIXTH GRADE NOW and the commute is again a large part of my life. But it has become more of a routine that I don't mind so much. I am back in class with all my friends.

My eyesight is perfectly normal and Dr. Rosenthal says I can stop the drops. The left eyelid remains red and puffy where the stitches were.

Stephen will be eight soon and I think he grew three whole inches in camp this summer, but he is still rib-skinny.

Miriam is ecstatic at being a high-school girl. I used to know all her secrets but now I hardly see her.

Even Twinkie is her old self and roaming the neighborhood on her own again. I worry about her but keeping her tied up is worse than poison.

The woman who poisoned Twinkie will think several times before she ever does anything like that again. What I had to give thought to was how to let her know that the destruction she incurred was related to her willingness to harm an innocent animal. Her two garbage cans were turned upside down with all the stinking garbage inside so when she lifted the cans up all the rotting food would spill out. And if she looked carefully, there on her lawnmower was a full Sunday newspaper page with ads of dogs for sale. It was a warning.

I have learned to be invisible when I choose. You get caught if you make mistakes and don't plan carefully and bide your time.

Dad looks much older this year. Last Sunday I worked in the store. The business continues to improve but I know he still has bills since Cottonland closed. He is moving faster than ever, trying to sell double time. He is also more short-tempered with Uncle Hy. Uncle Ira always glued to the cash register is making him visibly upset.

It is as though he can't depend on anyone so I also try harder to sell even more. I could urge him to send us back to public school but Stephen seems happy now and in truth I mostly like my new school. The kids are smart and I love playing chess with Kenny and I might be getting used to not fighting.

This week we have a holiday from school on Tuesday and Wednesday and I work both days. It is not as busy as on Sundays and I mostly help decorators. Helene is a blond woman around 30, tall and solid but not really fat with short-cut hair and lots of red lipstick. All her clothes are tight, with her two breasts crunched together. Her butt is so squeezed in the dress I think the seam will burst any second.

This is the second time I am helping her and when Dad tells her again to go with me she runs her fingers through the back of my hair and says, "You have grown so much. How old are you? Fourteen?"

"Eleven," I answer self-assuredly.

"Well, it's about time I am helped by someone good-looking," she says more loudly.

Dad ignores this and Uncle Hy gives me a flash wink.

Downstairs I ask Helene what she is decorating at the moment. She tells me it's a fancy apartment for a professional athlete.

After the first time I helped her Uncle Hy told me she has two front row seats at all New York Rangers hockey games and the penalty box is just behind her behind. She is the mascot of the team, which he didn't explain further.

"Perhaps he will like the new black sheets we just got in, a higher thread count," I suggest. "They are really smooth." She likes that idea and I also give her soft black bath towels and matching hand towels and washcloths.

Helene never asks the price, even though this new brand of sheets is twice as expensive as plain white muslins. Then I give her bathroom rugs and a toilet-seat cover. On the second floor I pull out a new king-size bedspread with a silky surface and a ruffle edge. She loves it, and soon there are pillows, comforters, and finally six pairs of 90-inch curtains.

As everything is piled near Uncle Ira I run and grab some dish-rags and potholders. Dad walks by as though he doesn't notice, and I check everything with Uncle Ira and the bill is $972, which goes on her account.

As it's being packed up she says loudly, "How about joining me at a Rangers game, Marc? I always have two seats, and then we can meet the players right after the game."

Dad glances coldly at me.

"Sure," I tell her. "That would be great."

Uncle Ira's head is buried reviewing the invoice. Bert passes me and winks. Dad is half turned away speaking to a customer, but he is listening.

I don't even know much about hockey. I have never seen a game. I only know that the players shoot the puck to get it into the opposite goal and that most of them are Canadian. And in every game there's at least one big fight, which is why none of them have teeth.

I am thinking it would be fun, first row, right on the ice, but Dad hasn't moved away. Helene runs her hand through my hair again and says, "With that red hair and brown eyes you are going to kill all the girls pretty soon." She looks toward Dad and says, "Sam, he would enjoy it, really."

Dad is engrossed with his customer and finally Helene says to me, "Well, let me know next time I come in. I always have tickets."

We are back in the Dodge Coronet and it's a slow ride to West Hempstead, so much longer midweek than on Sunday. Dad doesn't comment on politics for the first time. Politics might be just for Sunday. I know that Senator McCarthy is no longer a problem. But something is always going on that worries Dad. Dad really doesn't like Vice President Nixon. He calls him a snake.

At home he barely pays attention to his food and Mom has made really good soup. He finishes without comment and turns the page of the *New York Post*. Normally I would have had dinner well before him but as I worked at the store today we eat together. He says nothing and Mom quietly puts dishes in front of us then quickly takes them away. Miriam must be in her room and by now Stephen is supposed to be asleep.

Mom mentions to Dad that she sent the checks out. She means to the Temple and to Hadassah and a place I know is an orphanage because I saw their letter come in asking for money. Dad worries about kids brought up without parents and he worries about Israel and I heard him tell Uncle Ira that even if there's less money right now it doesn't mean those kids should suffer.

It is so dark outside that I can hardly see the pine tree in the back. Mom asks me to take a carton down to the cellar and I grab it from the kitchen and deposit it in front of the storage closet.

It is 8:15 p.m. and no one says anything about watching TV. Tonight is Milton Berle and usually Dad won't miss him. Dad is the loudest laugher on the planet but if it is possible to imagine he laughs even more loudly when it is Jack Benny or Sid Caesar.

No TV and I will read my book. I am trying to complete another one by Ernest Hemingway. Since *The Old Man and the Sea*, I have read two others but they are much slower. In one the main character has a bad war injury and the book jacket says that Hemingway was a newspaper reporter during the Spanish Civil War. Twenty years earlier he was seriously wounded in Italy during WWI.

Uncle Hy told me that Dad also wanted to volunteer to fight the fascists. "Stupid Americans," Uncle Hy added, "fighting the wrong war." And then just a few years later Uncle Hy was stuck on an island for three years fighting the Japs.

Dad turned 40 in February. Cottonland failed and then he was sick in bed two months and has diabetes and I thought he was going to die. He didn't recover like I did from polio. He has too many worries.

I see him go by my bedroom door and I hear the bathtub water running. In his undershirt he looks smaller. His shoulders are sloped and a piece of skin hangs from under his dark right armpit. I haven't noticed it before even though it's almost the size of a pencil eraser. His upper arms and shoulders are thinner and his belly protrudes. Like me he has no butt and really skinny ankles. The only thing that is still strong are his calf muscles, rippled and thick.

I go past the bathroom door, which is partially open, and knock. Water is still running in the tub and I think that maybe I will brush my teeth.

"Come in," he says quietly, and when I enter he is sitting on the toilet.

I am about to leave quickly but he says softly, "Brush your teeth. There is nothing to be ashamed of. It's natural."

He steps out of his underpants and gets into the tub, which is steaming hot and would scald me.

He lies back against the slope to the right side of the tub, not washing yet, and closes his eyes.

He has few chest hairs and very little hair on his legs even though his facial hair is so thick he has to shave every day.

If he knows I am here he doesn't say anything. I am thinking about Helene and how much I sold her. No one said anything to me. I know it's a big sale and maybe they think they could do the same. But except for Dad I don't believe they could. She had a sharp perfume smell that stung my nose when she leaned over me to touch a towel. I felt her hip right against mine and then in front of the rugs she leaned over further and her breasts were almost against my face.

In my grade some of the girls are starting to have breasts and one girl in eighth grade, Doris Feigelman, is really big. I was thinking about bumping her by accident in the hallway and then as we almost passed each other she gave me a vicious look. I guess I wasn't the first to think about it.

Dad is as still as a quiet lake. He had a terrible life in Poland and when he was exactly my age they didn't let him attend public school any longer. Aunt Essie once whispered, "Your daddy really starved."

"It's why his leg bones are a bit curved," Mom explained.

Why him? They didn't say that about Uncle Ira or Aunts Isabel and Anda, who are all older than he is. And certainly not his younger half-brother, Uncle Jan, who was already very fat as a child in an old family picture.

In the tub his skin looks as white as the porcelain around him.

Dad left Poland 24 years ago and now he has his own store. He is a worrier. He worries about Israel, about Jews anywhere, about the price of sheets, about Uncle Hy being too lazy, about Uncle Ira never leaving the cash register.

I don't think he has to worry about me. I sold $972 of merchandise to just one customer today and I didn't agree to go to the hockey game.

I go over to the tub and say, "Dad, do you want me to wash your back?"

He doesn't answer and I repeat my question.

Then he barely nods his head yes.

I take off my pajama top and ask him to lean forward a bit. I have a bar of Ivory Soap in my right hand and reach behind his back. First in slow circles I soap him and rub my hands up and down and across. Then with my right fingers I knead his neck carefully and firmly and ask him to lean further forward. My strong hands find his ribs and muscles.

Dad has many small black moles on his back which I never noticed before. Near the bottom of his hairline there are more white hairs.

I wash his hands and between his fingers and then his feet and lower legs. All the while his eyes are closed. Maybe he never had a bath in Poland. I heard he once didn't eat for three days and stole an apple from a cart. ▪

CHAPTER 30

Road Rage

I T IS LATE OCTOBER and this Sunday is no school. I am not sure why—there's no religious holiday. The long commute seems like a settled part of my life. As far as I know Stephen is never picked on. School is mostly good if one allows for the fact that Talmud is half the day. When it is too monotonous I am out playing handball and if they know no one ever seems to say anything.

Miriam loves high school and we see so little of each other.

I hate to think it, but I miss her dancing over my head. I miss her secrets. She loves being a teenager and it's boys now all the time but I am not around to keep up with who she hopes will call her. She told me a few weeks ago she let a kid put his tongue in her mouth. She wanted to choke but she knows that's what you're supposed to do when you make out.

I just don't see the sense of doing anything you detest. Just try having me eat cottage cheese. It tastes as bad as it looks.

I saw Miriam dressed up last night. I think she had a date and I almost didn't recognize her. She had on thick red lipstick, very pink makeup on her cheeks, and a thin pearl necklace above a pretty light-blue dress. Her shoes were patent leather, which she says is the style. She looked so happy.

This is Mom's last year as president of Hadassah at Temple Beth Israel and I am not sure what she'll do if she doesn't have a lot of people to boss around. I know she raised a lot of money, but you have to do every little detail her way. Dad raises a lot of money for the synagogue and Israel and UJA too but you never hear him talk about it.

Mom mentioned that she might start helping at the store and she is sure she can get a lot more done than any of those lazy union men. Dad said nothing. Everyone who works at the store is in the union except for Uncle Ira and him.

I hope she doesn't go. That's where Dad is boss.

Everything changes. The Yankees weren't in the World Series, not with Cleveland finishing with a record of 111 wins and 43 losses and the best pitching rotation in history. And then despite all expectations the New York Giants beat Cleveland in the series in four straight. No one I know is a Giants fan except Uncle Jack.

Another minor Jewish holiday. Dad avoids the Southern State and takes back roads across Elmont and into Queens.

I don't recognize this street, which is under a subway, with one lane on each side of the stanchions. Dad usually likes to drive in two lanes but here it isn't possible. He is listening to the news and commenting as always. Nasser was almost assassinated. Dad says that when Nasser is ready he will make war on Israel.

Dad is never wrong about these things. They should ask him to be on radio.

Ernest Hemingway just won the Nobel Prize in Literature. They cited *The Old Man and the Sea*.

The radio announcer says that 1954 has been the most destructive hurricane season on record, with storms like Carol and Hazel doing hundreds of millions of dollars in damage. I wonder why hurricanes are named for women.

There is tremendous traffic here with many large delivery trucks and vans. Dad is getting upset and suddenly he cuts across the stanchion and makes a quick left across the oncoming traffic. One car horn blares loudly and I hear a sharp screech behind. Dad drives slowly down this small street with warehouses on either side. It is just like him. He goes slowly now that there are no other cars. We are partway up the street when a long gray Chevrolet pulls along our left and a man with a sandy crew cut is screaming at Dad.

Dad doesn't turn around and the man honks and screams through his open passenger window. His face is red and he keeps raising the third finger of his right hand at Dad. Of course I know that's a swear but Dad doesn't react.

You would think from Dad that the man isn't there, which makes the man yell even louder, and suddenly Dad brakes his car and flings open his door and jumps out.

The man didn't anticipate that Dad would stop. He goes another 30 or 40 feet, slams on his brake, and is out the door.

The man is much taller than Uncle Hy, who is six foot one. He is about Dad's age and broad shouldered. His cheeks are red and pulled up to his wrinkled forehead, which stops at hair that comes straight across and looks like a wheat field.

Dad is half running toward this man. He swings his head around and yells to me, "Stay there!"

Dad is a full head shorter than the man, who must outweigh him by 50 pounds. This is like Willie Pep in the ring against Rocky Marciano and I really want to go help Dad but he points again at me to stay put.

Dad stops about three feet in front of the man, clearly within punching distance, and I am afraid Dad is going to get knocked out. The man is screaming and pointing right at Dad's face. I can't hear exactly what they are saying but now Dad is yelling as well. I have never heard him yell like this. The most until now was yelling at Uncle Hy that he is lazy.

Dad's shoulders and hips are jerking back and forth and then I hear him say, "I will beat you to a pulp. I will beat you like a rotten dog."

The man also keeps yelling but so far he doesn't punch.

Dad should stay out of punching range but he doesn't know this. Then Dad does exactly the wrong thing. He steps right up to the man almost bumping chests, his eyes even with the man's neck.

Then all at once the man backs off two steps, yells some more, and turns back to his car. He goes another two steps using more swear words.

Dad begins to walk after the man and yells, "You are lucky! You would have lost your life!"

The man is back in his car and holds his third finger high in the air. Then he drives away.

Dad stands there a while and finally turns back to me. His face is a dark pool of sweat.

"Get in," he orders.

In the car he drives even more slowly. The radio is off.

I wait for a few minutes then say, "Dad, but you cut him off."

He doesn't answer.

"Did you jump out because he gave you the finger?"

"No," he responds.

"He was twice your size, Dad."

He stares straight ahead as we turn left.

Maybe I got my fighting ability from Dad. But I am almost always thinking ahead.

Dad blasted off like a firecracker.

I never heard that he had an actual fight except once when I was little and Mom's brothers were over at the house and Mr. Easa's three sons from across the street. One of them said something nasty to Uncle Hy, and then everyone was out the door with Dad quickly behind. Uncle Bob later laughed and said it was pretty even until your pint-sized Dad showed up. He would have killed all three if we didn't drag him back home.

"Why were you ready to fight him?" I still wanted to know.

"They can say almost anything. Talk is cheap." He hesitates. "But I won't stand for that."

"What?" I press.

"Everything else is okay but not that," he says as if to himself.

By now I understand. Dad rarely gets angry but then occasionally something sets him off. Recently I saw a book next to him and I asked to look at it. He showed me the pages with old black and white pictures. "My Zionist group," he said. "Sambor." The kids were probably around 17 to 20. That was the saddest I ever remember him being. The wrinkles along his eyes were sunken into deep crevices. He was staring at the boys and girls standing on three rows of wooden benches all wearing white shirts and darker skirts or pants. Blue and white, I suppose. It was taken in the summer of 1935 and Dad had already left a few years earlier.

"All dead," he said slowly, and I could feel him trying to hold onto each face, as if remembering would keep them alive. After going back and forth with him to the store hundreds of times I know that he mostly speaks in silences. In that moment I knew he felt guilty that he was alive and they were dead. And it was too late to correct it. No matter what he did the ending would always be the same. What I read is almost all fiction, make-believe, but this is real and there is no forgetting the end.

Unlike me in many fights Dad got angry for good reason. It was more than calling him a dirty Jew. But he won't tell me. And he might have killed that man and then he would be in jail.

We are now many blocks away. Dad says nothing more and I am suddenly thinking of Tom Joad in *The Grapes of Wrath*, who kills Casey's murderer and becomes a fugitive. That was around 1938, during the Depression, the year Mom and Dad were married. I heard that one year before, Dad had hopped trains across the U.S. and like the Joads wound up in California. The Joad family got meager wages as farm pickers. Dad got a job selling textiles in Los Angeles and then after six months came back and married Mom. ▪

FAMILY PHOTOS

THE EARLY YEARS

My parents, clockwise from bottom right: Samuel Straus at about age 21 (Circa 1935); my mother and father as newlyweds, ages 20 and 24, in 1938; Dora Straus *née* Drattel at age 21 (Circa 1939)

Sam and Dora Straus, approximately 34 and 30, on a family summer vacation on Long Beach, Long Island, NY (Circa 1948)

My mother's parents, Katy and Max Drattel, approximately 58 and 62, about three years before Grandpa Max died (Circa 1945)

My sister, Miriam, and me, 5 and 2, with Grandma Katy when we all still lived in Brooklyn (Circa 1945)

My dad and me at a summer bungalow my parents rented in the Rockaways (Circa 1945)

Miriam and me, 7 and 4, in our house on Lindberg Street about a year after we moved to West Hempstead, Long Island (Circa 1947)

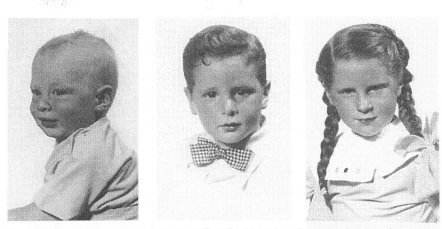

My mother took us to a photographer's studio in Brooklyn to have these portraits taken when Stephen was 1, I was 4, and Miriam was 7. (1947)

We went back to the same studio the next year. I'm wearing my Roy Rogers shirt, a birthday gift from my parents. Miriam's necklace was a birthday gift from our Uncle Bob. My mother always dressed Stephen strangely. (1948)

With my friend Charlie Aber (right) on the stoop of our house on Lindberg Street (Circa 1950)

Surrounded by family at the Nevele (*Neh*-vuh-lee) Hotel in the Catskills. (Circa 1952)

Stephen, 7, laughing after getting sprayed with cold water on a hot day (Circa 1953)

Twinkie the Wonder Dog (Circa 1953)

Grandma Katy with Stephen and me, 7 and 10, in our driveway on Lindberg Street (Circa 1953)

Miriam, 14, modeling her Doris Day haircut the summer before starting high school (1954)

Counterclockwise from bottom: My parents, Sam and Dora, with my dad's older brother, Ira; Ira's wife, also named Dora; and a woman I don't know (Circa 1953)

Sam and Dora Straus (Circa 1953)

Dad opened his store on the Lower East Side in 1943 with his brother Ira and his brother-in-law Sol Gold. Sol left the partnership and my dad changed the name to Roman Cotton Goods a few years later.

My hard-working father behind the counter on the main floor of Roman Cotton Goods (Circa 1955)

In front of my mother's bookcase in the basement of our house at age 12 (Circa 1955)

Rehearsing for my bar mitzvah at Temple Beth Israel with Stephen (left) and my teacher, Ovadiah Glass (May 1956)

Portrait of the bar mitzvah boy, Temple Beth Israel (May 1956)

Stephen and me, 11 and 14, in our bedroom. The bedspread came from Dad's store. (Circa 1957)

PART FOUR

TAKING CHANCES

CHAPTER 31

Totemanship

E VENTUALLY YOU KNOW everyone in your grade. You know
their friends and even who they avoid.

Unlike girls, boys don't tend to talk against one another,
which I really like.

In Yeshiva I am mostly judged by the fact that I am a good
student—most of the time—and really good at chess. Kenny, my
closest friend, has an infectious laugh. Even if what he's laughing at doesn't seem funny you almost have to laugh. And Pincus
Schwartzman is hilarious. He can mimic any teacher flawlessly. He
will be rich in a few years as a comedian in the Catskills.

Mrs. Rosenberg, my new sixth grade English teacher, gives me
many personal assignments. Not just books. Lately we are reviewing more history including the Magna Carta. I read everything I can
about the Holocaust. At the end Roosevelt and Churchill made a
deal with Stalin and look how that worked out. There are two Ger-
manys with all Eastern Europe now Communist.

Recently Mrs. Mahoney at Hempstead Library gave me *Lord of
the Flies* by William Golding and it made me think about camp and
how kids can be mean. In Chestnut Street School too there were
always some boys who picked on other boys. Some kids are always
tormenting other kids, pushing them, calling them names, and taking their lunch. Then they become adults and some are Nazis and
some have to hide.

There is almost no time for anything else but school, yet one evening Mom tells me that she wants me to go to Boy Scouts, which meets Thursday nights.

It is a frosty November evening. Scout Troop 300 meets in a small carriage house behind St. George's Episcopal Church on Front Street in Hempstead. I think Mom decided this because Morris Gerson's sons were Boy Scouts here and it is right near Temple Beth Israel. I guess she thinks that for a few minutes a week we should hang out with non-Jews. She forgets that's all I did my first five years of school.

But Mom and Dad know nothing about Boy Scouts or what they do. Three years ago I belonged to Troop 300's Cub Scouts and hardly ever attended. You wear a dumb uniform and a beany.

Anyway, here I am and except for Frankie Drummond, I don't recognize anyone from my Cub Scout troop.

I come in just after they start. My new uniform is actually a hand-me-down from Joshua Grodin. Fifteen boys are lined up in a row and the Troop Leader, Mr. McDonald, leads them in the Pledge and then they all say the Scout Oath together.

The assistant Troop Leaders are Jeff Murphy and Mike Sochak, both of whom have kids in the troop.

The troop leaders all have perfectly pressed uniforms and dozens of badges. Mr. McDonald is the oldest. His hair is wiry, salted gray, and buzzed off flat on top like in the army. He looks a lot like Uncle Hy, with very light ruddy skin. But Mr. McDonald's nose is too small for his face and turns up at the tip.

We sit around in a circle and Mr. McDonald introduces the three new scouts including me, and then a 14-year-old with a zillion badges on his uniform explains the rules for becoming a Tenderfoot. We have to know the Oath and the Scout Law and go camping, pitch a tent, and whip a rope, which I can't picture in my mind. He shows us the wrap and knot we have to make and it's simple, but I have never been camping.

Mr. McDonald says that Barry Thompson, the kid with the badges, has just exceeded 30 merit badges and is well past the number needed for being an Eagle Scout, the highest rank.

Hopefully for Barry he is not finished growing because he is short. His face has lots of new red acne spots. He has the kind of hair you can brush all day and as soon as you are done some hairs just stick up. Barry is asked to show off the patches on his shirt for woodcarving, cooking, cycling, first aid, community, and on and on, and I am still wondering why I am here when I get home so late and wake up early and what am I going to do with tying knots. I can't even be a Tenderfoot unless I go camping and when would that possibly be with school six days a week?

Mr. McDonald tells us enthusiastically there is a camping trip in three weeks and it turns out that Mom knew and already signed me up. It's Friday and Saturday overnight and we will return Sunday afternoon. So I'll miss school one day which is a big bonus.

It's at a campsite on eastern Long Island where we will spend Friday afternoon pitching a tent, preparing and cooking dinner, learning knots, and handling knives and axes, then make a campfire and sing, and we leave Sunday morning and everyone new always makes Tenderfoot.

Why not? I get off a day of school or maybe it's another little Jewish holiday I forgot about. Jews have so many holidays, mostly about disasters like the destruction of the Temple. I can't keep them straight.

Heckscher State Park is in East Islip, only 40 minutes by bus: 1,600 acres on the shores of the Great South Bay with a pool and 20 miles of paths and trails. Of course, it's freezing out now so no swimming.

Last Saturday Dad took me to a camping store in Mineola. It's the first time he has gone with me to buy anything except for clothes at his friend Harry's on East Broadway. I got a canteen covered with thick canvas, long thermal underwear, a knife with 12 blades, and a gray fitted cocoon-like sleeping bag with down feathers. The man who sold this to us said I would be hot sleeping in this even in northern Alaska.

The sleeping bag is rolled up tightly and attached to my backpack, which has my clothing, toothbrush kit, and some toilet paper. You need to bring your own. That was definitely on the list.

There are 12 campers and three scout leaders along and in no time the older boys have marked out an area for four tents and Stuart Harnett, a 14-year-old First Class Scout, has the first one already staked out using large steel pegs hammered into the cold ground. Then three boys help unroll the tent and begin to pitch it.

Two of them are dressed in camouflage pants and thick red wool hunting jackets and medium high leather hiking boots.

The kids here are mostly lean and seem used to being in the outdoors. Probably they all go on camping trips with their dads and already know how to make a fire and cook franks and beans and bacon and eggs for breakfast at sunrise.

No one in my family ever chopped wood. We don't own a fishing rod. Stephen knows much more about tools than Dad. I doubt Dad ever used a screwdriver. If we went camping Dad would shiver all night and by the next morning we would be in a motel or headed home.

Each of the large camouflage tents sleeps four with a mat covering the ground. I help with the next one and get one of the pegs in, which takes me as much time as it takes Stuart to hammer in three. I see how he figures out where all the pegs are going and if he's wrong we have to hammer all over again.

After everything is up I am assigned a tent where I leave my backpack. The troop meets in an open area where there are two large picnic tables. We do the Oath and the Law and hold our middle three fingers up in the Scout salute. We learn the left-handed Scout handshake which is supposed to be like a secret handshake, but the picture is in a library book so it can't be very secret.

Mr. McDonald talks about the troop history, about how many merit badges have been earned and the four members who have become Eagle Scouts in the last two years. He says that for the rest of the afternoon we are going to learn knot-making and Second Class scout tasks including use of a knife and ax and making a fire.

"When we are done here, boys, you will be prepared for Second Class and then I want you to think about planning for those merit badges. With hard work a boy can make Eagle even in two years."

Then Mr. Sochak, who made Eagle almost 30 years ago, tells us about the different merit badges.

"First Aid," he says. "That comes first. You have to know how to handle an emergency. Fitness. Everyone in Troop Three Hundred must pass this. We will start testing each of you. You will leave here as a Tenderfoot."

I wonder what you have to do in the fitness test. They have a badge in cycling and I can go three towns away. They want us to get a citizenship badge and that means knowing about the Declaration of Independence and Bill of Rights and I know them already. They have a badge in salesmanship and they want you to work somewhere for a day. Are they kidding? That's a freebie for me. They have a badge for collections. Like showing you can start a stamp collection and organize it. I have 2,212 baseball cards all organized. Another freebie.

But none of this seems interesting. They would be giving me badges for lots of things I already do. They didn't say anything about a badge for reading. And who cares about sharpening a knife? Or making a knot? When did I ever need a knot?

A merit badge for archery and exactly where does it come in handy unless you hunt, which Jews don't do? I think with all the running out of different countries we got practical. If you want meat go to the butcher. Save a day hiding in a forest waiting for an innocent deer.

What was Mom thinking?

AFTER THE TALK the group splits off to learn various activities. I am with Mr. Murphy. He has this intense look all the time with his eyes pulled together under brown bushy eyebrows. Although his hair is light brown I see he was a redhead from the wiry hairs sticking up on his hands.

"Are you in Chestnut Street School?" he asks, half looking at me while lining up some ropes for knots.

"No. I left a year ago and go a school in Queens," I say.

He whistles. "That's a big trip. Why are you doing that?"

"For a religious school," I answer. He loops a two-foot length of thick rope and lays it on the ground.

"This is perfect for half hitches," he says looking down. "But we have a great Catholic School in Garden City. My three kids went there."

"No, it's not a Catholic school," I say.

He looks at me like I am a new species that he has never seen before.

"What religion?" he says, very slowly.

"Jewish."

I see he is confused. It happens all the time. He thinks that I am Irish like he is and then, bam, he is surprised.

"Oh," he says cautiously. "We had two of your people in the troop in the past. One was Josh Greenberg."

"Josh Grodin," I correct him and suddenly I see my error. Mr. Murphy's face pulls in tightly and he grabs one of the lengths of the rope on the ground.

"Maybe you know better," he says. "Okay, Tommy," he says to a tall skinny boy near me. "Let's make sure you get all the knots right."

Mr. Murphy goes through five knots with two more boys and right now I am a phantom. He never looks at me though I am in the same place the whole time.

When he has finished he tells all the boys they have it right and will pass this part of Tenderfoot. The other three boys are joking around and he interrupts and says, "Okay, boys. Enough horsing around. Now we go on to knives and an ax."

To me he says firmly, "Do you know how to use an ax?"

"No," I respond truthfully. "I never used one. We don't have one."

"Of course not," he chuckles. "I didn't think so." He looks at the other three boys and says, "Shall we teach him how to use an ax?"

They don't get the joke and say nothing.

"Yes, let's do it. Jerry, bring over that ax in the leather sheath."

It's an ax about one and a half feet long with a curved wood handle and the blade in a buckled leather pouch.

"Show me the right way to take it out," he says to me.

Of course, I am going to get this wrong, but I take it and turn it over and then unfasten the buckle.

"No, that is wrong. Just plain dangerous," he says loudly. "Boys, you have seen exactly what you should never do. Which is what, Michael?"

Michael has the blondest hair I have ever seen. Yellow, really like thin corn stalks. He knows that the blade has to be faced away and you must always be a certain distance from anyone and I am wondering how he knows this.

I do this a few times and there is always something left they haven't told me. Finally, I get it right and Mr. Murphy says that even I will eventually pass Totemanship, which is required for Second Class.

"There is one final exercise," he says to the group. "You have to throw the ax correctly into a tree from twenty feet. Can you do this, Marc?"

Why not? I think. I am a good aim with snowballs and can throw a hardball pretty accurately. I nod okay.

"Okay then. That's great. Let's see you do it and if you get it right you pass Totemanship. Step away, boys," he orders. "No, more. Stand back there," he says pointing to a line of pine trees in the rear.

Mr. Murphy hands me the sheathed ax and takes about five steps to my right.

I move a little further from him so when I take the ax out I am at a safe distance.

It has a large curved shiny steel surface and the edge of the blade is very sharp. Mr. Murphy showed us before when it sliced a piece of paper.

I line up the tree and try to plant my feet firmly, left foot a bit forward.

"No, you are too close," I am told. "Two feet farther back or it's too easy."

It's just me and the ax and the tree in front. I am trying to figure out the best way to do this. The ax is heavy but when I do easy practice swings I realize that if I arch it back behind me with the blade faced away I think I can catapult it in one sweep and throw it like a slingshot.

I bring it behind me, elbow raised in front, and then with the blade straight and midline I gather momentum quickly and with the right arm fully outstretched I let it go.

The ax turns over like a wheel three full turns and hits the tree dead center, ax head in and deeply embedded.

The boys are cheering and cheering at this perfect throw and suddenly Mr. Murphy blows a shrill high-pitched whistle.

We stop instantly.

"What is the problem with the throw?" Mr. Murphy first asks Ronald, who shakes his head and then says, "I don't know. It's in the tree right in the center."

"And you, Michael?" he glares.

Michael is helpless and then back to Jimmy who says, "I think we are not allowed to throw an ax."

"We are not allowed to throw an ax," Mr. Murphy repeats. "Not allowed? Have any of you read the *Boy Scout Handbook*?"

They all raise their hands. Michael is already Second Class.

"You read the book and forgot. Right?"

They nod their heads sheepishly.

"It is dangerous, you dummies! Of course we never throw an ax."

They are looking at their toes.

"And Marc did and of course fails the test on Totemanship. Not just fails. He did the worst thing possible. He threw it."

Mr. Murphy has not looked directly at me for a while and now does.

"You won't make Tenderfoot. Maybe never. You might want to think about whether you really belong here."

I don't answer. I didn't want to come anyway. I have no time and I hate the uniform and the stupid little scarf we wear. I don't care about knots and oaths and mottos and the last thing I will ever do is cook.

Mr. Murphy continues to stare at me waiting for an answer.

I stare back and say nothing.

THE FIRST NIGHT HERE I lie in my cocoon down sleeping bag and the man in the store was right. I would be warm in Alaska. I am getting sleepy but the problems I had with the ax are rolling around in my head.

I think about *The Red Badge of Courage*, of 18-year-old Henry Fleming, a Union soldier fleeing from battle. Henry saw wounded and dying soldiers and wished he had a wound, a red badge, to indicate bravery. But the wound he received was accidental and when he returned to his regiment he was treated with respect.

It was a mistake to come here. I didn't ask for any badges. ▪

CHAPTER 32

One-Legged Mongoose

W E SPEND MOST OF SATURDAY chopping wood, tying knots, and cooking lunch over a fire we made. Mostly horrible stuff from cans. The pretend meat smells like sour dog food. Even the hotdogs are rubbery.

In the evening we all gather. Mr. McDonald pauses, adjusts his cap, and says it's time we talked about the One-Legged Mongoose. He allows a moment for the idea to sink in. Mr. Sochak mumbles, "I was against coming here."

I am thinking, me too.

Stuart Harnett makes a choking sound and says under his breath, "Harvey Ritter was never found."

Mr. McDonald says "That was a long time ago" but now every boy is shuddering, each with our own picture of the One-Legged Mongoose forming in our minds.

We are in a tight circle around the campfire. Mr. McDonald explains that he wants to dispel rumors about the One-Legged Mongoose. "The park is open again for scout camping," he says unconvincingly. "And there has been no Mongoose incident in the past six years. So not to worry."

Right now, every boy is on the verge of vomiting. For Jamie Cranbrook who is shivering next to me the Mongoose must be the size of King Kong but more ferocious. I know mongooses are mostly small. Like Rikki-Tikki-Tavi in Rudyard Kipling's *The Jungle Book*.

"Okay, boys," Mr. McDonald says to the troop. "I guess I opened this door and am obliged to tell you more."

It is only 6:15 p.m. and the last light is dipping beyond the big pines in Heckscher State Park. A blanket of fear drapes over us like a black cloth covering a coffin. "I am not sure," he goes on. "There are just a few people who claim to have seen him in the last thirty years. And a couple of boys went missing and were never found."

A few boys recoil in their seats and quickly edge closer to the fire. Then far to the right there is a shrill cry—OHHH, WAHH—and Jamie bolts from his seat as a torrent of vomit erupts, just missing three of us.

"He is reported to be half-man and half-mongoose," Mr. Mc-Donald says matter-of-factly. "Hairy, narrow eyes, and short tail and almost the height of a full-grown man."

He pauses so the picture is clear.

"This creature is said to live off the small animals in the park. But some think that once he rid the park of all its animals he began to attack humans. One leg was shot off almost twenty-five years ago by a man whose little daughter was grabbed late at night."

Mr. Sochak mumbles, "The girl is the only person known to have survived to tell about it."

"I bet she never came here again," Stuart says knowingly.

Mr. McDonald adds, "They closed the campsite for a long time but, like I said, there have been no incidents in six years so likely the One-Legged Mongoose is gone."

"Or dead," Frankie says, hopefully.

"Well we just don't know but everybody pay attention and stick together."

Mr. Murphy chimes in. "This is our time, Troop Three Hundred. What are we? Scouts or cowards?"

Looking at the boys' faces, I think the answer is pretty clear.

"Let's do this," he says. "Let's send out patrols and look for him." No one responds.

"Okay then," he claps. "On your feet. Any of you want to look for the One-Legged Mongoose raise your hand."

Stuart Harnett's hand of course is up in a second. Then slowly Tommy and Mike and Frankie and you could feel the electric ripple spread around the group—be brave, put your hand up—and then even Jamie shoots his hand up high.

That leaves me. Mr. Murphy grimaces in my direction and says, "I see that there is only one who is afraid to help find the Mongoose, to root him out, to make certain he never does harm again."

"Are you with us, Marc?" Mr. Sochak asks.

"Sure," I find myself saying, thinking it is no bargain missing school for this. Everyone seems relieved. Of course except for Stewart no one wants to go, but if one of us refuses then it is that much harder for everyone. There is strength in unity, some general said before a battle where everyone was killed. Maybe it was George Custer.

"Okay scouts," Mr. Sochak orders. "Let's go in groups of four. Stick to well-marked trails. No knives. I want no accidents."

I am assigned to Mr. Murphy, who gathers us around for final instructions.

"Probably we won't see him but if you do, report it as soon as possible. And make certain it doesn't see you. Use all the stealth tactics we've taught you."

I am not sure what stealth tactics he is talking about. All we've done so far is knots, tents, cooking, chopping wood, and my mistake throwing an ax. And if there is such a mongoose, which makes little sense, why would we be looking for him?

"Okay, fan out and stick to trails with clear markers."

We move east along the Ramapo Trail. Jamie, Mike, and Ronald step cautiously behind Mr. Murphy, Ronald wincing every time a leaf crackles under his shoe.

Here I am on this bogus mission on a freezing night with a half yellow moon. I wish I had two wool hats and two pairs of gloves. The other three boys can't disguise their fear, with plumes of breath shooting out rapidly from their mouths.

"Okay scouts," Mr. Murphy says stopping. "Let's do a compass check. Ronald?"

"Southeast."

"Correct, and what is the direction we must return?"

Neither Ronald nor Jamie have a clue.

"You, Marc. Our great axman. Do you know?"

"Northwest," I respond as the other boys look like I have a disease that is catching.

Mr. Murphy winces at me. "I guess your people had to figure that out."

I don't quite understand and say nothing.

"Okay then. We stop here. There are three branches of the trail going forward. We can spread out or stick together but sticking together we won't cover as much territory. What do you say?"

Jamie looks like he might vomit again.

"Come on, boys. We can be the ones to find the Mongoose and then report it to the Park Rangers and Troop Three Hundred will be famous. Someone start off to the right."

My hand goes up.

Mr. Murphy points to a tall light pole about 200 yards down the right branch. "You are restricted to go only as far as that light. Do you understand? Then come back."

Why not? I don't have to listen to this gibberish. The moonlight is enough to see the first set of trees along the trail and I have my small bright flashlight ready. The air is cold and I pull myself deeper into my thick jacket. There is no sense rushing.

I don't want to allow for the possibility that there may be a Mongoose monster out there. Even if it's a tiny thought you are undone by fear. When you fight someone much bigger you can't start thinking you might lose or you will.

I laugh a little to myself, pushing away that dangerous thought. If there is a Mongoose what's the use of trying to sneak around? It knows the hideouts. Like my hideout on Woodfield Road when I was five with our peashooters and little cement pebbles to hit cars going by. The few people who stormed in looking for us never could find us. Our bush covering was so good.

I am sorry I came. I will never even make Tenderfoot. They don't want me and what is the point.

I blow out a few large breaths and watch the cloudy vapors.

I near the light post, a thick tall pole painted black too many times. The bulb high above is yellow and oval and gives off little light.

I am about to turn back when I hear scratching sounds in the trees to my right. My heart races and then again the sound and now bushes being shoved aside. I want to run. That sliver of a chance there is a monster takes on a larger dimension. But somehow I remain rooted where I am and then suddenly the bushes and leaves move more loudly and branches snap.

I know what it is to tuck fear in and make it vanish. I can do this, and I can't go back and report what I heard and have done nothing. It is probably a deer.

I am past the first stand of trees into thick brush but I don't use my flashlight as it will pinpoint where I am. I check my compass in case it is difficult to retrace my path. I catch my breath and decide I will go just another 20 feet and return. Then the noise is much closer and slightly to the right. I take a couple of deeper breaths and move forward. No doubt it hears me and why would any animal not run unless it is as brazen as a bear or a One-Legged Mongoose?

But it's yes or no.

I quickly turn my little light on and ahead about ten feet away I catch a glimpse of what looks like the back of a man's head slightly lower than my height. I remain perfectly still and after a few seconds it pushes off in a hurry, the head raised almost full height and taller than me. The back of the head seems hairy but there is far too much foliage to be certain. I want to see if it moves on one leg and as bushes swirl for the briefest moment I think in fact there are four legs.

I am back. Mr. Murphy and the other boys ask me what I saw and I am silent. At the campfire hot chocolate is passed around.

"Well boys," Mr. McDonald says, "we need a report from each group."

One by one the leaders say nothing was seen and there is an air of incompleteness and disappointment. Of course they wanted the creature found. The wanted their troop to gain fame.

"Nothing?" he asks once more. And my hand is up.

"Yes?" he points toward me. "Let's hear it if you have something to say."

"I saw something," I say quietly.

"That is not helpful. Tell us what." I think he forgot my name and Mr. Murphy says, "It's Marc."

"I saw something."

"The Mongoose?" Mr. McDonald says expectantly.

"I think so," I answer.

"Well tell us."

I am a little emboldened and respond, "What I saw was a head like a man's." Around the campfire there is a collective breath sucked in. "It was really dark and hard to see."

"And?"

"A human head. I only saw the back. And I didn't see one leg." I hesitate. "I think there were four."

There is a gasp.

"Did it try to attack you?" he asks.

"No, it tried to get away."

"Well this is great. Shall we report that Troop Three Hundred saw the Mongoose?" he asks.

"I guess so," I say.

Mr. Murphy springs up and says, "We can't say maybe. Either we report it or not. You have to say one way or another."

Time draws out like a slow fishing line and in my head I know I am not sure.

"Yes," I say more firmly. "You can report it."

Several boys are joyful and then the talking dies down and the troop leaders are silent.

Finally Mr. Sochak begins. "Boys. Troop Three Hundred. Every year we take new scouts on an outing. We learn scout basics. We learn to work with one another, to help one another. The One-Legged Mongoose is part of this learning experience. Without fail every year one of us has seen it."

The boys all have a look of surprise and now I know where this conversation is headed and my stomach turns over.

"If there was such a creature we could never come here. Right? How could we take a chance? But it is an important part of how we begin as scouts. How we learn new things. Marc has told us he saw the Mongoose. There is no Mongoose."

They all turn toward me together and he continues.

"Mr. McDonald is our Mongoose."

Mr. McDonald laughs loudly and says, "I am the Mongoose. I left a bit early and went down the road and into the bushes on the Ramapo Trail just as we always have, near the light. That was me rustling around. I was freezing my butt off. Marc really took his time coming to the end and then sure enough he came into the woods. I shook the bushes a couple more times and he almost caught me. He had the guts to go in but he reported something that doesn't exist. Every single year someone does and always it had one leg. Marc saw three more."

Some of the boys are elbowing each other.

I said I wasn't sure. I know I saw something with a human head and that was correct.

I am the butt of their joke.

I will never outlive this.

I AM IN MY THICK DOWN sleeping bag. The day and evening rumple inside me. I won't ever come back. I was stupid to be fooled in their game. They tried to convince us there is a monster in the woods and mostly I never believed it. I was willing to face it. I know all about monsters. ∎

CHAPTER 33

The Vow

IT IS TOWARD THE END of our first semester. Chanukah and Christmas three weeks away. School takes on its own predictable pattern and color. I never skip English. I really like Mrs. Rosenberg, the only rookie teacher I am aware of who survived and she didn't do it with yelling or punishments. If the teachers can't control the classes here the kids are merciless on them.

She and I had a big discussion recently during recess about Queequeg, easily the most interesting character in *Moby Dick*.

He was covered in astrological tattoos, the son of a king of a South Sea Island, and the best harpooner. Mrs. Rosenberg said his story could be a modern morality tale. She pointed out that Queequeg comes from a society of cannibals and he looks different than British white men, but he is honest and hard-working. The book was published in 1851, 17 years after the British abolished slavery but ten years before the United States would fight a war about it.

Queequeg was different and people have difficulty with different, she pointed out, whether it's tattoos or color or beliefs.

Queequeg is the real hero to me. Now I think he is a greater hero than the Count of Monte Cristo. The Count waited over 20 years for revenge. But he lost those years in prison. Queequeg came from a tribe that practiced cannibalism, for which he showed no shame. He had discipline and frequently fasted and was silent. But above all he was a great harpooner, and on the whaling ship prejudices were put aside because his skill was recognized.

Dad thinks about the Holocaust all the time but he is not ashamed of being Jewish. I think sometimes he is ashamed of his pitted teeth and now he is talking about capping all of them. Maybe he won't be the same when they are all white and perfect.

Dad came here only four years older than I am now and owns his own store. I know he hopes Stephen and I will be doctors. It doesn't matter if a few people like Mr. Murphy in the Boy Scouts taunt me for being Jewish. What matters is to be the best—like Queequeg, the best harpooner alive.

I DON'T LIKE Rabbi Yitzhak Rosenstein and I am cutting more of his Talmud classes. For Rabbi Rosenstein only being Jewish and following Jewish law is important. Talmud is supposed to be about problem-solving and questioning, using a legal issue to uncover exceptions and conflicts. But Rabbi Rosenstein allows little debate.

I am back in class this morning only half paying attention. He asks a question and doesn't wait for an answer.

He paces nervously, stops, points at us and says, "What do we know about Jesus?"

Now he has my attention. Since starting this school over a year ago there has never been a discussion about Jesus. I would have thought otherwise since Christianity is an offshoot of Judaism and Christians outnumber Jews in the world close to a hundred to one. And without Jesus it would be none to one.

Johnny Applebaum answers, scoffing, "Jesus was a Jew who was crucified, and Christians celebrate when he was born on Christmas."

This is so basic. I think I am the only one who ever went to a non-Jewish school.

Rosenstein ignores him. "Who were his father and mother?"

Only Ira is willing to respond, "Mary and Joseph."

"Two simple Jews," Rosenstein says. "The father a carpenter. And Christians say that Joseph was the father of Jesus but then they say Jesus was the son of God. Which is it, boychiks?"

No one says anything and I have no idea what this has to do with Talmud.

"Does this make any sense? Either Joseph is the father or not."

Most of the boys nod their heads as if they are following the argument.

"And they say his mother, Mary, gave birth without having a father plant a seed in her? Do you know what that means? Pregnancy with no man except Hashem in heaven. Is this possible?"

Shakes of the head no in unison.

"And they believe this *mishigas*, this utter nonsense. Hundreds of millions believe. And that he was killed on a cross and three days later rose from the dead. And for *that* they left Judaism?"

Now I am understanding, and anger wells up. In West Hempstead Stephen and I were taunted so many times for being Jewish. Now in the Jewish school it's the same, only here all Christians are wrong.

Rosenstein fully extends his right arm, aiming his finger at us like a bayonet. "And do you know who the worst was? Saul of Tarsus! Do you know who he was? After Jesus died Saul called him a false prophet and then he becomes Saint Paul. He gets a new big title. Where is this wonderful loving Jesus now, boys? Has he come back as promised? What did he do for anyone by dying for their sins? The Christians! What they did was kill six million Jews, *alav ha-shalom*."

I am sitting in the back as usual. "There were plenty of good Christians too," I blurt out.

"What!" he yells. "You *apikoros*, nonbeliever."

"The Danish," I continue. "They protected their Jews."

"They kill us in the Crusades, the Inquisition, the pogroms...."

"Where was God during the Holocaust?" I exclaim.

Rabbi Rosenstein takes me in like a diseased rat. "What? What did you say?" he shouts.

"Did God stop six million Jews from being killed?" I say.

"How dare you!" he screams, taking two quick steps towards me, and stops.

I stand up and walk out.

I am outside a block up on Jamaica Avenue where a subway screeches by overhead. I don't know where I am headed or what I will do. It is cloudless. A man on the far corner is hawking wool hats and scarves.

MOM AND DAD had no idea what school was like for Stephen and me in West Hempstead and now it is the same. They make us change schools and travel so many hours but we never discuss school.

It makes no sense. I suppose Dad doesn't know about sixth grade. That's when he stopped school.

I mostly like Yeshiva, but this is the same kind of hate teaching I used to see in public school. In second grade my teacher asked me to explain Chanukah and the eight-day miracle. Of course it sounded like the same nonsense to my non-Jewish classmates that Jesus does to my class now.

After this episode Rabbi Rosenstein and I ignore each other. Days later I am back in class and he is on a new topic. He is talking about different types of Jewish laws. There are First Level laws that must be followed though God doesn't explain why. Like not working on the Sabbath. But a doctor is an exception if there is a life at stake. Second Level laws are less strict and also come with exceptions. For instance, if certain fast days fall on Shabbat, they get postponed. Then the Third Level laws are things one is expected to do but there's no strong prohibition if one does not.

I am beginning to lose interest when he mentions that eating only kosher food is a First Level law. As expected, no one challenges him. What if there is a new animal discovered and it is not certain whether its foot is cleft or if it chews its cud, which are necessary for it to be kosher? What if some day we can clone animals and pigs that chew their cuds? Ha, I would like to ask him that one!

Rabbi Rosenstein tells the class Jews who break this law say they don't need to follow it anymore because it was really only about cleanliness, but the Bible doesn't explain the reason so we must accept it.

I am really tempted to interrupt. Next he talks about charity. A First Level law is that all who can must give away at least ten percent of their income every year. There is no trade-off, nothing they are permitted to do to avoid this law.

I wonder how they determine who can afford to give and how income was measured 2,000 years ago compared to today.

The money can be given to a poor person or to a charity such as a synagogue. And it's also a First Level law that a recipient of charity must genuinely be poor.

The next discussion has my attention. "Vows are also a First Level law," Rabbi Rosenstein says. "If a man makes a vow there is no retreat. If he says, 'I vow to give Feinstein one-third of my business,' there is no option to back out. 'I vow to give Goldberg one hundred and fifty shekels as part of my charity.' The donor must follow through or violate a First Level law, which is almost as bad as killing someone."

I am immediately struck by a conflict in his argument. I really hope I am right. If I am, then Rabbi Rosenstein will be stuck. If I am wrong—well, there is hardly much worse he could think of me.

I raise my hand, which I haven't done in months.

Rabbi Rosenstein ignores me.

I keep it up. Several of the boys are chuckling now and Rabbi Rosenstein has no choice but to call on me.

"What?" he says, as if brushing me off.

"I have a question."

"Yes, yes, I see that," he responds with annoyance.

"So in order to accept charity a man has to be genuinely poor?" I ask.

"Yes, of course. I think you weren't listening as usual."

"Let's say a rich man says to a poor man, 'I will give you charity as part of my required gift. I will give you one hundred and fifty shekels next spring around Passover.' Can the rich man do this? Defer this a few months?"

"Yes, sure," he waves dismissively. "So long as it's within a year."

"And let's say the rich man goes to the poor man and says, 'I make a *vow*. I am going to give you one hundred and fifty shekels.' Right? Can he do this and make a vow?"

"Yes, he can make a vow. Where is this going? I think if you don't pay attention for three months I should vow not to answer."

Everyone laughs.

"But here's my question," I say before he can turn away.

"Finally, boychiks, he tells us there's a question."

Everyone laughs even harder, which he clearly enjoys.

I won't let this go. Not now. "Let's assume the rich man says, 'I make a vow. I will give you one hundred and fifty shekels just before Passover.' The charity and the vow are both First Level laws. Right? He can't withdraw it."

"Okay."

I take a slow breath. "And the poor man accepts. He is truly poor."

"Yes, yes, yes," he squints, perhaps beginning to see the scythe hidden behind my back. "So the rich man vows to give the poor man one hundred and fifty shekels in a few months and the poor man accepts and in that interim the poor man has an idea for business and is immediately successful and makes a lot of money. By the time the charity must be paid he is not poor anymore. He is now rich."

Rabbi Rosenstein frowns deeply and begins to pace.

"Now the poor man must not take the charity since it violates a First Level law."

"Go on," Rabbi Rosenstein says hurriedly pulling on his beard in long strokes.

"But the rich man must give him the charity since he made a vow. He must!"

Rabbi Rosenstein stops and rocks back and forth looking down. The class is deathly silent. A thin smile crosses Kenny Siegel's face.

"So we have two First Level laws in conflict. Neither one may violate them and both break the law if they adhere to them."

Rabbi Rosenstein doesn't look up and rocks rhythmically right to left. We all wait and wait.

Minutes pass. Then he looks at me and says, "Yes, this is a *shaila*, a question. I am going to see Rabbi Charny. I demand quiet until I return."

I suppose he will ask Rabbi Charny to finally kick me out of school. He will tell him that I don't even come to class half the time and now I ask questions just to make trouble.

I commute four hours a day and I can't work in our store on Sundays. I like my English classes but half the day is this nonsense and all I am getting better at is handball.

The door swings open and Rabbi Charny takes large steps to the front of the room and a much smaller, wider Rabbi Rosenstein follows.

"Moishe," Rabbi Charny says, sternly. "Rabbi Rosenstein is in my office to tell me you are asking a Talmud question."

Rabbi Charny has given up on me. I know he doesn't want to but he is the principal.

"Rabbi Rosenstein tells me you have asked a true *shaila*. I want you to repeat it."

I begin slowly, then more eagerly and finally come to the end.

Rabbi Charny has his eyes lifted as though the answer will dance down from above. I know he is this way when he is thinking really hard.

Finally, he says, "I have to give this question a great deal of thought. Next week I will come back to the class."

Class ends and there is great excitement. I realize Rabbi Charny really likes my question and even Rabbi Rosenstein is in a good mood. Kenny pats me on the back. He is always unhappy for me when I am in trouble. He prefers I am here every day so we can play chess over lunch.

IT IS LATE the next week and in a few days Chanukah begins and then it ends eight days later just before the 1955 New Year.

I have been in Talmud class every day. I am actually enjoying the arguments. Now Rabbi Rosenstein is calling on me constantly. Halfway into the class today Rabbi Charny comes in.

"I promised last week I would report to everyone on the question posed by Moishe Straus. I gave it many hours of thought, but I cannot see a solution. He has two vows in conflict. One must be broken. I took this question to the Talmud Assembly, which I serve on. We hear questions and then we debate and offer our opinion. Almost always we can answer them. We have no answer. We are still discussing it.

"Boys," Rabbi Charny goes on. "Talmud is a direction, a living tool, to teach us to be good humans, to think. This is cause for a celebration. It shows us that as Jews we celebrate thinking. Soon it is Chanukah and then after we return from the break, in the second week of January, we will have an assembly for the entire school. Moishe will be given a prize for asking this question. The head of the Talmud Assembly will join us. Okay, back to your studies."

I think he winks at me. Everyone seems to think I feel special but inside I feel empty, as though I have won a hollow victory.

What does it all lead to? The debate, the disagreements? That's what Jews do. Dad hopes I will be a doctor. So people can look up to me? He once said that Maimonides was a great philosopher but even more important he was a great doctor. He was the physician of Saladin, the emperor of the Muslim world. I think Dad's idea is that if you are a great doctor non-Jews have to ignore that you are a Jew. Everyone worries about their health.

I was born during the Holocaust, which no one in this Jewish school ever discusses, not Rabbi Rosenstein or Rabbi Charny. Or in Temple on Saturday. Like it's a secret. Like it never happened. Like those piles of dead bodies are just pictures in books. I read about the ghettos and expulsions and all Jews know whether they admit it or not that the Holocaust will be the single defining moment for us for at least a thousand years. It follows Dad like a constant shadow.

You can't make bad things go away by ignoring them. It is a rabid rat that will bite again and again unless you face it. Some Jews convert. They change their names.

I think if someone raises a fist you hit him first. That's what Israel does and maybe I will go there. ▪

CHAPTER 34

Hosea

WHEN I FIRST CAME to this yeshiva school in fifth grade it was like landing in Mozambique or New Guinea or a remote island in the Pacific where the natives dress differently and speak a different language and have customs and organizations completely unfamiliar.

The boys in Yeshiva wear saggy blue or gray wool pants, black leather belts, and black leather shoes. The shirts are simple white or blue dress shirts. Girls wear long skirts and long-sleeved blouses. No sneakers, cotton chinos, or polo shirts.

I guess there is conformity everywhere. In the time of *The Three Musketeers* the noblemen wore powdered wigs and in British courts judges still do though I am not sure why.

Every class here elects its own president every month, while in Chestnut Street School there were none. Last year, at the beginning of fifth grade, Ira Bernstein was president. I guess they knew him and no one else was nominated so everyone voted for him. But Mrs. Sonnenberg said you can't be president twice in a row. So in October she asked for nominations and someone said Paul Slater and then Kenny Siegel nominated me. Then it was mostly Ira alternating with me as president.

Now in sixth grade Mrs. Rosenberg told us the elected presidents have certain jobs to do. They make certain everyone is seated when class begins and, most important, they decide whether a classmate will not be permitted to go to recess because of misbehavior.

Ira Bernstein and I are alternating again. He has never held anyone back from recess, not even Hosea Lowenstein when he shot spitballs and hit Ann Cohen in the face, and Mrs. Rosenberg did not override Ira.

The kids know if they are still horsing around when class begins Ira will look bad. So usually they comply.

I have a much harder time figuring out what to do. It's always the same kids who make trouble. Johnny Applebaum is often out of his seat when class begins and no amount of warning him has worked. Taking away recess is a big deal and I haven't done it thus far.

It's near the end of January and I am finishing out my month as president. Stephen turned eight in November and I bought him the January 1955 issue of *Scientific American*. It has a feature on helicopters, but he is already glued to the story about magnetism. I was planning to read James Michener's *The Bridges at Toko-ri* about Navy pilots in the Korean War after seeing Grace Kelly in the movie last year, but Mrs. Rosenberg advised I read more biographies, perhaps a biography of Albert Einstein, who is 75.

Something is going on with Hosea. More than ever he is getting into arguments and gets really loud. He is tall with black hair and a square jaw. He's good-looking but I know the girls steer clear of him. Maybe it's because he says things so unexpected and can suddenly become explosive.

Most of the time I think he doesn't mean to misbehave. It's as though he has no choice. He is big but he gets picked on nevertheless. Often size means very little. If you are different enough, you will be teased and you will want to crawl into a hole and stay there.

I think at times he says things that at first seem ridiculous but are actually very intelligent and clever. Once Mrs. Rosenberg was teaching current events and said that President Eisenhower is an example of America electing war heroes who are not equipped to lead a democracy.

Hosea blurted out that it was Truman who got us into Korea and Eisenhower who ended the war.

Mrs. Rosenberg turned red, but she ignored the comment and went on to another topic. Mostly the class laughed. They often laugh when Hosea has an outburst, but I thought his comment was interesting. Truman also dropped two atom bombs.

I like Hosea. He would be a very good chess player if he could stick it out to the end. He can think seven steps ahead but then suddenly he loses interest.

I think something is inside him, a big secret, and I know how that feels. His father is a well-known rabbi and perhaps Hosea is a big disappointment to him. As soon as any adult knows who his father is they are quick to say how great it is to have a father that brilliant. But maybe it's not so great for Hosea.

This morning in Talmud class I can see Hosea is going to have a bad day. He is fidgeting with something in his desk at the back of the room and is getting very upset. When he gets this way, he turns red and sweaty and just now even his hair looks soaked. I am not sure who has been kicked out of class more often, Hosea or me.

Rabbi Charny must know about Hosea's problems and I can tell that he feels bad having Hosea come to his office.

Hosea always looks awkward and partly it's because his pants are too big and tightly cinched by a belt. He wears blue corduroys like you see in movies from the 1930s. His shirt colors are always a complete mismatch.

I doubt that his family is poor but I don't know of any kid who has ever been to his apartment. He never speaks about his family and I am not even sure if he has siblings.

During lunch today he watches Kenny and me play chess and suddenly gets angry and knocks over the board, yelling, "Kenny if you are going to make a move that stupid you should quit!" Kenny takes it all in stride and shrugs after Hosea leaves.

It does not take long for Hosea to act up in Mrs. Rosenberg's class. We are discussing U.S. history again and we are at the time it appeared that George Washington's army would be defeated.

"And how did the French help us?" Mrs. Rosenberg asks.

Hosea is talking to himself and says aloud, "They gave us French fries."

The kids chuckle and Mrs. Rosenberg quietly asks him not to interrupt. "Without Washington's courage it is doubtful we would have ever had our own country," she says.

"Washington and Franklin had syphilis," Hosea says loudly, then twirls his pencil like a baton.

Mrs. Rosenberg stops abruptly. I have never heard her yell at any student but I think she might now. Then she obviously reconsiders and is about to continue when Hosea says loudly, "Washington and the cherry tree is bullshit."

Mrs. Rosenberg's face is beet red. She points to Hosea and says, "Stand up, young man. You will not use language like that in my class."

Hosea slowly stands and doesn't look directly at her, which seems to make her even angrier.

"If you have something to say about the lesson then raise your hand and share it."

Hosea seems to shrug and I am still thinking about what he said about syphilis. I know it's a terrible disease but not much more. I think the seafarers got that after a long voyage but maybe that is scurvy.

"Now sit down. If you interrupt again you will be suspended and I will ask Rabbi Charny to consider removing you from the school."

There is a rumor that Hosea was in BTA, an all boys' yeshiva in Brooklyn, and that they expelled him. If he is kicked out of here where will he go?

The first half of the afternoon session ends and most of the kids are quickly headed out for recess. Hosea is slow to get up. He is looking through something in his desk.

By now everyone has left and he notices that I am standing just a few feet away. He looks at me in a way that makes me feel he is seeing me but doesn't completely know it's me. As he is about to stand I say, "Hold on, Hosea."

He stops.

"You have been really too much trouble today."

He hesitates and his mouth wrinkles around.

"I can't allow you to go to recess."

Now Hosea is staring at me really hard and I wonder if he will try to hit me but I don't see that in him.

"You can't go. You can't make this much trouble."

Hosea continues to stare and says nothing.

"Really I have to. It's my job."

Then slowly he lowers his head and tears begin to roll down his cheeks.

"I'm sorry about this, Hosea, but there is a limit."

He starts to cry and buries his face in his sleeve. I guess he really looks forward to recess even more than I ever knew. I am sorry I have this job, but they elected me and if I don't do it now it is meaningless.

He looks up briefly to see if perhaps I will commute his sentence and when he sees I can't his head squashes down again.

I am outside standing in the cold a block from the school. I feel terrible. Hosea can't help himself. He has to deal with things far worse than me. I sense that. Worse yet, I am not so sure he can overcome his problems. I have friends and he doesn't. I am having no fights and I cut class out of boredom. But I could easily not do so.

Somehow after recess everyone seems to know that I punished Hosea and yet no one says anything. Mrs. Rosenberg knows. She begins the lesson and suddenly Hosea bolts from his chair out the door.

I am on the Long Island railroad with Stephen heading back to West Hempstead.

At night in bed it is turning around in my head. I am starting to feel sick to my stomach. I am shaking a little inside. I read all about the Holocaust. The Nazis used Jews in the concentration camps to help control things. Kapos, and if it was possible Jews hated them even more than the Nazis.

I will never let them elect me President again. ▪

CHAPTER 35

Subway Ride

A T THE END OF JANUARY there is a three-day school break and I work at the store. Business is so much better even though it's generally a slow time. I wish I could figure out how these business ups and downs come about.

I can see Dad is more energetic. I will know he is doing really well when I see a new car in the garage.

Mom got a new game called Scrabble. You get seven letters and make words on a board and you get points depending on how many letters you put down, what each letter is worth, and where you place them. Anyway over the holidays Mom decided she wanted to play and of course with me as she needed a challenge. Goodbye 1,500-piece puzzles.

I think Mom is going to be a Scrabble nut. She makes all these seven-letter words and who could ever compete with her. So what I've learned to do is block all the good places for her to go, jam up spaces with little words, and she really gets frustrated. Then I wait for her to give me an opening and down goes something good.

I've beaten her now a couple of times. And I will keep beating her from time to time because I am far more patient.

W INTER SLOGS ON. Same teachers, same commute, and by now I am pretty much used to it. Stephen seems pretty happy here though you never expect him to say much.

It is mid-February. I really like my English classes. Gym class is a joke at this school. Mr. Birenbaum loves prancing around in his shorts blowing his brass whistle and yelling at us like we were the New York Giants football team. He is taunting Barry Sonnenshein now for faking push-ups.

What I don't like about Mr. Birenbaum is that he will smack a kid across the head from time to time.

It is amazing how quickly kids have changed. Some of the boys' voices are an octave lower. Mitchell has half the old voice and half the new voice, which is hilarious.

The change that I can't help noticing the most are the breasts on some of the girls. I think they used the one-week February break to buy bras.

Ann Cohen looks entirely different. She is taller now, probably two inches more than me, slim, with even darker straight hair and breasts regular woman's size. Ann, who is best friends with Ruth Kallor, our spelling champ, has always steered clear of most of the class except me and Ruth. Ann seems older than the rest of us and has told me numerous times that she goes to high-school parties.

Ann is not a good student, though I suspect it's simply that she doesn't care. She says after eighth grade she is going to public high school and will be away from this awful school.

In English thank goodness Ann is seated toward the back or I might be staring at her all the time. She wears tight silky, colored blouses even though it's not allowed.

How could I not stare with her breasts almost pointing up at me?

We are in our third week and during recess Ann confides that she likes petting and French kissing.

I haven't even kissed a girl yet much less had my tongue in her mouth.

Ann says she tells me this because I am more mature than the other kids. But I have a sense that's only part of it. She also enjoys the tease.

I have a straightforward way of asking questions I get from working at the store. I ask her how she decides what the boy can touch.

"Just over the bra for now," she says.

That would be pretty good for me, I think.

Yesterday she told me she is going to another bar mitzvah party and she always spends her time making out.

She winked. "Maybe we'll go."

Once that door opened I wasn't going to let it close.

"Okay," I said, "as long as it's us making out the whole time."

She laughed. "Sure, why not."

Today in class she comes by my desk and leans over with the top buttons of her blouse unbuttoned to pick something up and I can see all of the space between the breasts and just where the slope starts up. She knows that I'm looking, and she says, grinning, "Want to touch a tit?"

Mitchell Cooper overhears and Ann smirks at him. "Too bad. You will never have a feel."

Mitchell tries to say something and it comes out in broken squeaks.

Ann, Ruth, David Pincus, Mitchell, and I usually take the same subway after school. For me it's only three stops to get Stephen.

It might be winter but the train is sweaty hot with people packed in. Ann stands behind me pressing against my back and I can feel her hard breasts and hope I never have to move.

Now almost each day she sashays past me with a knowing grin. Ruth sees and giggles.

During recess I find Ann standing by herself and finally have the courage to tell her we should make out. She can teach me all about petting.

"I like you a lot," Ann says. "You're the only boy here who isn't a moron."

"That doesn't say much for me," I respond.

She laughs. "You are more grown up. Pretty good-looking. But I only date boys at least two years older than me."

"Make an exception," I tell her. "Or maybe not a real date. Just making out."

"My boyfriend now is sixteen but don't give up."

Ruth walks by and as if she could read my mind says nastily, "I wouldn't give you a feel in this lifetime."

I never had an issue with Ruth though we almost never speak to each other. "Ann and I wouldn't be seen dead with any of you," she goes on. "You probably never even had a hard on. And you too, Cooper," she yells across to Mitchell.

I am trying to hide my anger and act nonchalant. Ann seems embarrassed and when Ruth walks away says, "I don't know what happened except she broke up with her boyfriend and Ruth was really putting out."

Ruth is even a few inches taller than Ann, big-breasted and slightly overweight. She has no friends in school except for Ann.

IT IS FRIDAY and the subway car feels like an inferno from everyone's body heat. The door finally closes and it is not possible to speak to Mitchell and Ann, who are on my right. My back is pressed against a pole and my brown leather briefcase in my right hand is painfully squeezed against my leg.

Ruth is standing facing me on my left, just past a young man facing the other way and as the car rumbles side to side I slowly reach my left arm behind the young man and using the car motion inch further, and then with just one more effort my hand is on Ruth's large left breast. I cup it all around and squeeze before I finally let go.

At the next stop I am off.

The next day in class Ann has already accused David, Mitchell, and me of feeling up Ruth and she threatens to tell Mr. Birenbaum and Mitchell is panicking. Before lunch Ann and Ruth walk by. Ruth glares at me and says, "If you weren't such a pig I would give you a free feel."

Lunch is served in the gym. As I am leaving Mr. Birenbaum comes by and says, "You and Pincus, to the library now."

It's not really a library. It is a room toward the right rear first floor with high ceilings and thick wood-paneled walls lined with empty shelves. I think girls' homemaking meets here.

Pincus and I walk in with Birenbaum close behind. Mr. Birenbaum closes the door and plants his sneakered feet wide apart. Mitchell Cooper is already here, frozen just four feet to his right.

"Come right here!" he demands. "I want to see you lowlifes up close." His lower lip is pulled up and his chin pushes down further into his neck.

"This is going to be doomsday for you disgusting beasts."

Mitchell is shaking badly and David Pincus is staring at his own shoes.

"You scums. Sneaking a feel on the subway! You want to deny it?" he yells in Mitchell's face.

Mitchell mumbles something incoherent that sounds like high-pitched grinding wheels.

Smack! An open hand against his temple and Mitchell nearly falls over.

"Go ahead and deny it, you creep!"

Mitchell starts to cover his head and he gets a slap even harder across the other side.

"Pincus, tell me," Birenbaum says turning to him. "If you don't admit it I will break you in two."

"Wait!" I yell.

"Who said this?" Birenbaum swivels left to me and takes one step forward almost in arm's reach.

"You are next then, Straus. Good, I have had my eye on you."

"You dare touch me and I will be in Rabbi Charny's office in one minute."

Birenbaum's body pulls into a tight coil.

"I am going to beat the shit out of you, you bastard."

"They teased us about touching their breasts."

"It doesn't matter," he answers, "You have no right—"

He stops, glaring at me, lower lip curled up.

I suddenly realize I am provoking him, but I can't contain my anger. I want to hit him with both my fists against his disgusting face.

"Go ahead and ask them," I say.

The weight down on his front foot lightens.

"How dare you hit Mitchell. Mitchell didn't do it. Just look at him."

"So you admit it," he seethes.

"I admit nothing and you already hit Mitchell twice. Explain that to his mother and father. Explain that to Rabbi Charny."

"You piss ass!" he yells, raising his right hand.

"Hit me, you bully. Just try it."

"You dare—"

"Come on, Mitchell," I say pulling his arm. "David, you too, now!"

Birenbaum is starting to say something indistinct.

"Ask those girls," I say turning back. "Hit them."

Mitchell, David, and I leave. Mitchell can't stop shaking.

In the hallway Ann comes by. We glower at each other for several seconds. Her blouse is cinched tightly and I stare directly at her chest.

I am outside on a bench two blocks away.

In kindergarten, in Chestnut Street School, I was punished by having to sit under the piano but never got hit. Some of the kids I knew in West Hempstead said the nuns hit them all the time.

Rabbis, nuns, and Mr. Birenbaum. I saw Robbie Davis's father slap him very hard across the head. But kids never talk about whether they are hit by their parents. And if Yeshiva parents know that the teachers are hitting the students maybe they don't care.

I think to go back now but my hands are shaky. After the holdup in the store I didn't realize I was frightened until many hours later. I detest being afraid but just now I feel so jittery. Not because I was close to being hit.

I try to force my mind to drift down to that place of calm but the longer I sit here the worse I feel. Slowly I begin to realize it is my own rage that frightens me. ■

CHAPTER 36

Studebaker

STEPHEN AND I GET OFF at the Lakeview Station, the days much longer. The last light lies easily behind us as we walk along Woodfield Road. Past Colony Street and for a moment I think of Howie, my best friend who moved away to Plano, Texas, when we were five. Spruce Street.

There are two new houses across Woodfield just before Lindberg. Well, not so new anymore. It was where Mr. Generelli taught me to nail two-by-fours.

I live here at 268 Lindberg Street but with my long commute for one and a half years sometimes it feels as if it's not my home but a stopover.

Tonight, though, I expect a special dinner. Grandma Katy is over.

On the corner of Lindberg, I tell Stephen, "Do me a favor. Take my briefcase and coat. I want to stay here for a while."

Stephen looks puzzled. With two briefcases he will be carrying over half his weight, but he asks no questions.

I love the cool air at this hour. A slight breeze catches round my face and infuses me with lightness and energy.

There are things I could never do well no matter what, like catching fly balls in the outfield. Like running fast. But once in a while when I'm all by myself I run the length of Lindberg Street like a tornado. It is as if something enters me and lifts me up and my short legs can churn like pistons. Like the great Jesse Owens.

I am about 20 feet in from Woodfield Road looking down Lindberg. Black macadam and I know every inch, every house, mine at the end of the block next to last on the left, just after Mr. Mitchell's. The night gray drops in like a song on a breeze. Cars going along Woodfield have turned their headlights on and I will run in my leather shoes and thick wool pants like Citation winning the Triple Crown.

I plant my feet and lean over, left foot forward. The count begins in my head and then there's a noise. No, I have to run, but something is behind me.

I look back over my right shoulder and see nothing in the gray dusk. Then I hear it again and look again and coming quickly around the corner of Woodfield there is something barely visible.

I freeze with growing understanding. Larger and faster I begin to see a car, gray with no lights. In the moment between moments I know exactly what it is, a Studebaker, a Champion model, the unmistakable round headlight rims that look like mournful frog eyes set wide apart, a hood sloping down low to a thin fender below.

I am frozen in place knowing it doesn't see me and I will be hit with no chance for escape. And then from deep in my mind I instantly react. I swivel 90 degrees right and crouch slightly and relax.

And then everything slows down so much I think I am dreaming. I am about to run down Lindberg Street. I will break every record in the book. If only they could measure what is about to happen but there is no use telling anyone. It is enough that I will know.

Time moves in minuscule increments and inch by inch the car comes nearer, and I relax and soften and then the front hood is against me, against my upper right thigh and lower right abdomen, and slowly I am weightless. I am thrown up and to my left and I see the hood so clearly, and the window, behind which is a man, hatless in a wool coat, face contorted and drawn in.

He knows now he has hit someone but for him time moves at breakneck speed and fear has gripped him.

I angle my body farther left, raising my legs and hips like a swimmer, and just barely, barely, by a fraction of an inch, as I soar up and left I miss the hood and the windshield.

I am flying and see everything in tiny moments as I ascend above the roof of the car, but it is mostly past me now and I don't look back.

I am looking ahead and to my left and I know what must be done.

At the peak of my flight where up and down are suspended, I tuck my head to my chest and bring both arms and elbows up and wrap myself, and then in the descent I turn further to the left. The tree is a large maple to the right, leafless. The sky and the road are almost one color but there, just below and ahead, is a patch of green. A green rise from the road's edge to the sidewalk behind. I am drifting down and I complete my half flip as though I am a swimmer racing at the start of the turn. I can't allow the knowledge to intrude that I could never do this well.

Now only perfection is possible.

And then I'm down and the grass catches me blade by blade against my arms and shoulders, each one a tiny cushion.

I sink down and roll around and begin to open my arms and slowly lie back.

And the dream begins again but is interrupted.

Noise very close behind.

"Marc! Marc!"

I would rather sleep just now but the noise intensifies.

"Marc!"

My eyes flutter open and someone is leaning over me on my right.

"Wake up!" I think he says.

Dark hair and some kind of uniform with letters above the jacket pocket. What?

"Look at me."

I try to focus. He is clearer and close to my face and beyond him only sky and some tree branches and now lights, more lights whirling around, and a sharp horrible noise coming closer.

"Come on. You can do it. Look at me."

A really nice face. Younger than Dad. Something around his neck and more lights and maybe more people in a half circle.

"How are you?" he asks.

"I dreamed I was hit by a Studebaker," I say.

"Yes, but please tell me what you feel and don't move anything."

Behind him two more people in uniform are pushing through.

I look a little more to my right and Grandma Katy is there without a coat, her hands completely covering her mouth, rivulets running down her face.

"Let me just try to check you first," he says.

At the edge of a thick circle of standing people who look a little like monsters circling their prey a woman ducks down next to me on my left.

"Did you check him?" she asks.

Behind her Miriam is standing frozen as though she can't breathe.

Where is Stephen, I wonder.

"I am going to check you carefully," the nice man says.

I stare at him, in full focus now. Blue eyes, wide nose, and a dimple in his chin.

I concentrate on my toes and wiggle the right ones and then the left. Now just my fingers, each of them a little bit.

"I am okay," I say quietly. "I guess I wasn't dreaming."

He doesn't answer. It's true. It wasn't a dream, but it was so slow motion.

"A gray Studebaker," I repeat. "A man driving it."

"Yes, he stopped finally at the end of Lindberg."

Someone behind me says, "Hit and run."

"Do you have pain anywhere?" he asks.

"I am not sure," I answer. In truth I have no pain but it might be that just as I was hit I shut it out as I have learned to do. But if I say I have no pain he might assume I am not hurt.

"I want to check your legs first."

"I can move everything," I say.

I like his smile.

"You are a pretty smart kid. We are going to get you on a stretcher and take you in the ambulance."

Now I can see to my left and behind the crowd. Miriam hasn't moved a muscle. Grandma is choking from so much crying.

"I am okay, Grandma," I say toward her.

It's true. I know this. If I am alive now, then I will stay alive. I think I am hurt really badly but I protected my head.

I am on the stretcher and the woman in uniform and another man I didn't see before lift it up and then I am rolled into the ambulance. There is so much stuff in here right and left.

They quickly pull over an IV bottle, roll up my sleeve, and stick a needle in.

"We are off in a minute," the second man with a thin face says. "I will be back here riding with you."

I lift my head slightly and Grandma Katy is standing near the open door.

"Let her come with me," I insist.

This makes her cry even more and the man says, "It's against the law. She will come later."

Wa Waaaa. Piercing siren and I think we are on Hempstead Avenue blasting through red lights. The ambulance leans left then right and I yell, "Slow down or you will kill me!"

The man in the uniform laughs.

The ambulance pulls under a canopy, the door opens, and two people in long white coats wheel me down a corridor, half trotting. The woman with a tight hair bun yells, "Pressure and pulse?"

"Stable."

"Bleeding, neuro?"

"Looks like full motor. Huge abdominal contusion, likely fractured right leg and more."

"Time unconscious?"

"Around fifteen minutes."

In a room with large overhead lights two of them use a blanket underneath to pull me off the stretcher onto a hard table.

I am surrounded by four people all yelling at each other. A doctor in a white coat leans over me. "Try to keep your eyes still," he says and aims a sharp light in my right eye and dials a wheel. Then the left. "Can you move everything?"

"I think so," I say, starting to lift my left leg.

"No, not now. Don't move anything. Let us look first."

It is 7:42 p.m. on the round wall clock. Soon I have an IV in each arm, a blood pressure cuff attached. A nurse whose name tag says Mary cuts my pants from the top to the bottom on each leg and carefully removes the lengths. Then my shirt and undershirt come off. She shines the light on my lower abdomen and says, "Doctor, you had better take a look at this."

"What is it?" I ask.

No one says anything and now they are cleaning my belly with cold liquids, first something white and soapy and then maroon. Then a couple of small needle pricks which sting for a moment. The doctor holds a long thick needle aimed at my belly.

"What are you doing?" I want to know.

He says, "Just a procedure. It won't hurt at first."

He didn't mention the second part when it feels like something is ripping inside me. I guess my blotting out pain is over.

"Hold still," Mary orders.

I don't like the needle and then he pulls it out part way and pushes it back in and uses a large syringe on the other end to withdraw something.

Thick red blood.

"Another unit of O positive," he demands.

"Is it active?" Mary asks.

"Can't tell yet but I bet there are three units in here. Gonna need some portable films fast. Have to see if the liver or spleen ruptured."

8:25 p.m. Dad and Mom are here. He is wearing his best suit. His thin red tie is hanging down and his white shirt is soaked through. I remember now that United Jewish Appeal was honoring him tonight for his support of Israel. There was a dinner at a big hotel in Manhattan and Dad had been grumbling about having to give a speech. He looks like he is hoping this is a bad dream and he will awake and it won't be true.

Mom is studying me. She would know how badly I'm hurt better than any doctor. She is staring hard into my eyes. I can't hide anything from her when she does this. I stare back hard and then the nurse tells Mom and Dad they must wait outside.

The worst part is when they put a urine tube in me and attach it to a bag.

A second needle in my abdomen and another unit of blood.

It is 1:24 in the morning. I have had tons of X-rays. I hear them say they are going to cast my right leg.

The activity slows and less often a nurse or doctor come in. They are different people now.

I feel like I am in someone else's dream.

It began when I was about to run down the street. Now I am in Meadowbrook Hospital.

Sounds of ambulances and screams. Two bays away people behind a curtain have been crying.

When I was younger I sometimes imagined that when bad things were happening to me it was a dream, my dream where all the characters are my invention and if I concentrated I could make new ones and eliminate those I didn't want. At times I thought the world is only what you imagine it is and you can change it in your head.

I am almost 12. In this hospital. It's me in the bed. It's me with five tubes coming out of my body. I am so tired but I want to think more about this.

I almost died. I begin to think about Grandpa Max and just now I ache from missing him.

He died suddenly of a heart attack when I was five.

The pain on my right side, just above my hip, is pulsing in and out. Knowing it hurts is not dreaming. I think now it is better to be able to feel pain. But I will take the pill when the nurse comes around again. ▪

CHAPTER 37

Flying

IT IS SNOWY, I AM FIVE, and the last sunlight is glassy and speckled with frost. Two third graders are coming down the middle of Lindberg Street almost by the Davis house and hooting at me. They will surely catch me before I can make it home. Not just because they are four years older or I can hardly run in these rubber galoshes. It's that I have no ability to move.

One is Grayson Turner, who has been threatening for a year to thrash the daylights out of me. I have beaten up his younger brother, Simon, and it doesn't matter to him that Simon is two years older than me.

They want to beat me up for sport. I guess when you fight as much as me there are some kids who are like new gunslingers in town. They want to kill Wyatt Earp or Billy the Kid and gain bragging rights.

I don't move and the two boys are just 15 feet away and calling me names, most of which I've heard a hundred times.

I can't win where I am. I need dry ground and I have no chance unless I can fight one at a time. And they understand this as they mock me further.

Then I lift my arms and slowly begin to flap them up and down like whooping crane wings, like the ballerina in *Swan Lake*, her elbows sinking as her wrists and hands are raised and then everything reversing.

Faster and faster and I am up, at first just levitating, and as the boys are about to grab me I accelerate up and away. It is beautiful, hovering near the treetops, which seems the midpoint between last light and darkness. I take a quick look at the boys, so angry and amazed. Then I extend and take off, climbing rapidly and rotating and nosediving down. On days like this I am a fighter plane, a streak of light zig-zagging through enemy gunfire and annihilating the boys at will.

In the last few years my flying dreams have become increasingly rare and it is a good thing because at their worst they are terrifying. My arms can hardly move and I am exhausted from trying and the boys are readying to pummel me. They are always older boys and always on Lindberg Street. On such nights I am really frustrated because by now I know it's a dream and I know I can fly faster and higher. But then it turns out the dream has its own story to tell.

I AM WIDE AWAKE lying in this emergency room bed at 4:00 a.m. They pushed a long thick needle into my belly again and changed my urine tube, which was clogged with blood. Another doctor pops his head around the curtain and says I should really try to get some sleep now. That's with the overhead lights, all the noise, and new people getting wheeled in, one in a serious car accident but in his case he was in the car.

Mom went home and will return in the morning, when they say they will be moving me upstairs.

At last I am feeling drowsy but am afraid to sleep. I heard them say I was unconscious for 15 minutes. Those 15 minutes were for me a recurring dream. All so slow motion.

When I went aloft after the car hit me it was just like in my childhood flying dreams. And in this flight I was weightless as though time was still, and just at impact everything ended and down on the ground the entire episode replayed again and I was hoping that I had gotten it right this time and that I had flown with precision.

The sounds are more distant—the lights are less harsh. It is my own heartbeat I hear most loudly. Ba bump.

What I know now is that my flying dreams saved my life tonight and this time I was magnificent. ▪

CHAPTER 38

Wheelchair

THEY HAVE CAST MY RIGHT LEG and put me in a 40-bed male adult unit, this egg-shaped room where all 40 beds are out in the open and everything is heard and smelled and seen, except when nurses or doctors come in and pull a curtain.

I was moved from the emergency room up here to the second floor just after 5:00 in the morning. I expected to go to the pediatric floor with the other kids, but I overheard a doctor tell a nurse that with my trauma I am best treated here.

Twenty-eight beds ring the wall. Inside, where I am, are another 12 closer to the entrance.

The beds are completely full. I would say that about three-quarters of the men are Negro and no one but me is under 30.

There is nothing to do. I have no books as yet. I have one IV in each arm and a tube in my abdomen and another in my penis. No breakfast for me.

Mrs. McCaffrey is my nurse on this shift and she says I am going down soon for a new X-ray on my right leg. I heard the doctors say they aren't sure if a pelvic bone broke but there is nothing they can do about that.

A thin Negro technician who smells of cigarettes pulls over a cart and takes out a bunch of empty vials for blood: one blue cap, one orange, and two red. With badly shaking hands he sticks me four times, poking the needle in and out.

Emily Johnson is a nurse in training and she says she needs to take some urine from the bag and check the tube going in. "You aren't going to look at me," I warn her. She blushes and walks away and then Mrs. McCaffrey returns with her and says this is what they have to do. She doesn't wait and pulls the blanket back without even pulling the curtain around.

While they are doing what they are doing, I see my lower abdomen for the first time since the accident. A thick yellow tube, held in place by black stitches, enters to the left and below my belly button. My skin is deep orange and purple and badly swollen from the top of the cast almost up to my ribs.

"We need you to use the bedpan," Mrs. McCaffrey orders. "Miss Johnson will bring it over. Just slide onto it."

They think I am going to have a bowel movement lying back and everyone standing around. They might as well ask me to jump from the Empire State Building to the Chrysler Building. It won't happen.

Then the technician wants more blood. José. That's his name. It's going to be at least four sticks again.

If I had a chess set I could play against myself and practice different defenses. Even a book. Right now I think about Santiago in *The Old Man and the Sea,* with the marlin pulling him and pulling him and he has no idea how long it will go on.

AT 10:15 DR. HAYWOOD and Dr. Jones come by with five younger doctors. Mrs. McCaffrey and Emily are there, too, so they can't all fit around the bed. One nervous doctor with acne looks at my chart. "The primary impact from the car was to his hip and lower abdomen," he explains.

Dr. Jones asks him, "What about head trauma?"

"Minor abrasions."

Dr. Haywood asks, "What is the status of this morning's lab tests? Urinary output, further bleeding. Come on, everyone! Let's get focused."

There is more back and forth and I am losing interest. It feels like I'm outside their semicircle watching them in a boring movie. Then Dr. Jones adds, "What about the abnormal kidney values?"

"What's wrong with my kidneys?" I ask. They ignore me. And then they are speaking about blood numbers again and X-rays. "Is my leg broken?" I demand.

Dr. Haywood, barely looking at me, says, "Everything in good time, young man. Just hang in there."

More discussion about how much blood I lost. I have already gotten three pints of blood and there is only a little blood in my urine. In the emergency room, I asked the doctor who put in all the tubes whether I needed surgery to stop the bleeding in my belly, and he said he wasn't sure yet. Since my blood count hasn't dropped any more this morning, it sounds like they aren't going to do surgery.

W HEN THE NURSES aren't around, everything is different. The men fart and tell dirty jokes and most of all they complain about the hospital, the food, and their wives. Many were in the war and I hear stories about Normandy, North Africa, and Anzio Beach. One patient was part of a group that liberated a concentration camp. When I wanted to know more, he told me it's not for kids.

Some of them have been on the unit over a month. Mr. Chillington to the right of me is here six weeks. He has bad diabetes and his kidneys aren't working.

Arnie Bickford, a large Negro man with a shaved head and massive forearms says, "It's crazy, man, that they put you in here. This be no place for a boy. How old you be? Twelve?"

"In a few months," I tell him.

I think he's taken on the job of watching out for me. So has Jobie Casey, a very old white guy who says he can repair any car on the planet. Jobie adds, "If you got a problem you tell me."

Marvin Daystrom's wife comes in around noon and then three hours later another woman visits with lots of makeup and a very tight dress. Jobie winks at me.

By 4:00 p.m., I think the cast on my leg weighs more than me. They checked whether it is too tight but now it itches like crazy and how do you scratch? All the itch is unreachable. Maybe I can steal a wire hanger and scoot the end down to scratch.

Dinner is at 5:00 p.m. and I am only getting IVs. I have no appetite but with all the blood loss I think they should give me steak.

Dad and Mom arrive exactly at 6:00, evening visiting hours. And soon it's crowded. But I see that Jobie and Arnie have no visitors. Dad is so white he looks like he lost more blood than me and says almost nothing. Mom asks me a few questions and then goes to find the doctor. I know what will happen. They have no choice.

They will tell her everything and then she will tell them what they need to do.

I wonder what my classmates heard. Maybe that I died. Kenny Siegel might visit me because he lives in Westbury and if he does he will bring his chess set. But no one else in my sixth-grade class will come. They live too far away, in Queens.

A T NIGHT THERE ARE two TVs on. The men are waiting for a big boxing match, a middleweight or welterweight comeback. John Verplanck predicts that Kid Gavilan will win. "He isn't powerful but he's cagey and wears down his opponents."

"He's a bum," Manny Rosso argues. "He threw that fight to Saxton."

Another man three beds to the right has been coughing badly all day. He leans over and spits in a small steel tray and now there is blood. Jobie looks at me, shakes his head, and quietly tells a night nurse this is no place for a boy. "Move the kid out or move that sick guy out of here."

They don't allow TV on after 9:00, so Mr. Verplanck has his portable radio turned up loud. I try hard to follow the fight. Second round, Gavilan back in the corner takes a right and left. "Cut that shit out!" Mr. Verplanck yells at his radio. "This guy is peach toast and no time for a dive."

The fight is in the ninth round and by now almost everyone is asleep. The man spitting blood is coughing continuously and starts to gasp, trying to suck in air. Vinny Delmutto yells, "Nurse! Nurse! Get in here!"

Then the man rolls over on his back and the horrible air-sucking suddenly stops. Vinny yells again and tries to get out of bed, but just then Mrs. Ponte marches in.

"What is going on here?" she demands. "Everyone is sleeping."

Vinny glances quickly at me and then looks over at the man who was coughing and raises his eyebrows. Mrs. Ponte hesitates and then goes over. She takes a long time with the pulse then listens to his chest with a stethoscope and leaves.

By now half the men are awake and Arnie Bickford starts talking to me. He asks about my family, my brother and sister, and tells me he is originally from Alabama and his father was a sharecropper. Do I know what that is? I'm about to tell him that I've read *The Grapes of Wrath* when two young men in clean white coats wheel a gurney into the room. They go right past me to the bed with the cougher.

They lift the man onto the gurney and cover him completely with a clean sheet, even his face, and then they wheel him out. Almost immediately, two nurse assistants come in and remove everything from his little stand and put it in a bag. They take off the sheets and pillowcases and put new linens on.

Jobie and Arnie are chatting. Finally Jobie says, "Look, little guy. It happens. He was really old."

Arnie adds, "You be young and will be out of here in no time flat."

The night clock grinds almost to a stop. Every snore is louder than a train engine. Mr. Verplanck sees me wide awake and says, "You get used to it, kid. I could sleep in a damn foxhole."

In the morning, more rounds of doctors and more talk about my blood and urine, and they take blood twice more and X-ray my abdomen, maybe 15 pictures.

In the afternoon, when I see the doctor walking by, I tell him I have a question. "Yes, what is it?" he says nicely.

"There's no blood in my urine," I say. "Can't you take this tube out?"

"I'll discuss this with your mother," he answers and walks away.

I want to tell him that she won't be here until the evening.

My belly is now much more yellow, but it is slightly less swollen. I think I heard the doctors telling each other that the color is from all the old blood in my belly. I know that the nose of the Studebaker hit me right there, the top of my leg and right side of my lower belly, because I turned that way at the last second. I had this instant thought that if I was going to be hit then take it where I was softer.

Dad and Mom are in again, but not Grandma Katy or Miriam and Stephen. It looks like I am staying on this unit. Mom says they are thinking that in about a day they will start to feed me but first with only soft food.

Tonight all the belching and coughing seem further away. I ask Mr. Verplanck when the next fight is and he says not until next week. I forgot to find out if Kid won.

NOW IT IS MID-MORNING the next day and at this moment there are no nurses in the unit. I want to go to the bathroom, a real bathroom. I need both hands to lift my fully casted right leg to the right and scoot my butt to the edge of the bed. My leg drops too quickly and I have to stand immediately or I will fall over. I remove the urine bag strapped to the side bed railing and attach it to my left ankle.

"What the hell you doing?" Arnie asks.

"Bathroom," I say.

"You're too banged up. Just get yourself back in bed."

Jobie snorts and says, "Let the tyke be."

I lug the IV pole past the nursing station. There is lots of traffic going by and no one looks up.

I have no idea where the bathroom is. Maybe it was that door in the rear of the unit but now that I am out, I like walking. I walk past six rooms, dragging my heavy casted leg. It's like a dance. Step, slide. Step, slide. The names of the patients are on stickers on each door. At the end of the hall there's a window and it is so sunny. I see the overhang of the emergency entrance just to the left and beyond a large parking lot and past that a street with trees, and houses on the other side.

Down the next corridor there is a wheelchair against the wall. I maneuver into it as quickly as I can. As I position the pole in front of me, I realize that I can wheel the chair and maintain the pole between my feet.

Near the end of the hall are two elevators. As four people get on I wheel in. I look like I know what I am doing. Three are visitors and the fourth has a hospital badge but he isn't medical. Maybe the electrician or something.

On the first floor I follow the signs to the Emergency Room and as I pass an empty gurney I grab two blankets onto my lap.

There was never a plan and you wouldn't think it would be this easy, but I am outside.

It is beautiful out. Crisp and almost cloudless. I love the hum of car engines and birds. The parking lot is almost full, many De Sotos and Dodges, one just like Mom's, the '51 Wayfarer. A sharp breeze washes over my face and I arrange the blankets, one covering my chest and the other across my lap and partway down my legs. I wheel through the parking lot to the wide street, watch closely and wait. No cars coming. I hurriedly wheel across to the sidewalk.

I sit here a few moments. I think about riding my bike when I get home. Grandma Katy will be there and at least for a few days I can eat anything I want. Maybe roast beef for breakfast.

Miriam saw me lying on the ground. She is going to cry like a big baby when I am back.

I don't know how Stephen is getting to school without me. Maybe Mom is driving him.

My right leg itches a lot. Nothing I can do. I look around and make a decision. I am going home. The IV pole in is front of me. It could use a flag on top.

From here in East Meadow I will wheel this chair all the way to West Hempstead. I can figure it out. I am used to biking many miles and this really isn't very hard.

I'm almost to the next corner when suddenly two men are shouting at me and running really hard. Then another man with a badge is in front of me. I don't think he is a policeman.

They are yelling loudly.

The smaller one with big white hands grabs the handles of my wheelchair. "What the hell do you think you are doing?" he shouts.

"I left," I say.

"You can't do that!" he says. "It's not allowed."

I try hard to push away their hands.

I AM BACK in the Emergency Room, curtain closed, wrists tied down with straps. One of those white clocks with black letters clicks hard every second.

It's useless. They may keep me tied up for now but eventually they will make a mistake and I will get free.

I might have slept a little. I hear Mom. They must have called her because I got outside.

A man and a woman are telling her about the wheelchair and danger when she yanks the curtain aside. She has almost the same look as when I broke the top of the lavender toilet tank upstairs. It shattered into a thousand pieces. But this is different.

She stares at me, white-faced, with a stony concentration.

Then she abruptly turns to the doctor and nurse, "Next time," she says, "when he asks you a question, you will answer him! And take those damn straps off immediately."

Mom knows I won't go back to that big floor. She has to take me home.

Santiago went to sea 85 days in a row and caught nothing. Then he went back to sea and returned after three days with an 18-foot marlin skeleton attached to his boat. ▪

CHAPTER 39

Reckoning

MOM COMES AROUND and opens the car door to let me out. I like this.

Late afternoon and Lorraine Plant across the street waves. Mr. Mitchell next door walks cautiously toward us and sizes me up. No hat today. A green-gray scarf over a light tan jacket.

I think he doesn't want to ask how I am in case the answer isn't good.

"I'm doing good," I wave heartily to him while trying to plant my weight on my left foot. The full cast on the right must weigh 20 pounds.

Mom gathers my crutches and hands them to me. Mr. Mitchell must have used a supersonic transporter because by the time I look down and look up he is next to me.

"Let me help you," he offers cheerfully.

"Naw," I say. "I need to build up my strength so I can get around in these."

"Thank you, Jim," Mom says, and a hint, we are going in now.

I wave and half hop toward the house. No tubes. All my blood counts are good, the doctors said, and I have an appointment next week with the orthopedic specialist.

Two steps up and right into the kitchen, 4:22 p.m. on the clock.

The sink seems so much smaller, the kitchen narrower, and the refrigerator small. It is not that I was away that long. Nine days. So I can't account for it.

I read that some survivors of the *Titanic* came back and had a different perspective. For a few their food tastes even changed. But there is no chance I will ever like oatmeal.

I was hoping Grandma would be here. She needs to see how well I am doing or she will be stuck in Brooklyn worrying and knowing Mom won't tell her everything.

Stephen and Miriam have not returned from school. I didn't ask how he commuted on his own. Probably Mom and Dad dropped him off and picked him up.

I hobble into the den past the rectangular gray Formica table, the four rear windows and the windows on the left facing the Mitchells. The leaf buds are opening on the tall oak past the rear fence. But the hammock isn't up.

"Twinkie," I say loudly to Mom in the kitchen. "Is she still out? It's a little late for her."

The sink water runs. A glass is out of the cabinet and filled and Mom is in the den and places it carefully near me. A tall 12-ounce glass almost full.

She quietly begins to turn and leave.

"Twinkie," I say.

She slowly rotates left, her head partially lowered.

There is an instant in which you know something without hearing, without smelling, without touching, and even without seeing.

I am sinking inside. I have a little tremor that starts somewhere in the middle and radiates out in rolling waves and my mouth tastes like clay.

I already know and then what I see makes the impossible a certainty. Her eyes are teared and her nose and cheeks ruby red.

Everything is up and down in me and finally I say, "How?"

"Poisoned again." She waits. I am staring right into her brain.

"I tried to save her. I knew you would want me to do everything. But it was impossible. I had to... I mean you had the accident and—"

"When!" I half yell.

"Last week Tuesday."

"But I was awake. You should have asked me first before you put her to sleep."

"We couldn't be sure how you would do," she pleaded. "You were badly hurt and no one wanted to upset you at that moment."

"It's not your decision!" I scream. "Mine!"

"I did not want to take a chance."

"Mine! My dog. My decision."

"I know. But I did the best I could. I got her to the vet, but it was too late, I promise you."

"The lady around the corner?"

"No one knows, and you can't go making assumptions."

I wait. Thin tortuous charged wires are running around in my head and the shaking inside is worse.

Slowly Mom turns and is back in the kitchen. The refrigerator opens and closes twice. The stove is lit. A metal pot put on.

I am inside the garage, Stephen's refuge. My bike—but where will I go with a cast on my leg? I feel my face redden, my throat draws together and twists like a necktie knot. Wetness under my eyes; my cheeks are soaked. I want to shriek. My chest heaves. I can't remember the last time I ever cried and now it pounds in and out of me. My 16-pound proud dog.

Mom is wrong. She should have told me and then I would have spoken to the vet myself. I wouldn't want Twinkie kept alive if she was only going to be in pain and never recover. You see pictures of people who they say are brain dead and still on IVs. If you are going to die, it's better to get it over with.

But I can't be sure there was nothing they could do and Mom made the decision for me. That is never going to happen again or she will find me in San Francisco or maybe not find me ever.

I need to carefully plan. I will find out who did this.

Eleven years ago the Allies made plans to invade Normandy. It was to be the first army to cross the Channel from England to France in five centuries.

And the key was not to let the Nazis intercept the plans.

The Allied Forces did some trial runs elsewhere. They needed a full moon. And then on June 4, 1944, two days after my first birthday, the weather prediction for the invasion set for June 5th was really bad and the invasion was put on hold. German meteorologists predicted the weather would stay bad for weeks and the Nazis let their guard down. But British forecasters predicted a brief break in the storms on June 5. Eisenhower took the gamble and the next day they went.

It doesn't pay to think about why anyone would kill a dog. Twinkie had a tag. They could have called us. Warned us.

People will kill a dog. People kill whales for sport. They whip slaves. They hang Negroes from trees.

And that isn't even half of it. In Sambor, Dad's town, the local people lined up 2,000 Jewish men, women, and children along a long high brick wall in the Jewish cemetery and made them dig a ditch and then murdered them and they all fell in.

But if that lady killed Twinkie then there will be a consequence that she can't even imagine now. What I did before will seem mild in comparison. She is a coward because she does this believing that no one will know. She murders in private. What does she tell her children when they come home from school? "I have really good news for you. I murdered a Wirehaired Terrier today."

General Eisenhower waited only 24 hours to begin the invasion. The Count of Monte Cristo waited 20 years for revenge. This too shall happen when the time is right. There will be a reckoning. ∎

PART FIVE

TURNING POINTS

CHAPTER 40

Uncle Hy's Gifts

UNCLE HY HAS SO MANY FRECKLES on his arms it looks like cooked carrots stuck together. We are both redheads and both have brown eyes but Uncle Hy has long legs and a shorter torso, just the opposite of me. I know he would like to quit Dad's store but if he waits it out a few years as a Local 65 Textile Workers Union member he can retire with half pay.

I am busy helping him put away Springs Mills sheets in the basement as there are few customers.

"Winston Churchill resigned," I tell Uncle Hy.

"I told you," he says, from the other side of the rack of sheets. "Everything comes to an end."

I convinced Dad to let me work in the store both Thursday and Friday as the school is closed to celebrate Israeli Independence Day.

"Twelve soon," Uncle Hy says with a laugh.

I nod my head in agreement.

"I never asked, how long did you have that big cast on your leg?"

"A few weeks."

"I don't get it," he says with a worried look and the way his face crinkles reminds me of Mom's face. "It was supposed to be on like three months."

"They said the bones were never broken. They did that to stabilize everything."

"Doesn't make sense but it's nice seeing you fit as new. It pays to be young, believe me."

The discoloration near the top of my right leg is almost gone. I remember when I first returned to school Kenny Siegel and Mitchell Cooper were overjoyed to see me and the class had a chocolate cake.

"Hey Uncle Hy," I say, flipping open another dozen lavender sheets. "This is a new color."

"Yeah, that's what your Dad bought. We will see who buys it."

"Elston Howard started yesterday, the first Negro on the Yankees."

"Yeah," Uncle Hy says in his most quiet distant voice. "They were in no hurry. An old white boys' club. Eight years after Robinson joined the Dodgers."

"They might as well get used to it," I tell him.

Uncle Hy is unusually quiet this morning. I wanted to ask him if he'd heard about the problems with Jonas Salk's new polio vaccine, kids getting sick from the shots. I could have used a vaccine last year and even more so, Janie, the little girl across the street who died in an iron lung when I was five.

"I am really sorry about Gary," I say.

He turns and looks away like he is trying to remember which carton should be opened next.

Uncle Hy and Aunt Betty have one child, Gary, who is 18 months younger than me. Gary doesn't look a bit like Uncle Hy, whose hair remains bright red and curly. Gary has black hair, black eyes, and skin even darker than Dad's.

I haven't seen Gary in a few years. Mom and Dad and Uncle Hy and Aunt Betty don't get along. Maybe because Hy hates working in the store and Dad would fire him if he wasn't Mom's brother. That's how it always is with a border war going on.

Two weeks ago, I heard Mom and Dad say that Gary has a bone cancer in his knee.

"Does Gary have cancer?" I ask Uncle Hy.

"Yes," he says looking down.

"Where is it?"

"His right knee," he answers.

"Does he have to have his kneecap taken off?" I ask. "I read that we don't need kneecaps just like we don't need an appendix."

Uncle Hy leans over and slaps me gently on the shoulder. "Well, Buddy," he says. "I wish I knew. The docs aren't sure. They are going to give him radiation to the bone."

"They think it's going to work, right?"

"The docs are optimistic. They said it was caught on the early side."

"He's going to be better, Uncle Hy. I know it."

I know that Uncle Hy has nothing else on his mind now. I would go see Gary if I could but when I had polio I resented everybody visiting me who I hardly ever saw. It made me feel even sicker.

When I am back in the store two weeks later I want to ask Uncle Hy how Gary is doing but it hurts Uncle Hy to discuss it and what if Gary's treatment isn't working?

I looked it up at the library. It must be osteosarcoma. It usually starts in a leg bone in kids and teenagers and often the doctors amputate the whole leg and many patients still die from the spread of disease to the lungs.

Uncle Hy never works fast but today he is at half speed.

I try to get him talking to get his mind off things.

"Hey, Uncle Hy, I have a question for you."

"Sure Buddy," he says like slow-poured orange molasses.

"Why did Mom stop playing the piano?"

"Well Sis is Sis."

"I saw the medal when she was second in the whole city in the piano competition."

"Yeah. I think she was about the age you are now."

"She was twelve. I have two weeks to go."

"She was great."

"Were you there?" I ask with a chill running through me.

"I was. Me and Pops."

I take a deep breath. "Not Grandma Katy? What was Mom like playing on the stage of Carnegie Hall?"

"Grandma Katy had no interest. Sis was like a tornado blasted through the hall. A redheaded girl on fire. No one had ever seen anything like it. Sis was in her own world."

"But she didn't win."

"No, and there were even boos when she didn't."

"But then, why did she stop playing, Uncle Hy? She could have been the greatest."

"I don't know, Buddy. She was a crazy stubborn girl and in nineteen thirty Pop lost his job and Mom had Sis cleaning houses."

"I wish she'd kept playing," I say almost tearfully.

Uncle Hy walks very slowly to my side of the rack and points behind me. "Let's sit down," he says. "We need a break."

I want to say that I have one more case of sheets to put away, but I sit down on a large carton across from him.

He reaches behind his carton and retrieves a long thin package wrapped in plain blue paper and Scotch taped along a fold at the top. "A present for you," he says extending it.

I don't know why he is giving me a present. When I was sick with polio he gave me a baseball mitt but he's never given me a birthday gift. The only other thing he ever gave me was his army hat, a green-brown color.

"Go ahead and open it," he says smiling, his lips thinning out like rubber bands.

I hurry the paper off and inside is a gray velvet case, also long and thin, with a smaller zipper on top.

"What do you think it is?" he asks.

I have no idea. I run my hands along the velvet and inside there is something hard and thin, actually two things side by side. It might be metal but because of the weight it is probably wood. What could it be with two short wooden poles? I once saw a karate movie where they fought with two short sticks with a few inches of leather holding them together at the top. A nunchaku I am thinking, a dangerous weapon when you know how to swing it quickly.

"I don't take karate," I tell Uncle Hy.

He laughs and takes the case and opens the zipper. Out come two long wooden sticks just as I imagined, but then I realize that one stick screws into the other. It is very light-yellow wood, shiny and smooth.

Uncle Hy connects them and the pole is slightly taller than me. Where they come together two thin black stripes are painted around near the middle. One end is thicker and it gets thinner along its length to the other end, which is flat-tipped and covered with a thick round piece of gray felt.

"You know what this is, right?" he asks.

"A pool stick?" I answer hesitantly.

"Of course a pool stick. A really very good one."

"I never played pool," I tell him.

"You will," he responds, "and when you do you must have your own stick. It is like Mickey Mantle. Do you think he just uses any bat? He has each wooden bat made to his specifications. I think his is a thirty-five inch since he is so strong. Little guys like Rizzuto use a much lighter and smaller bat."

"I don't even know where to play," I say.

"Not a problem now, Pal. You are getting there faster than you realize. You are almost a teenager now."

I nod.

"You put this away somewhere safe and then practice. When you walk in that pool hall this is your weapon. You know how to win."

"Thank you, Uncle Hy," I say leaning across to hug him and quickly realize I had never done that. Not even with Dad. It's that way I guess with men and boys, though I have also never hugged my Mom even once. But Grandpa couldn't wait to hug me. Those were my last hugs and he died six and a half years ago.

Uncle Hy wraps his long arms around me and gives me a huge squeeze.

"You are nearly my size now," he says, half pushing me away.

"I am nine inches shorter than you," I correct.

It's not possible I will ever be as tall as him, not with Dad's side of the family so short. But I have gotten much thicker and filled out and my voice has changed a lot, so I think my growing days will end in just a couple of years.

"You are built like a wrestler," he says, winking at me, "and the girls are going to fall down at your feet."

I try to picture that. I can immediately think of one girl in my class with big brown eyes and medium-size breasts.

"You will be a lady-killer," he goes on knowingly. "And with that crazy brain of yours and a memory like no one has ever seen you will punish them."

It is like he can read my mind. I have one girl or another in my head all the time. Sometimes I can't even pay attention to classes I like. They are there swirling around in my head with nice legs and puffy butts and breasts that angle up. I think about kissing them and....

"So I have one more present for you."

He reaches into his pants pocket and retrieves something in his hand, obviously small. Without giving me a chance to guess he reaches to me, opens my palm, and places a small square blue packet in it. I reflexively curl my fingers against it—something thin rolled up inside the wrapper with a slightly thicker edge.

"Do you have your wallet with you?"

I shake my head no. I never bring my small wallet to work. At school I have it for our train tickets and some money for a snack for Stephen or in case I need to call home.

"Well then put it in your pocket and don't let anyone see it and don't open it until you use it or you can get an infection."

I turn the wrapper around. On either side in large black letters on a white background it says "Trojan" with a profile of the head of a warrior in a helmet.

"When you have sex with a girl," he says firmly, "you can't go out bare. Know what I mean? You always have to be ready because you never know and then if you don't use this little guy you can get the clap or even worse get them pregnant and then it's curtains."

I don't know what to say.

"Didn't anyone tell you about this? Guess not. You are going to get lots of action and this thing is going to be very handy."

I am almost 12 and after that I am a teenager. No one ever spoke with me about sex and exactly who does what and when and how. But some of the boys talk as if they know all the answers. Johnny says he already fingered two girls, which was hard to imagine why that would be so good. But I know that it's what adults do in secret. I know that teenage boys always want to have sex.

There isn't anything in the library that really helps but I guess that sooner or later you figure it out.

"Well, what do you say?" he asks, arms widespread.

I can't help the big smile on my face. "Thanks so much. I'll keep it with me."

"All the time," he points at my chest with a long index finger.

"All the time," I point back with a scrunched-up look. ▪

CHAPTER 41

A Person's a Person

IT'S A REALLY HOT DAY. Just two weeks till school ends. I think I am about fully recovered from the car accident but I know I had better avoid a fight. In any event it's been almost two years without a single fight except in April shortly before I was hit by the car.

Stephen is curled up with a new book, *Horton Hears a Who*. I would tell him he should stick to serious books. He is eight and a half and hasn't even read *Tom Sawyer* or *White Fang*, but he is laughing so hard he begins to cough.

"There's a whole planet on a little speck," he tells me, grinning ear to ear.

I have always known that Stephen imagines the greatest power in small things. He might become a nuclear physicist. He might be the next Albert Einstein, who died recently. At age 26 Einstein imagined the relationship between mass and energy. He predicted the atom bomb.

"Horton is begging the people of Whoville to make noise before the kangaroo and monkeys burn up the speck," Stephen says, and then looks up. "Are the people in Whoville going to die?" he asks fearfully.

"Just read on," I tell him.

"I don't want them to die," he says almost crying.

I want to tell him that it's only make-believe, that there's no such thing as Whoville. Of course he knows this but still he is really frightened. He is even more frightened after what happened.

It was last Easter Sunday. But so much of it remains foggy. It's as if that time keeps rerunning and erasing in my mind. It feels like the dream I had while being hit by the Studebaker, but this one isn't as clear.

Joey Connerty came home from church, hopped the cyclone fence on the side of our driveway and found Stephen hammering planks of wood together in our garage for one of his new inventions. Joey came up behind Stephen and hit him across the shoulders and back with a baseball bat yelling, "Christ Killer!"

I didn't see it. I only saw Stephen later when he was upstairs in bed sleeping on his side. Dr. Fallis helped clean the wounds and gave him an injection. It was still sunny out and a slight breeze came through the window near my side of the room, the window overlooking Joey's house on the other side of the fence.

Mom was sitting by the side of the bed with her face buried in her hands. Dad wouldn't be home for a few hours. I can't remember if the store was open or why I had stayed home. Maybe it was to watch Stephen because Mom had to be at a meeting. But I must have gone off for a while and left him to his hammering. Had I been there he would never have been hurt. No one will ever hit him when I am around. The neighborhood boys all know the consequences.

It is my job to protect him. I knew it the first time I saw him, when Mom brought him home from the hospital and put him on the kitchen table for me to see. He was so small and helpless. He is not meant to fight. He is meant for dreaming of tiny things and building huge things no one ever understands.

I wasn't there this time and he was hurt so badly he will never forget. He was frightened to begin with and after this beating by Joey, a boy two years older, Stephen will be forever changed. Once you have experienced something like this it never leaves you.

I can remember almost everything. I even remember down to the tiny things that happened a few years ago, even a whole day from beginning to end when I was two. Even the faces of people walking by on the boardwalk.

But the day Joey Connerty hit Stephen with a baseball bat is all a blur, like someone took a big eraser to the blackboard in my head, leaving only traces of chalk, only smudges with no chance of understanding a single word. And since that afternoon nothing further was ever said to me about it, not by Mom or Dad.

I was hit by a car just a few weeks earlier. And Twinkie died. Maybe that's why I have trouble remembering.

Now two months later Stephen's wounds have healed. A thin red scar like a strip of neon remains on his right shoulder. I am left with only a few small scars where they put tubes in my abdomen.

I was 12 on Thursday. Today is Saturday and I bike to Hempstead Lake State Park and go by the stables. It is so clear out, only one small dazzling cloud almost the color of a pomegranate. A group of horseback riders about my age are returning to the stables. Maybe a class.

I sit down on a park bench. The hazy memory of that Easter Sunday again roils around in my head.

I am back out on the street after seeing Stephen. I vaguely recall the cement sparkling in the sun tilted over our house to the west. Maybe a small draft. Maybe Grandma is staying over. Across the street and one house down loud music is coming from the Plant house. Humphrey Plant is outside. They were also in church for Easter Mass. Most of our neighbors were there. In Hempstead, the large Catholic church is not far from Temple Beth Israel.

I think I am yelling at Humphrey, coming for him. I think he is shaking his head and pointing. Not him, he swears. Telling me who did it.

The garage, a broom. I might have unscrewed the stick. Or broken it off. The thick wire of the cyclone fence seems to melt in my hands.

Then there is more floating, a feeling of scratching and tearing. A terrible noise that would probably be loud, as loud as a roar, except it is covered in so many rags and the rags are red and dripping, the sound is rippling.

Sometime much later that day I am inside lying on my back. Stephen is asleep five feet away. I hear talking outside our window along Mr. Mitchell's house, then everything disappears.

Dad is here pushing on my shoulder. I brush my eyes and at first can't remember where I am.

"Come down," he says very quietly glancing over at Stephen.

I can't respond. It is dark out and the lights are on upstairs at the Mitchells. "Put on this bathrobe," he says, handing me his oversized flannel robe with brown patterns swirled around. "Come on. Some food."

I am most of the way down the steps, the kitchen one more turn to the right. To my left the living room, the front door. Vague music from outside.

I think I sit down. My throat feels like I have swallowed a bottle of sour milk.

Grandma. Is she here?

I hear Mom, not Dad. On the phone.

Her loud sharp voice pierces my mind, soaked over, flattened down into itself.

"You make the biggest mistake you can imagine with any kind of threat!"

It's about Stephen. That much I know. But why would anyone be threatening Mom? I can't recall anyone ever doing that.

There is a long pause or maybe it's another slice of memory discarded.

"The hospital," she seems to repeat. "A broken jaw...stitched over...more surgery... intensive care...."

I can almost hear Mom breathing. It is as if I can hear it deep inside her.

Then her voice is much softer, words coming out as if in single letters. At least that's how I hear it.

"Apology? Is that what you want?"

And spaces of time.

"Then let me tell you something, Mrs. Connerty..." and a rush comes in my head quickly trying to retrieve lost time. A huge scratch inside my brain shaking some thoughts loose.

"Broken jaw? You should feel lucky my son didn't kill him."

I don't remember dinner. I vaguely remember being back upstairs lying near Stephen again. He's breathing more softly and I want to cry.

It was my fault. I should have been there. I have this extra sense when it comes to Stephen. But not that day.

I want to be done with fights. I don't want to hit anyone ever again but I know this is different. It was necessary.

THAT WAS APRIL. Now we are a few days into June. Stephen is reading the book and laughing again. We are finishing our second year in this yeshiva which I believe has been good for Stephen. They don't pick on him and someday they will be proud he graduated from their school.

"They got that Who always in trouble to use his big horns," Stephen yells with glee. "He did it." I look over at him so thin, his blue eyes like two big sparklers.

"A person's a person no matter how small." ■

CHAPTER 42

Pool Stick

IT'S TWO WEEKS after my 12th birthday, a Saturday afternoon, and this might be a good time to bike all the way to Queens, 9.8 miles to school as the crow flies. Dad isn't home. He has a meeting about a new synagogue in West Hempstead. A small Orthodox group has rented a house on Hempstead Avenue and they want Dad to help them. I don't understand why since Dad has been on the Board of Directors of Temple Beth Israel since they opened the new building over five years ago, and a year from now I will become a bar mitzvah there. Mom says that next week I will begin bar mitzah lessons with Mr. Glass and I will be the first boy in the Temple to chant the entire Torah reading.

It's the same. First they decide Stephen and I have to commute almost four hours a day to the yeshiva and now weekly bar mitzvah lessons are starting, and to do the Torah reading you have to memorize the musical intonation.

Miriam is off to visit a new friend in her high school. They will spend the entire afternoon gossiping about boys. Last week Miriam secretly told me that she had kissed Peter McIntosh.

"I know you always keep my secrets," she said in a Bette Davis voice. Her face was sparkling as she just went on without waiting for my response. "He stuck his tongue in my mouth and at first I almost gagged. I know you are supposed to close your eyes and roll your tongue around."

I told her again it's ridiculous to do something you don't like.

I have never tasted coffee because I don't like the smell and I will never eat mustard. It stinks like vomit.

"He tried to feel me up," she said, wrinkling her nose. Miriam's strawberry blond braids are long gone. Now her hair is straightened in yet another hairdo of an actress. "Don't you dare tell anyone," she whispered in a voice like Lauren Bacall in a movie with Humphrey Bogart. Then she tapped my shoulder and was off.

It is nice out and Stephen has a new pail of nails I got for him, but I warned him that this is the last building site near us, so he has to make them last.

I decide to bike all the way to my school. It will be different on back roads and everything at bike pace. From the train window it is monotony, the same thing every day.

I'll need my hat from the basement. I will put a large bottle of water in the basket because this is going to be a long trip and then if I time it correctly I will be home before dark.

Downstairs in the basement is a red tile floor and a large pantry closet filled with extras: cans of tuna, canned peaches, huge boxes of Tide, light bulbs. Then the wooden bookcases which extend 90 degrees left, filled mostly with Mom's books, different than mine. No Conrad and Melville. Thick books on the Spanish Inquisition, the Dreyfus Affair, Henry the Eighth and Ann Boleyn, Plutarch's Lives. Nonfiction with lots of killing.

I see my hat on the small table near the brown leather couch across from the TV. In the laundry room to the far left Mom must be ironing as I hear the whir of the mangle she uses for pressing sheets.

This is my Yankee hat. Uncle Jack took me to a game just after the season started. The field there is so green. We were up in the second tier halfway down the first baseline. Uncle Jack was smoking one cigar after another, first biting off the tip and spitting it on the ground. Whitey Ford was pitching so there was no doubt who would win. I hadn't realized Yogi Berra is so short. It's his head that is so big and his arms are long and thick. He is the best catcher in baseball and even though he is the same height as Dad Yogi can hit a ball over the deep left-field fence.

Mom pops her head out the door and looks at me, her face all sweaty and red from the laundry heat. I don't know why she doesn't just wait for Christine, her new cleaning lady, to do all this.

I pick up my cap and am about to turn and leave but there is a prickle in the room like a sharp breeze that doesn't move but sits against your face.

Mom takes a step toward me. She is wearing one of her thin cotton housedresses, this one a dull white with small blue flowers. It has a tie around the waist where Mom is thick even though she is thin. She's all thick waist and forearms and long limbs and massive hands always raw from floor-scrubbing, always with a thin gold wedding band.

I feel anchored now where I am as a memory wafts in like salt on a wound. I am 12 and I thought we were done with this. I had promised myself to be fully prepared if it ever happens again now that I am this big and this strong. There is simply no one in my school nearly as strong, not even eighth graders.

She takes two slow steps toward me from about ten feet away. Her sharp blue eyes seem so liquid and unseeing. Perhaps if I just scream out she will awaken from some lost place in her head. But I remain mute and a little fascinated in a way that I can't explain.

I have no sense of fear. What I feel though is different. It is more like curiosity.

Then from behind her back—I had not really noticed that her right hand wasn't visible—something comes forward not easily seen in the dim basement light. A sharp slant of sunlight from the upper transom window hits the floor like a scimitar, a dividing line of yellow right between the two of us.

My pool stick in its gray velvet case. From Uncle Hy.

I am perplexed. I thought I left it on the upper shelf of my closet, not to hide it, just to keep it safe so when I am ready to play pool I will have it.

Still staring at me she unzips the top with her left hand and removes the two poles so slowly and evenly as though she is holding onto a B sharp note with the middle foot pedal of the piano.

The case drops quietly to the floor and now she screws the poles together, around and around until they are fixed, as though they can never again be taken apart.

I am watching this as if I am outside looking through that transom and Mom is in a play, or more like she is a slow-motion mime on the street, face and limbs painted all gray.

Then the pool stick rises slowly in her left hand and is transferred to her right and she begins floating toward me, liquid moving across glass.

I know what the outcome will be, and it doesn't matter, yet again I can't think of anything I have done that would provoke her so. There is the slightest thought in my head that I am wrong to have the pool stick. That I didn't mention it to her. If she knew it was a recent gift from her brother, Uncle Hy, things would surely be different.

I have no thought of turning and running out. I stay perfectly still.

Now she lifts her arm and the pool stick looks like a thin samurai sword in the hands of a skilled warrior.

The pool stick hovers inches from the ceiling and when it comes down it will increase in speed in tremendous intensity. No one can play Chopin as quickly. She murders those keys.

The bottom of the pool stick, which would be placed in my right palm, fingers cupped around, leaning low, is now in her strong right hand and then the long rod begins to move. It will hit the middle of my face from the left. All this is known the way Ted Williams knows exactly what pitch is coming the moment the ball leaves the pitcher's hand.

My face will slice open. The stick will fracture my jaw just as I think I fractured Joey's jaw in April.

Splayed out to the right where the light shimmers across it. And whipping across.

And then my left hand is up as though by itself. Not to shield my face. I catch the end of the pool stick inches from my face as though snagging a hard line drive down third base with a bare hand. One hundred twenty miles an hour. Just like that. With no pain whatsoever. Hands with reflexes as quick as hers. A ninja.

In my left hand it's fully stopped and we are glaring across the pool stick. We stare as though we might stay this way for a century.

I think my eyes are open double size and I am so calm I could play a game of chess in my head at the same time.

Then suddenly she yanks back quickly with all her might and the pool stick doesn't move. Her eyelids flutter, her upper lip curls up, as she yanks with both hands.

Nothing.

And her face begins to change ever so slowly. Some life comes back into the blue eyes, the red chin, and even the red hair rumpled above. She looks at me as if recognition is only beginning.

We seem stuck like this and my hand remains implacably and

firmly around the stick. There will be no chance to withdraw it. It is mine and will remain mine.

Her head now tilts down a bit and to the left.

"It is over now," I say. "It is over."

I tug slightly on the pool stick and easily withdraw it from her hand. I pull it toward me and around and unscrew it and place the two poles together again.

I retrieve the gray case, put the pool sticks in, and zip it up.

I look hard into her eyes and turn around and walk out. ▪

CHAPTER 43

Under the Pine

A FTER TEMPLE WITH DAD in the morning I bike to see Mrs. Mahoney at the Hempstead Library.

"I am just so happy to see you, Marc," she says. "I hope your school in Queens takes good care of you."

"Yes," I say, thinking that in September, seventh grade, I will have Mrs. Ginsberg, known to be the toughest English teacher in the school. I am already prepared for the fact that my handball days may be over.

I am glancing at the display of new best sellers. On the left is *Bonjour Tristesse*.

"No," Mrs. Mahoney says, shaking her head. "Lightweight but still remarkably written by an eighteen-year-old French girl."

Near the counter I spot Irving Stone's last best seller, *Love is Eternal*. Mrs. Mahoney shakes her head no again. "But come here," she says. "I have a few I have saved for you."

I mean to tell her that I never got around to reading *Oliver Twist*, about a boy with a long hard-luck story who gets to be happy in the end.

Mrs. Mahoney goes behind her desk and retrieves several hardcover books. Looking up she says, "I am glad you are here. I wanted to tell you in person I am retiring in July. Forty years in the library system."

I can't help feeling really sad but I suppose she must be happy.

"Yes," she goes on, "and I plan on more travel and time with my four grandchildren but what I will miss and never forget are the very special people like you."

She comes around the counter and holds out her hands, which I take, and she gives me a double squeeze.

"You always give me great books, Mrs. Mahoney," I say. "Except for that one by Brontë." And we both laugh and then keep laughing.

"It is impossible to believe that you first came here when you were what? Five?"

"Yes."

"And now. Almost fully grown and that wonderful mind."

"Thank you so much."

"I have told Mrs. Lester to look after you but I hate it not being me."

"Well just send me some ideas by mail," I tell her.

She laughs even louder. "I never asked if you have even begun to think about what you might do someday although for you I can't even guess."

"I don't know. I love working in my dad's store, but I've started reading about scientists and physicians like Paul Ehrlich and Jonas Salk."

"Ah, yes, the Salk vaccine was re-approved, thank goodness."

I am thinking it's already too late for many kids who needed it and I am luckier. I have no after-effects.

I AM IN THE STORE today. In four days, on June 30th, I am off to Camp Massad—this time I expect for the entire summer. I could easily skip the Hebrew, but I am surprisingly looking forward to camp. I will try out for junior lifesaving and as soon as I really think about camp a girl pops into my head. Andrea has black curly hair and a fun smile and loves to dance.

It is a beautiful day on Grand Street, the clouds moving like thin whispers across blue sky. The streets are filled with shoppers and in our store we are backed up trying to take care of eager customers.

Dad is enjoying the bustle. He knows which customers to focus upon. Still Uncle Ira doesn't move from behind the counter. Uncle Hy tells me it is like this now every week. Retail customers are flooding to the Lower East Side for bargain shopping.

In the few times I have been able to work at the store over the past two years I realized our most frequent customers are mostly gone, the jobbers who buy and then sell the goods door to door.

That is for greenhorns, Uncle Hy said—refugees—and none of this generation will do that backbreaking work. It's almost over.

Now our largest sales are to smaller retail textile stores and we sell to them as far away as Kansas and Miami.

I see the pricelists are disorganized again.

At the end of the day Dad and I are back in his car headed for West Hempstead. It is time to campaign.

"I have two more years of yeshiva," I say.

He doesn't answer of course.

"It takes you so long to drive to work now, why not move to Queens or Brooklyn?"

Dad barely glances at me, but I know it takes time to plant an idea in his head.

"Stephen and I commute so many hours and if we lived much closer I would have more time for studies."

Perhaps that is a hollow argument especially if he only knew how much time I spend out of class.

"Yeshiva of Central Queens only goes through eighth grade and then I need to go to a good high school and it isn't West Hempstead."

"You won't go there," he says as though to himself but then Miriam has been there a year now and this makes little sense.

I won't get further today but hopefully one day he will wake up and decide we are moving to the city and he won't even remember I started this idea.

West Hempstead has so many more Jews moving there now but it is too late. School was terrible and I admit grudgingly that it was really good I left even if it was to go to a religious yeshiva.

The kids there have parents like mine. They want their children to succeed and that means a strong education. I wouldn't like to admit it but on many days my favorite course is Talmud. The math is too easy, and history is reading about things that already happened.

Talmud is not about cows goring cows anymore. It is about how ideas branch out to more ideas and just when you might be considering what seems fair for one person you realize how that decision might impact someone else. Fairness is a delicate balance without absolutes.

I weigh almost 120 pounds and have thick arms and legs. I plan to do more sit-ups in a row than Charlie, our camp counselor. He attracted girls like flies.

The thing about Camp Massad, once you get past how much

food they serve, how bad the baseball field is, the Hebrew lessons, is that many of the kids are super smart. And nice, except for a few. Which makes me wonder if Mark Spilkowitz will return—chief bully of Bunk 13.

And what about Freddie? He was tortured almost the entire summer. If only he could return and have things be different. Otherwise he will only remember the bad.

I hope David Meyers comes back, spittle-talking and all. And Bonnie Breitman lights up everything around her.

If I had my choice, I would work in the store all summer, but Dad has decided it's camp again. I know it's not just being Jewish full-time. It's not just because as an impoverished kid he had no such opportunity. It's because it's American. That seems too simple but I am sure that's what he sees on TV and in magazines and it's what his friends have done—their kids go to camp.

I see that. People come into the store and it's where does your boy go to school? Oh, that's wonderful. Which camp? Where is that?

Massad. That's the best orthodox camp in America.

Anyway, that's what they think on the corner of Grand and Eldridge.

For Dad and Mom too there is a thread that inevitably leads to medical school and law school, and my older cousins Marty and Herbie now have both gone to NYU law school. And their dad, my great uncle Mendel, might be very wealthy with the buildings he bought on Broadway, but to hear him speak, with the same Eastern European accent as Dad, it's all about his boys in law school.

Two years without a fight in Yeshiva. Just one fight in West Hempstead.

Now I hope no more.

There are times when I feel threatened and this surge begins inside that I am so familiar with and it's hard to cut off. But by now I see that my reaction is usually exaggerated. I am expecting the worst so I can't see past the threat. Still I am wary that I might miss something and be blindsided by being trusting. Mom loses control. I never want to be like that. But I will remain vigilant. I will work out hard and become even stronger.

Things are so much better for Stephen, but I have to be watchful without him realizing it. As far as I know no one has picked on him. He doesn't really want me hovering around him any longer. He has good friends and he is better off not being a fighter.

Tomorrow morning, I will do 40 push-ups in a row and then another 40 after a five-minute rest. Because you just don't know for sure.

Mom is different. She speaks to me more and occasionally wants my opinion.

I am about the same weight as she is. She tells me what's going on in Hadassah. Now she tells me her political opinions. She knows in six years I will go away to college and I think she feels it's just around the corner.

She gave up the piano and she was a genius at it. It is so sad. She knows she was the best and knowing that isn't good enough. It's what you keep doing.

I can sell textiles but not as well as Dad. No one can. But I am good at it.

I will never run fast and I don't care.

If I want to go to medical school, then I will. If I don't go it will only be my fault, which means cutting class will end. Maybe not just yet.

If I am a doctor, I want to treat people who are really sick and then if I give it my best I can make many of them better.

SANTIAGO IS MY HERO, a poor old fisherman who has true courage. Santiago never thought about defeating the marlin. He simply did what he had to do.

I have been thinking more about Henry Fleming, the Union soldier in *The Red Badge of Courage* who abandons the fight and tries to convince himself he was justified. Later in battle he grabs the regiment flag and without any weapon helps lead a charge against the Confederates.

It is seen as a moment of great bravery.

Now I am not so sure that when he ran away he was a coward, or that when he charged the enemy he was brave.

He was frightened in war and he thought everyone from his side was quickly retreating. His instinct was to save himself from a hopeless situation in a war where in some battles over half the soldiers died. It isn't wrong to be frightened and he wasn't abandoning a fallen comrade. But then when his act seemed brave maybe it was foolhardy, taking a huge risk at the wrong time and without much gain.

I am in Dad's hammock, my hammock too, under the thick pine. A big slice of sunlight crosses my polo shirt. I smell the sap. A bluebird is pecking away at the fresh grass. I think about Twinkie. I let her roam. I knew the risks. Maybe it was the neighbor lady. Maybe not.

It'll be good to be away all summer. It will give me time to think and try a different way, try to change. I want to find balance. I want to be very strong and defend myself and Stephen if I have to. But not have so many accidents and not have unnecessary fights. I think I have been running and running with a flag daring everyone.

Not everyone is the enemy. ▪

REMEMBERING

Poems by Marc J. Straus

Green Dust

An old man arcs his slim wooden fishing pole.
A boy skims a stone across the water. I am

seven thousand miles from home. In this river town
south of St. Petersburg, tiny wooden shacks

are capped with tin roofs. A sallow-skin man
in coarse woolen slacks sells cigarettes, homemade

vodka, soggy tomatoes. A woman wearing
a yellow babushka scrapes gristle from the bone.

This could have been me. My father's mother
died of typhus when he was one. He left school

at age eleven. There's a picture of him, age
fifteen, slender and sinewy, dark eyes glistening

as if dotted with iron ore. As a young boy
I worked in his store in lower Manhattan.

At the end of the day he spread a thin layer
of green dust on the old wooden floor. He swept

in hard even strokes until the oak glowed
like winter moonlight on a Russian lake.

Grandma Katy

The sky a July coconut haze,
the blue and white enamel sign:
49th Street and 14th Avenue.

The two-family brick house, one in
from the northeast corner,
is a small religious school now.

Its concrete stoop, four steps
(I would have guessed six), is painted over
yellow too many times, and the chink

in the balustrade to the left
against which I fell, is sanded smooth.
My memory is frozen into still frames.

In one, I hesitate at the top step
on my new red tricycle. In another,
a cold rag is wrapped around my wrist.

A pea-green cotton housedress
with small white flowers billows like a tent.
Steam lifts off the clear soup filling

a broad maroon bowl. A thin stick of celery.
Two carrot chips. A chicken foot
with puckered skin and three large toes.

The Day Stalin Died

I leaned my back behind the mower:
wooden wheels, thin metal blades in need
of sharpening. Earlier in the day
I was in a spelling bee - stumped
on appetite - forgetting the second P.
After school Kenny Teuton asked me
if it's true that Jews drink blood

on holidays. I looked at his wide face,
large spaces between his teeth. Had he
not asked so innocently, I would have
smashed his lower lip, just like I did
to Frankie Robinson on Lindberg Street.
Dinner on Thursday was always string beans
and lamb chops. Grandma Katy was there.

She baked potatoes with fried chicken skins
mashed inside. Sunday we'd be visiting
Grandpa Max at the cemetery. I'd taken
a pail of nails and two wagonloads of lumber
for Stephen from Woodfield Road.
Miriam was on the phone with Rhoda
Stopnick. I turned the Dumont on.

Edward R. Murrow was talking
with a cigarette dangling from his mouth.
I heard my father come home. I was supposed
to be doing homework. Instead,
I was reading Freddy the Pig. Freddy
had just unionized all the animals
and was planning a nonviolent protest in town.

Steam Bath

My younger brother stood in the center
of the huge tiled room–the Turkish
Steam Bath at Brighton Beach. He was
thin and white as an oyster shell
surrounded by bulbous naked men
dripping puddles of sweat.
I can't breathe, he cried. It's good for you,
my father said, as my brother bolted
for the door.

Now I wonder how my father knew
it's true, that breathing in the viscous heat
is healthful. So much of childhood
is offered in rote: this is good,
this isn't. So little room
for reflex. And yet at the moment of birth
the diaphragm descends. A breath's
drawn in. A breath's pushed out.

Shoe Box

Sooner or later it returns to
    my cards fastidiously kept
age five to fifteen five-cent packs
    with flat pink bubblegum
won with dexterity two and half turns
    from the hip a leaner a used
Mickey Mantle for Mel Ott
    a mint Honus Wagner today
worth $600,000 thrown away
    discarded by my mother
when we moved to Ocean Parkway
    apartment 6F with a terrace
rear room facing the alley because
    a man offered my father $46,000
for our house a size 8 ½ double E
    shoe box 2,000 cards catalogued
ten years and now I tell my wife my
    two children my dog my poet
friend who plays left field my
    analyst that my childhood
vanished in that box.

Before That

Synethesia, metaplasia. Before that
my language was acquired on the corner of East 10th Street,
Alice Singletary lip-synching every song, Archie
Grover starting every sentence with "Hey." Somehow
an occasional three-syllable word entered my vocabulary.
My tenth-grade paper was on Hemingway
and Mrs. Clara Mann wrote across the top in bold red,
"Needless to say you missed the symbolism entirely
in *A Farewell to Arms*–C minus." For the next exercise
she asked us to write a poem in class. I sat the hour
and angrily penned a dark and pessimistic verse. God
had disappeared in fear (and this was a religious school).
"This is an A Plus," she wrote in red in the margin,
"but you must pay more attention to Yeats."
That may have been asking too much, but soon
I had found Rilke, Bishop, William Carlos
Williams, and Stanley Kunitz, who wrote about a slap
his mother gave him across the face when he was five
that still stung sixty years later. Words were pistols
and fireballs lined up like dominoes across a line. Words
etched out the cilia in my throat and held my ankles down.
Later, in college and medical school, language stretched
on an unending yardarm. It became convoluted and specific.
Sometimes I yearned for simplicity, Joe Applebaum
tapping the top of a garbage can–do wop, do wop,
hey everybody, just do the hop.

Breathing Spoons

Breathing spoons. That's what my grandmother
called them—wooden ladles she dipped into
the thick vegetable soup. Not as thick as your wrist,
I teased. And I could tease her. I could say her potato salad
was sour, the coleslaw was stringy, that she always

grabbed my food away before I finished. I could tease her,
even when she touched my hand and said, you forgot
your old grandmother. And you're getting a little senile,
I'd joke. But it was true. She forgot her second son's name,
Joe, who died fifteen years earlier. And it was true

her wrists were thick. I only lied about the potato salad.
It was warm and delicate with sprigs of fresh parsley.
Today, my daughter straightens my bow tie just before
we start down the aisle. She smiles. I cover her face
with a veil. You're so elegant, she says.

The Green Dodge

I was about to call my father. I know
it's impossible–he died ten-and-a-half years
ago, but I almost picked up the phone.
I stood up and looked out the window
of my study. It was the first sunny day
in weeks. The lake edged over its bank
and the ice had shiny circular pockets
as if someone had scattered its surface
with silver dollars. We first came here
in his Dodge, a sleek green car
with an oversized motor that made the rear end
fishtail in bad weather. The house is too isolated,
he said, too big a financial risk. The last time
he visited he wore his blue running suit
with a red and white vertical stripe.
He'd been losing weight again and refused
further chemo. I helped him up
to look out the window. It was early April.
A late freeze flounced the shoreline
with thin ripples of ice. I never noticed before–
it looks like whipped cream, he said. A deer
incautiously stepped off the shore. Its foot nearly
broke through before it quickly leapt back.
My father smiled. I walked him to his chair.